The Spirit of Earnest Inquiry

The Spirit of Earnest Inquiry
The Statistical and Social Inquiry Society of Ireland 1847–1997

Mary E. Daly

Index by
Helen Litton

First published in 1997
by the
Statistical and Social Inquiry Society of Ireland

© 1997   Text with Mary Daly and index with the
         Statistical and Social Inquiry Society of Ireland

British Library Cataloguing in Publication Data
A catalogue record for this book is available from the British Library

ISBN 1 872002 29 3

Publishing consultants: Institute of Public Administration, Dublin

Cover design by Creative Inputs, Dublin
Typeset by Wendy Commins, The Curragh, Co. Kildare
Printed by ColourBooks, Dublin

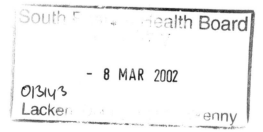

For

Nicholas and Alice

Contents

Message from President Robinson

When the Statistical and Social Inquiry Society of Ireland was established Ireland was experiencing the worst period of the Great Famine, by far the most catastrophic event of our history and one which has left its mark on Ireland and the Irish people to this day. I am sure that the plight of those bearing the brunt of its effects was very much in the minds of the Society's founders in 1847.

Those early years saw the beginnings of the social service system which was to continue with the setting up of public health, employment, housing, education and welfare schemes. The Statistical and Social Inquiry Society of Ireland, with its membership drawn from people of diverse professional backgrounds in the public sector and in the legal, medical and business professions, provided a forum where contemporary issues and developments could be examined and new ideas and concepts could be aired. The Society's great strength lay, and still lies, both in the diversity of its membership and in its capacity to act as neutral territory where the interconnectedness of the professions can be explored to exchange valued reactions, opinions and advice and where professionals can bridge the gaps which sometimes exist between people operating in compartmentalised disciplines.

These characteristics have ensured that it has not only survived but has proved to be an invaluable asset to the formulation and examination of policies and proposals which have had a significant impact on the evolution of the Irish social and economic system.

I would like to commend the Statistical and Social Inquiry Society of Ireland on its great work over the years since 1847 and I am very happy to wish its members continued success in their important and fruitful deliberations for many generations to come.

Mary Robinson
President

Acknowledgements

My thanks to Dermot McAleese the current president, and to his predecessor Padraig McGowan, for asking me to write the history of the Society. To Dónal de Butléir for his interest and involvement in many of the practical details of publication. Kieran Kennedy and Tom Linehan read the entire text and made many helpful comments. Bill Keating and the librarians at the Central Statistics Office placed the minute books of the Council of the Society at my disposal and Claire Devaney tracked down two missing volumes. Brendan Whelan, director of the ESRI, and John Roughan, the secretary, gave me access to the Institute's archives. My thanks also to Michael Casey, David Dickson, Garret FitzGerald, Paddy Lynch, Louis Smih and Jonathan Williams; to Helen Litton for compiling the index, and most especially to Tony McNamara for overseeing the production. Last but not least, my thanks to P.J., Paul, Elizabeth, Alice and Nicholas for sustaining me through yet another book.

All references to the Journal of the Statistical and Social Inquiry Society of Ireland are cited in the text in the following style: (Geary, 358). The number refers to the attached author index.

Introduction

The Statistical and Social Inquiry Society of Ireland holds a
unique place in the study of the Irish economy and Irish society.
Since its foundation in the autumn of 1847 the Society has
analysed the major changes that have taken place in population,
employment, legal and administrative systems and social services.
The one hundred and fifty years since the Society's foundation
span the closing years of the famine, the transformation of post-
famine society, the years when the land question was resolved,
and the entire history of the independent Irish state. Seventy-five
years of this history relate to Ireland under the Union, the
remaining seventy-five are concerned with the experience of a
native government. Through the Journal of the Society we can
chart how major issues such as emigration, crime and the
management of the economy have been evaluated by successive
generations of members. No other single source provides such a
comprehensive picture of social change over such a long period.

The period since 1847 can be neatly summarised in one phrase:
Ireland since the Famine, and the Society affords an unparalleled
window on this critical phase in recent Irish history. Many of the
earliest papers set out to analyse the causes of the Famine and to
make recommendations as to how the Irish economy could be
transformed in the future.The founders of the Society believed
that statistics and economic analysis would provide scientific
answers to the major problems of the time. If this seems naively
optimistic, it is important to note that no political grouping
provided a coherent plan that would have protected Ireland from
the consequences of the potato blight, and that by the 1840s Irish
society was deeply divided by politics and religion. The supposed
scientific nature of statistics, and their apparent ideological

neutrality seemed to offer a better way forward. The Society's constitution precluded discussions of any topics that related to politics or religion. During its early years the reforming agenda was extensive: changes in land law, reforming the poor law, more humane treatment for needy children and promoting temperance. In many respects the Society can be seen as an Irish variant of the many moral and social reform movements that were so typical of mid-Victorian England. It maintained a relatively low profile: insofar as it lobbied for changes in the law, it did so through direct contacts with senior politicians and administrators, or by sending leaflets to all Irish MPs, as opposed to organising mass petitions or public meetings. In the early years this was an effective way of working. The political complexion of the government of Ireland was determined by the electorate of England, Wales and Scotland, rather than the Irish voters. Many of the key decisions relating to Irish legislation rested with a small group of politicians and senior officials based in Dublin Castle; men, who were often members of the Society, or their close acquaintances.

Most papers read to the Society until at least 1870 were in favour of assimilating the laws and practices in Ireland to those applying in England and Wales. There is little doubt that until the 1920s the overwhelming majority of members were much more in sympathy with the British administration in Ireland than with the movement for Home Rule or the more radical wing of Irish nationalism. By 1924 however the Society had begun to enrol a substantial number of senior officials from the new Irish civil service. One of the most interesting aspects of its recent history has been its close relationship with the administration of the new Irish state. The Journal of the Society provides one of the few opportunities to penetrate the official anonymity of the Irish public service. Senior civil servants have spoken more freely on crucial aspects of government policy at its meetings than in any other public forum. The most significant papers in this regard were undoubtedly given by T.K. Whitaker during the late 1940s and the 1950s. Through these it is possible to trace the evolution of the key ideas that evolved in the 1958 publication, *Economic Development*. For many civil servants the Society has provided perhaps the only forum where they could discuss their work openly with academics, businessmen and interested members of the general public. However there were undoubtedly limits to this freedom of speech. In 1932 Joseph Brennan, chairman of the Currency Commission, withdrew a proposed paper following the return of a Fianna Fáil government. From the 1960s most of the papers presented by civil servants have tended to concentrate on technical statistical matters, though often the comments made in the course of discussions following such papers can prove extremely enlightening about the broad direction of government policy.

When the Statistical Society was founded in the mid-nineteenth century, societies that used statistics as a mechanism for investigating social questions were very much in vogue in Britain, continental Europe and in the United States. Most of these no longer exist; others have evolved into strictly professional bodies which tended to be dominated by full-time academics. The Statistical and Social Inquiry Society has not only survived but thrived, partly because until recently the small size of Ireland and the relatively undeveloped nature of professions such as economist and sociologist precluded the emergence of specialist representative organisations. On the whole, the papers presented to the Society have been concerned with practical problems, such as crime, poverty and economic progress, and by a common concern with the condition of Ireland. The Society has thrived as a result of the perennial fascination with critical aspects of post-famine Ireland, such as population decline, emigration and the state of the Irish economy.

During the nineteenth century it frequently provided an important platform for people who were concerned about major social problems, such as the care of orphans and neglected children. Indeed the key figures associated with the founding of the National Society for the Prevention of Cruelty to Children in 1889 were prominent members of the Society. Many of the topics that were of concern to members in the mid and late nineteenth century, such as law reform, the treatment of young offenders, adoption and child welfare, are now handled by more specialist agencies, and by trained professionals as opposed to interested amateurs. Yet the investigative methods that the Society members employed during the nineteenth century: the emphasis on statistics and on empirical research, and the tendency to base recommendations for administrative and legal reform on precedents derived from other nations, remain the basis of modern social policy.

The modern Society is dominated by statistically-minded economists and sociologists, many of them employed within the public service and private business. Although academic members have always been prominent it is ranks, the Society has provided a particularly useful platform for people from outside the universities who are interested in research. The growing technical complexity of the papers read to the Society, their use of elaborate econometric and statistical methods, reflect the evolution of the economics profession within Ireland, and the more professional approach adopted to economic and social inquiry. Regrettably the membership of the Society and its concerns have narrowed. There are few interested amateurs among the members in the 1990s. Lawyers were prominent until the 1920s and numerous papers focused on legal reform; such topics have since disappeared. Until the 1940s the Society provided an important forum for investigating public health matters; such research is now more likely to be presented in a specialist journal. While there are benefits from this growing professionalisation, the loss of an interdisciplinary audience is regrettable, and the major challenge for the Society is to find a mechanism for maintaining and strengthening this dimension.

In his introduction to the centenary history of the Society, Roy Geary, its president, noted that 'it is fascinating to observe how in each generation the studies under Society auspices reflected the public interests of the time'. While acknowledging the merits of Geary's remark, it is important to understand that the Society presents us with an unconventional insight into the history of Ireland since the Famine. The Journal says little about nationalism, republicanism, unionism, the Ulster question, the role of the catholic church or the revival of the Irish language, the topics that dominate most historical narratives. The Society's constitution precluded it from discussing matters that related directly to politics or religion, and a historian who was solely dependent on its Journal as a source would be unable to explain the reasons for the success of a grass-roots movement such as the Land League. However the Journal provides an invaluable insight into the thoughts of a professional and intellectual elite on some of the most important aspects of Irish society. It is extremely informative on topics such as emigration or rural economy and it enables us to explore many neglected subjects such as the early history of social work in Ireland, or comparative mortality in rural and urban areas in the 1940s. Many of the views expressed in its Journal on emotive subjects, such as emigration and population decline, provided a valuable corrective to the popular rhetoric of the time. One case in point is Roy Geary's 1935 paper which showed that it would be utterly impossible for the Irish population to return to its 1841 level of 8.1m. during the twentieth century. His assessment was correct, but he was roundly criticised at the time for his pessimism (Geary, 358). Papers such as this, and earlier papers by Charles Oldham (Oldham, 1017, 1020, 1022) and Chart (Chart, 144) on Irish industrial history deserve to be ranked among the classic revisionist texts in Irish history, despite the fact that they predate the founding of the journal *Irish Historical Studies*, which is generally regarded as the beginning of the revisionist movement.[1] The Journal also published data on agricultural prices since the famine: those compiled by Richard Barrington (Barrington, 39, 40),[2] Thomas Barrington (Barrington, 42) and Hans Staehle (Staehle, 1165), that remain a vital source for modern scholars and the key papers by Austen Bourke (Bourke, 83,84) relating to the potato crop in pre-famine Ireland.

Writing a history of the Statistical and Social Inquiry Society of Ireland presents a number of difficulties. The surviving sources consist of the minutes of the Council of the Society from 1863, together with the Journal and some other published papers. Although the minutes provide occasional glimpses of ideological and personal differences, they often conceal more than they reveal. It is regrettable that the practice of summarising the main points made by discussants following each paper did not begin until the 1920s, because these occasions provide a rare record of debate. In an ideal world it would be possible to supplement these sources with the private papers and correspondence of members, and with more direct evidence of the Society's impact on policy from official files. Neither source is available to any significant extent, so that at times we can only infer the extent of the Society's influence. Anybody who is interested in the history of the Statistical and Social Inquiry Society owes an immense debt to Professor

R.D.C. Black. His centenary history, published in 1947, provides a narrative of the first hundred years, together with invaluable profiles of the most important members. The flavour of the Society is best captured by dipping into the attached cumulative author and subject index of the Journal compiled by Helen Litton.

NOTES TO INTRODUCTION

[1] Ciaran Brady (ed), *Interpreting Irish History. The Debate on Historical Revisionism 1938-1994* (Dublin, 1994).

[2] Richard Barrington, author of these papers, was a member of the family that funded the Barrington Trust lectures on economics that were organised by the Society.

CHAPTER ONE

The Origins of the Statistical and Social Inquiry Society of Ireland

THE DUBLIN STATISTICAL SOCIETY

The Dublin Statistical Society, the ancestor of the Statistical and Social Inquiry Society of Ireland, was founded in 1847, a year which most Irish people associate with the Great Famine. By 23 November 1847, the date on which the Statistical Society was founded, Ireland had endured two successive years of potato blight, which had resulted in the probable doubling of the death rate, and an unprecedently high level of emigration. Although the potato crop was generally blight-free in the autumn of 1847, the acreage sown was small, and distress persisted because many families could not afford to buy alternative food. Evictions were mounting and attacks on landlords and their agents appeared to be on the increase. Six landlords and land agents were assassinated during the months of October and November 1847, the most sensational being the murder of Roscommon landlord Major Denis Mahon.[1]

Despite the apparent easing of the blight, the Irish crisis showed no sign of ending. By September 1847, the British government had terminated all special famine-relief measures, such as public works and soup kitchens, leaving the newly established Irish poor law (previously Ireland was regarded as part of the English poor law) as the sole provider of relief; this meant that the full cost of relieving distress fell on owners of Irish property and their larger tenants. Many Irish estates were heavily encumbered even before the Famine, so rising rents arrears and unprecedented tax demands forced numerous landlords into bankruptcy. During the autumn of 1847, the collapse of speculative investments in railway shares led to a major financial and business crisis in Britain, which forced the British government to suspend the 1844 Bank Charter Act, the act which regulated, and indeed limited, the right of banks to issue notes. The repeal of the Corn Laws in 1846 had marked the triumph of free trade throughout the United Kingdom, though the Tory party was split as a consequence. In the light of such economic and social turmoil, it is not surprising that the 1840s were characterised by highly charged debates on economic issues in both Britain and Ireland.

Any scrutiny of Irish newspapers and periodicals for these years confirms that this was also a period of considerable political activity, though, in contrast to the decision to found the Statistical Society, most of what transpired had little long-term impact. In January 1847, the second famine winter, Irish peers, MPs and gentry were invited to attend a meeting in Dublin shortly before parliament resumed, with a view to reaching a consensus on how to resolve the severe problems, that Ireland was facing. Although nothing worthwhile transpired, in the early summer of 1847 – at a time when up to 3 million people were receiving free or subsidised food from soup kitchens – an Irish Council was established with the aim of uniting influential Irishmen from all walks of life. The council held another much-publicised meeting in November 1847, on the eve of the new session of parliament, in order 'to stress yet again the need for union if the crisis created by the famine were not to be perpetuated in national bankruptcy'.[2] This meeting failed to agree on how to tackle the problems facing Ireland; in fact it attracted a much poorer attendance from peers and landlords than the previous meeting. Tenant-right and land reform proved the most divisive issues. Indeed the uncompromising attitude shown by representatives of the landlord class at this meeting led John Mitchel, a radical member of the Young Ireland movement, to adopt a much more revolutionary stance. Earlier hopes of uniting Irish landlords and people in a common cause, which had been expressed by Young Irelanders such as John Mitchel, Charles Gavan Duffy and James Fintan Lalor, had rested on a common opposition to free trade – which intensified following the repeal of the Corn Laws in 1846 – and to the Irish policies of the Liberal government, led by Lord John Russell. However, whatever consensus existed on these issues proved insufficient to overcome fundamental divisions over the respective rights of landlords and tenants. Before the Famine, Irish society was already deeply divided on matters such as Repeal of the Union, the British government's grant to Maynooth College, and the proposed Queen's Colleges. Far from obliterating these disagreements, the Famine years only aggravated them.

The founding of the Dublin Statistical Society must be set against this background of Famine, economic crisis and deep divisions over political and economic questions. The Society aimed at 'promoting the study of Statistics and Economical Science',[3] and it expressed a determination to reject all communications 'involving topics likely to produce discussions connected with religious differences or party politics' (Millin, 867). As in the case of the Gaelic League, another avowedly apolitical organisation, which was founded almost fifty years later, this was undoubtedly an impossible objective. However, rather than belittle the aspiration, we should recognise that it reflected a widely held belief at the time that statistics and statistical inquiry could provide an objective and scientific basis for discovering the truth.

When the term 'statistics' – a translation of the German term 'Statistik' – was first used in the English language in 1770, it apparently meant 'the science which "teaches us what is the political arrangement of all the modern states of the known world"'. The word was derived from the term 'statist', i.e. a politician or statesman.[4] Many so-called 'statistical' works of the late eighteenth or early nineteenth century would not be deemed statistical by modern scholars. Examples of early 'statistical' works, which tended to describe socio-economic and often political conditions, include the statistical surveys of Irish counties, which the Royal Dublin Society commissioned at the end of the eighteenth century. These were designed to examine the 'actual state, capabilities and defects of agriculture, manufactures and rural economy' in each county. Between 1801 and 1832 the Royal Dublin Society published twenty-three county surveys.[5]

By the 1820s however, the word statistics had come to be associated with numbers in Britain, France and Belgium,[6] though as late as 1842 the British economist J.R. McCulloch rejected the idea 'that everything in statistics may be estimated in figures'.[7] In a similar vein, James Anthony Lawson, a founding member of the Dublin Statistical Society, who held the Whately chair of political economy at Trinity College Dublin during the years 1840 to 1845, defined statistics, in 1848, as 'the contents of all the blue books which are issued to both houses of Parliament', or 'the collecting of facts which relate to man's social condition' (Lawson, 680). This definition of statistics was reinforced by the proliferation of quantitative data, mostly in the form of censuses of population, and statistics relating to crime, mortality and public health. In France, the Bureau de Statistique, established under the Consulate, was expanded by Napoleon I. By the 1830s, in addition to carrying out a population census, the Bureau was collecting judicial statistics, together with data on topics such as the health of army recruits. In Britain, the first census of population was taken in 1801, in order to estimate manpower needs during the Napoleonic wars. In 1832, a statistical office was established at the Board of Trade; in 1837 a General Register office was created to collect vital statistics and to take charge of an expanded census of population in 1841.[8] By 1847, although Ireland lacked a General Register office, the process of counting people, animals and crops was underway, following the success of the 1841 population census (which is generally regarded as the first scientific census) and the first official returns of agricultural output, which were collected in that year.

Statistical societies were very much in vogue by the 1840s. In June 1833, the British Association for the Advancement of Science, which had been founded in 1831, established a statistical section. September 1833 saw the foundation of the Manchester Statistical Society, the first such society in Britain or Ireland. In March 1834 the Statistical Society of London, now the Royal Statistical Society, held its first meeting, and by the mid-1840s statistical societies (some short-lived) had emerged in the majority of English and Scottish cities. In 1838, some members of the Belfast Natural History Society who had attended the 1837 meeting of the British Association founded the Statistical Society of Ulster. Within a year, this society could boast over a hundred members, mostly in the Belfast area. Thus the Dublin Statistical Society was a rather late arrival by United Kingdom standards.

The founding members of such societies were drawn from various backgrounds. Charles Babbage, the famous scientist, and John Elliott Drinkwater, an assistant commissioner for the 1833 Factory Commission and a municipal corporations commissioner, were responsible for founding the London Society. Most of the founding members of the Manchester Society belonged to the city's industrial and commercial elite. Medical practitioners were prominent in many provincial societies; their involvement was prompted by the environmental health problems associated with urban and industrial growth. Government officials and economists outnumbered mathematicians.[9] Few members of these early statistical societies were interested in statistical technique as an end in itself. They believed that statistics, whether quantitative or non-quantitative, would provide scientific, i.e. objective, answers to the great social questions of the day, and would either provide evidence of the need for reform and the direction that it should take, or alternatively – though this appears to have been a minority position – that statistics would justify the status quo. This belief in objectively determined facts is epitomised in the motto of the Dublin Society: 'Our Pole Star is Truth'. Practitioners contrasted the impartiality of statistics with the divisive speculation and opinions that were characteristic of party politics, and the Dublin Statistical Society was typical of the nineteenth-century statistical movement in excluding such matters from its meetings. Thus the first rule in the prospectus for the London Society was 'to exclude all opinions' – a rather sweeping objective; the Manchester Society banned 'party politics' from its discussions.[10] Abrams notes that the 'implicit purposes of the Society [the London Statistical Society] were at once to bring political economy into policy, in the sense of generating relevant administrative intelligence, and to end politics, in the sense of obliterating conflicts of principle'.

In practice, most men who were active in British statistical societies at this time appear to have been liberals; Abrams claimed that the Council of the London Society in its early years 'often looked like a subcommittee of a Whig Cabinet'.[11] This was equally true of the statistical movement throughout Europe. In Italy, it has been claimed that statistics and political economy were employed 'as a means to further a discourse of opposition to the political order established by the Congress of Vienna [1815], to promote and direct the formation of a liberal public opinion, and to lay claim to an increased participation in government'. Porter noted that 'Statistics reflected a liberal temperament and a search for reform that flourished not during the years of repression following the Congress of Vienna, but the late 1820s and especially the 1830s'.[12] British statistical societies concentrated their attention on the adverse consequences of rapid urbanisation and industrialisation and on investigating the inadequacies of public health services, the poor law, education and an apparent crime wave. Although the Dublin Society discussed poor law reform and crime, it was more concerned with problems which seemed to have greater relevance for Ireland, such as the land question.

The founders of the Dublin Statistical Society were drawn from the city's academic, professional and administrative elite. This reflected Dublin's character as a legal and administrative centre, a city with an active university, where commercial and industrial interests generally took second, or even third, place. Richard Whately, the first president of the Society was Archbishop of Dublin, a former Drummond professor of economics at Oxford and the founder of the chair of political economy at Dublin University that still bears his name. Thomas Larcom, Commissioner of Public Works, and a vice-president of the Dublin Society, later served as undersecretary for Ireland (the highest post in the Irish civil service) from 1853 to 1868. As the man responsible for carrying out the 1841 census, and for organising the compilation of agricultural statistics, Larcom can be described as the founder of Irish official statistics. Mountifort Longfield QC, another vice-president, was an established lawyer, a former Whately professor of political economy, who subsequently became a Judge of the Landed Estates Court and a Commissioner of National Education. A third, Sir Robert Kane, was the author of *The Industrial Resources of Ireland* (1844), president of the Museum of Irish Industry and a professor at the Royal Dublin Society. In 1845 he became the first president of Queen's College Cork. The three remaining vice-presidents were Rev R. MacDonnell, DD, a Fellow of Trinity College Dublin, Samuel Kyle, Church of Ireland Bishop of Cork, and the Earl of Rosse, a distinguished scientist, who is best remembered for erecting what was then the world's largest telescope.

Three future Lord Chancellors of Ireland (Joseph Napier, Thomas O'Hagan and Hugh Law), two future Attorneys General (James Anthony Lawson and George Augustus Chichester May), and one future Lord Chief Justice (the same Chichester May) were among the eighty-one founding members, as were Sir William Wilde, father of Oscar Wilde, a distinguished member of the medical profession and an antiquarian, who compiled the statistics relating to death and disease in both the 1841 and 1851 census – he was one of seven medical members – and William Mulvany of the Board of Works, who was later to make his fortune developing coal mines in Germany.[13] There was a strong Quaker presence, a characteristic which the Dublin Statistical Society shared with several English provincial societies. Like their English counterparts, the Quaker members were drawn from the world of commerce. Three members of the Pim family, Jonathan, Joseph Todhunter and William Harvey, read papers to the Society during the first twenty years. William Haughton, a Quaker grain merchant, was another active member; his daughter married William Neilson Hancock, a stalwart of the Society for over thirty years. Charles Bianconi, who established an inexpensive coaching service throughout Ireland in pre-Famine years, was also a member, though, unlike the Pims and William Haughton, he did not play an active role in the Society.

The men who founded the Dublin Statistical Society undoubtedly assumed that statistics meant social statistics, not a branch of mathematics, and they regarded the subject as a form of applied economics.[14] In 1863, when John Kells Ingram reminisced about the Society's foundation, he noted that 'it was the pressure of social problems then imperatively demanding attention that led its youthful founders to attempt the establishment of such an institution', adding 'it has not occupied itself with dilettante statistics, collected with no special purpose, and tending to no definite conclusion. It has from the first applied itself, in the spirit of earnest inquiry, to the most important questions affecting the condition of the country' (Ingram, 590). This belief that scientific investigation would help to achieve a better society was very much in keeping with the philosophy of Henri Comte, the founder of positivism. Many of the founding members were probably familiar with Comte's views; in 1845 they were summarised at length in the *Dublin University Magazine*. Several contributors to the magazine were active in founding the Statistical Society; indeed, early papers read to the Society often expressed opinions that are remarkably similar to those found in the pages of the *Dublin University Magazine*.[15]

Despite the obvious similarities between the Dublin Society and its counterparts in the English provinces, the term political economy appears to have featured more prominently within the Dublin Society, and economists were more conspicuous among its early members.. The meeting that discussed the proposal to form a Statistical Society took place in the rooms of William Neilson Hancock, the Whately professor of political economy in Dublin University, and the four previous holders of the Whately chair became important office-holders of the Society. R.D.C. Black, author of the Society's centenary history, suggests that its foundation probably resulted from a series of lectures on the condition of Ireland which Hancock gave as Whately professor. This interpretation is supported by Whately's statement in 1851 that the Society 'had its origin in the lectures of the Professors of Political Economy'.[16] Richard Whately, the Society's first president, who held office until 1863, firmly believed that 'next to sound religion, sound political economy was most essential to the well-being of society … [and] …to the prosperity of the nation'. According to Whately, economists were destined to become the new governing elite: 'the world must be governed, has been governed and will be governed by Political Economists, though many of them are bad ones' (Whately, 1292).

The foundation of the Dublin Statistical Society must be seen as part of Whately's wish to teach political economy to all levels of Irish society, 'even to ploughmen and the children'. In 1832, he was instrumental in founding the Whately chair of political economy at Trinity College Dublin.[17] Whately also used his position as the 'invisible president' of the Board of National Education[18] to have political economy included in the curriculum of the national schools, and he wrote the prescribed text, *Easy Lessons on Money Matters: For the Use of Young People*, which was published in 1834.[19] He referred at length to both these projects in his 1848 presidential address to the Dublin Statistical Society, when he emphasised that 'A science so important as that of Political Economy was not to be confined to a few' (Whately, 1292). In 1849 the objective of preaching the gospel of Political Economy to the masses gained further impetus, when the Society undertook the task of administering the Barrington bequest. John Barrington, a Dublin businessman and a member of the Society of Friends, had left money in trust for the purpose of hiring 'a fit and proper person or persons, duly qualified to give lectures on Political Economy in its most extended and useful sense ... in the various towns and villages of Ireland'. From the 1850s, the Barrington Trust financed lectures in many provincial towns. At the beginning most sessions were organised by local mechanics institutes or by literary and scientific societies. Although interest appears to have peaked during the 1860s, the practice continued until the 1980s and a roll call of Barrington lecturers includes many well-known Irish economists.[20] A similar concern with educating the masses is indicated by the fact that, in 1854, the Society had 28 corresponding societies (mainly mechanics institutes) throughout Ireland, and it assisted these organisations in having the Public Libraries Act extended to Ireland.[21]

When the Dublin Statistical Society was founded in 1847, the relationship between statistics and political economy remained uncertain. Whereas economics was primarily based on induction, statistics relied on empirical evidence, from which arguments as to causation could be deduced. Most of the early classical economists made little, if any, use of statistics; as Cullen shows, Nassau Senior, the first Drummond professor of economics at Oxford, appears to have found statistics rather confusing.[22] Archbishop Whately may have been more conscious of the value of statistics than many of his fellow economists. Whereas the 1834 English Poor Law Report made no attempt to count the numbers in the various categories who were in need of poor relief,[23] its Irish equivalent, which was chaired by Whately, estimated that the number of people and their dependants who were out of work and in need of assistance for thirty weeks of each year numbered 2.38m, roughly 30 per cent of the population.[24]

One man who addressed a meeting of the short-lived Statistical Society of Ulster predicted 'that the study of Statistics, will, ere long, rescue Political Economy from all the uncertainty in which it is now enveloped'.[25] In December 1847, at the second meeting of the Dublin Statistical Society, James Anthony Lawson argued that one of the functions of statistics was to supply facts, that could be used to test economic theories, and to correct the errors that might result from hasty generalisations. As an example, Lawson argued that the theory that population tended to outstrip subsistence (the so-called Malthusian trap) had been shown to be 'contrary to experience', a comment that is of particular significance because it was made at the height of the Irish Famine. Lawson regarded the relation between both disciplines as a two-way process. While statistics could indicate the existence or coexistence of certain factors, 'it required a philosophical mind to determine whether [or not] there be the link of causation'. Economics constituted only a part of the Society's interests. Lawson, for example, was at pains to emphasise that 'statistics suggests matter for the investigation of the statesmen, politicians and philanthropists, with which the economist has nothing to do' (Lawson, 680). In 1852, Denis Caulfield Heron, professor of jurisprudence and political economy at Queen's College Galway, referred to the study of sociology, rather than political economy, in the opening section of a paper dealing with landlord-tenant relations (Heron, 549).

In 1850, the Dublin Statistical Society decided to organise an associated 'Society for Promoting Scientific Inquiries into Social Reform' – a decision that eventually led to the words 'and Social Inquiry' being included in the title of the present Society. Whereas meetings of the Dublin Statistical Society consisted of members reading papers, which they had volunteered, the Social Inquiry Society collected subscriptions, which they used to commission paid research into topics that were regarded as too 'complicated and difficult' for individual members to investigate on a voluntary basis.[26] During the 1830s, the Manchester Statistical Society had financed an ambitious series of surveys into the living conditions and educational standards of the working-classes in their area; similar surveys, with a particular emphasis on education for the working class were commissioned by statistical societies in Bristol, Birmingham and Leeds, though enthusiasm for such expensive activities soon waned.[27] By contrast, the eight reports commissioned by the Social Inquiry Society between 1850 and

1855 dealt with legal matters, such as limited liability, wills, contracts pertaining to land, and the law relating to debtors and creditors (Millin, 867). Enthusiasm and financial support for this undertaking did not last, so in 1855 the Social Inquiry Society and the Dublin Statistical Society merged by mutual agreement. It was determined that the remaining funds of the Social Inquiry Society would be allocated for further 'scientific inquiries into social questions of public and general interest'.[28] The objects of the amalgamated Society were extended to include 'the promotion of the study of Statistics, Political Economy and Jurisprudence'.[29] The Society did not entirely abandon its commitment to collaborative research projects; in the late 1850s it established several committees to investigate topics such as the civil registration of births, marriages and deaths, the operations of the jury system, and the question of legislation by Provisional Order in England, Scotland and Wales. In 1871, it commissioned four further (paid) reports on aspects of Irish jurisprudence (Millin, 867).

During the early years, the affairs of the Dublin Statistical Society were closely intertwined with those of the Royal Dublin Society. In 1848, the annual meeting of the RDS rejected a proposal for a merger between the two societies, because it refused to reduce its subscription for associate members in order to bring it into line with the Dublin Statistical Society. In 1858, the RDS made an attempt to bring all scientific societies in the Dublin area under its umbrella: RDS members would be permitted to join the associated societies at a reduced fee, while members of associated societies would receive some of the privileges open to members of the RDS. Although the Dublin Statistical Society and the RDS came to an agreement in 1858, which initially appears to have worked well, it survived only until 1862. In that year the Dublin Statistical Society became the Statistical and Social Inquiry Society of Ireland; ladies were permitted to join as associates, and the objects of the Society were extended to include 'all questions of Social Science'. Business was to be divided into three departments:

> Jurisprudence and the Amendment of the Law including the subject of Punishment and the Reformation of Criminals.
> Social Science, including Education; Political Economy,

including the principles of Trade and Commerce.
Public Health and Sanitary Reform.[30]

The venue for meetings of the Society was changed from Leinster House, the home of the RDS, to the Friends Institute in Molesworth Street where the Society's expanding library was also accommodated (Millin, 867).

Although the accounts given, both by Shannon Millin and by R.D.C. Black, suggest that disagreements between the Dublin Statistical Society and the Royal Dublin Society related mainly to be provision of refreshments after meetings of the Statistical Society,[31] it seems probable that other factors also came into play. In many respects the objectives of the founding members of the Royal Dublin Society in 1731 anticipate those of the founders of the Dublin Statistical Society more than a century later. Both societies wished to use science to improve the condition of Ireland, and both expressed a determination to disseminate scientific knowledge among the Irish people, though the remit of the RDS was much wider, and it was in receipt of government grants. The series of Irish county surveys commissioned by the RDS were forerunners of the concept of statistical inquiry. By the 1830s, according to Meenan and Clarke, the RDS seemed to have temporarily lost its sense of purpose. However the lecture series on the industrial resources of Ireland given in 1844 by Robert Kane, Professor of Natural Philosophy at the RDS and a founding-member of the Dublin Statistical Society, indicates that RDS had an interest in economic development.[32]

In 1835, and in 1857, the RDS hosted the Dublin meeting of the British Association for the Advancement of Science.[33] The 1857 meeting appears to have given a boost to the activities of the Dublin Statistical Society. However, when the Statistical Society proposed to invite the National Association for the Promotion of Social Science to hold its annual meeting in Dublin in 1862, it discovered that the RDS had already issued an invitation for 1861. Although Black comments that both bodies co-operated in ensuring that the meeting was a success,[34] there is little doubt that the Social Science Association had much more in common with the Statistical Society than with the RDS.

POVERTY, FAMINE AND POPULATION: THE CONDITION OF IRELAND QUESTION AS SEEN IN THE PAPERS READ TO THE DUBLIN STATISTICAL SOCIETY

The proposal to found a Dublin Statistical Society appears to have been prompted by W.N. Hancock's series of lectures on the condition of Ireland. They were published in 1847 under the title, *Three Lectures on the Question: Should the Principles of Political Economy be Disregarded at the Present Crisis?*[35] The crisis was of course the Famine, and in Ireland it had led to serious questions being raised about the dominant tenets of political economy, in particular the assumption that market forces would automatically bring about economic prosperity. The aspect of the British government's policy which came under the most sustained attack during the Famine years was the failure to prevent food being exported from Ireland;[36] such criticism was often linked with a condemnation of absentee landlords (it was generally assumed that the grain was exported to remit rents due to the latter). Proponents of these views, such as the Young Irelander John Mitchel, argued that even at the height of the famine Ireland was producing sufficient food to meet the needs of more than double the population. From reading Sir Robert Kane, the Young Irelanders also tended to derive an unduly optimistic picture of the extent of Ireland's natural resources.[37] In 1847 Mitchel published a series of extracts from the writings of Jonathan Swift and George Berkeley in favour of government intervention in the economy. The book was entitled *Irish Political Economy*.[38]

At the Dublin Statistical Society's second meeting in December 1847, W.N. Hancock read a paper on the *Use of the Doctrine of Laissez Faire in investigating the Economic Resources of Ireland*. He began by describing the extent of Ireland's natural resources as 'a favourite topic for the indulgence of national vanity', adding that the 'unsound arrangements' which might hamper their development should be blamed on 'a want of reliance on private enterprise'. Most of Hancock's paper was devoted to presenting the case for free trade in food, in the light of the 'calamities of the past year [1846]'. Hancock asserted that there was 'no foundation in fact' for the argument that *laissez-faire* had resulted in increased deaths during 1846. Indeed he argued that the policy had not been tried in the west of Ireland, because the government had operated food depots, a policy that was 'at variance with Political Economy'. Anticipating the 'entitlements' argument presented by the present-day economist Amartya Sen,[39] Hancock claimed that 'the people of Ireland died from want of *money* not from want of *food*.' According to Hancock, Ireland experienced high mortality during 1846, because the Irish people were poorer than the English; poverty also explained why food was exported. Interfering with the food trade would not have helped, because the people had no money.

Hancock appears to have regarded the interests of provision dealers as being identical with the interests of the community, a somewhat naive argument – even within his terms of reference – if we accept the existence of local monopolies and barriers to trade in the form of high transport costs, lack of information on the part of consumers, and indebtedness to a particular trader. He also refuted most of the prevailing explanations for Irish poverty and distress, such as the subdivision and subletting of land, the pro-liferation of middlemen, combinations, over-population, absentee landlords, the racial inferiority of the Celtic race, and over-dependence on the potato. According to Hancock, the Irish people lived on a diet of potatoes because they were poor; they were not poor because they lived on potatoes.

Conacre, subdivision and other shortcomings of the rural economy were indicative of weaknesses in the Irish land market which could be removed by ensuring that market forces operated effectively. His recommendations for improving economic conditions concentrated exclusively on what we now term the supply side: introducing a free market in land at all levels of society, including removing the privileges which Irish farmers possessed over their cottiers; removing aspects of the landlord-tenant code which interfered with private enterprise, and giving tenants full security for improvements (Hancock, 488).

Hancock expanded on these ideas in a succession of papers to the Society. In February 1848, a paper on the *Condition of the Irish Labourer* developed the argument that the interests of Irish labourers were best served under a system of free trade and an unrestricted market. Irish labourers were poor because Irish agriculture was backward, and their condition would worsen rather than improve, if Irish manufactures were protected. Hancock assumed that the Irish labour force was perfectly mobile, both between the agricultural and manufacturing sectors, and between Britain and Ireland. Demand for labour depended on the 'well-being of the population'; increased wealth would result in a greater demand for labour. Anticipating the convergence theory,[40] he argued that 'every improvement in the condition of the labouring class in England would provide a permanent effect in Ireland', because it would result in increased emigration to England and consequently in higher wages for those remaining in Ireland. Agricultural prosperity in Ireland would raise the general wage level, whereas protecting Irish manufactures ultimately would reduce wages in both Ireland and in England (Hancock, 418).

Part of this paper was devoted to refuting the argument that Ireland suffered from overpopulation. Hancock also dismissed the suggestion that Irish distress was the outcome of divine providence – an argument that was influential among the British political elite at that time, and has come to be regarded as exerting a vital (or perhaps a fatal) influence over British policies towards Ireland during the Famine years.[41] According to Hancock, the problem was a deficient demand for labour, (owing to market imperfections), not excessive population. Turning the providentialist argument on its head, he condemned statements which asserted that unemployment was proof that a country was overpopulated, as 'a sinful expression of discontent with the dealings of the Almighty'. A country might be described as overpopulated, 'if the supply of food was deficient and every instrument of wealth was employed to the utmost of existing knowledge'. Asking whether this situation applied to Ireland, he continued, 'If not, then vainly shall we endeavour to conceal from ourselves the consequences of human folly, by representing the misery and distress produced by man's neglect as inevitable dispensations of the beneficent Authority'.

Hancock claimed that the growth of emigration 'affords the strongest proof of the energy, industry and foresight of the Irish labourers'. This was an implicit refutation of the cultural stereotype of Irish indolence much favoured by Sir Charles Trevelyan, the undersecretary to the Treasury. Trevelyan firmly believed that the Irish peasantry did very little work: 'a fortnight planting, a week or ten days digging and fourteen days turf cutting suffice for his subsistence. During the rest of the year he is at leisure to follow his own inclinations'.[42] Trevelyan blamed the potato economy for Irish indolence. In *Notice of the Theory 'That there is no hope for a Nation that lives on Potatoes'*, which he read to the Society in April 1848, Hancock refuted, by name, Trevelyan's argument that the Irish population's reliance on the potato reflected its debased tastes, and suggested that higher wages would automatically result in a more varied diet (Hancock, 461).

In a book which draws heavily on the economic theories of Archbishop Whately and on the opinions expressed by early holders of the Whately chair, Tom Boylan and Tadhg Foley argue

> ... that political economy was partisan, prescriptive, tendentious. Claiming to be non-sectarian and non-political, it performed a vitally important ideological function for the political and religious establishment in defending existing socio-economic relations, including landlordism, property rights, and in attacking trade unions.

They also suggest that the Dublin Statistical Society was founded 'not so much as a humanitarian response to the Great Famine, though it would be unfair to deny the presence of such an impulse, but in order to defend the laws of political economy then seen as under unprecedented attack'.[43] Much of what they say is undoubtedly true. Whately's presidential address at the conclusion of the first session of the Dublin Statistical Society, in June 1848, referred to the value of political economy as a bulwark against revolution:

> It was a mistake to suppose that religion or morals alone would be sufficient to save a people from revolution. ... A man, even of the purest mind and most exalted feelings, without a knowledge of Political Economy could not be secured from being instrumental in forwarding most destructive and disastrous revolution (Whately, 1292).

Whately's remarks should be seen as a reaction to the revolutionary wave, which began in France in the spring of 1848 and swept through Europe in succeeding months. Although the farcical revolt by the Young Irelanders at Ballingarry did not take place until the autumn, the authorities in Ireland were extremely nervous during the summer months, because several leaders of the Young Ireland movement were on trial for sedition.[44] Whately's paper referred to the potential revolutionary effect of some current economic ideas, 'that a landlord with a limited number of acres should support and feed an unlimited number of mouths', or the detrimental effect of the ten-hours bill.[45] His description of Ireland as a free country 'where every one might be said to take part in the government of the state', and the laughter in the audience when he noted that 'he had heard so much about the enslavement of Ireland that he was thereby convinced she was a free country', appears to confirm the views of Boylan and Foley – that the Dublin Statistical Society was an institution which defended existing political and socio-economic relations.

For Mountiford Longfield, writing in 1856, the survival of the Society was 'proof of the possibility of uniting Irishmen of all creeds and parties in one common object' (Longfield, 726). He believed that the objectivity of statistics offered a middle ground between polarised positions. Longfield's language echoes the United Irishmen of the 1790s and anticipates some of the discourse of so-called constructive unionists of the late nineteenth century, such as Sir Horace Plunkett. Yet Longfield's hopes of uniting Irishmen of all creeds and parties presupposed that authority would remain with the Anglo-Irish elite. Few catholics, and even fewer nationalists, were to be found among the Society's members during the nineteenth century, and most papers read to the Society before the 1920s assumed the survival of the Union.

Nevertheless, the opinions expressed on the condition of Ireland by the first-generation of members were quite diverse, and they did not invariably provide a justification for maintaining the status quo. After all, during the 1830s Archbishop Whately had chaired the famous Royal Commission of Inquiry into the Condition of the Poorer Classes in Ireland. Because it recommended a major programme of public investment to provide employment and develop Irish resources, this report has consistently attracted approval from Irish critics of *laissez-faire* economics. Its conclusions were very much at variance with the ideology, which Boylan and Foley see as dominating the Society's agenda. Although Hancock had dismissed the argument that absentee landlords damaged the Irish economy by robbing it of potential opportunities for employment, two other founding members of the Society, and former holders of the Whately chair, Mountifort Longfield and James Anthony Lawson believed otherwise.[46] Even Hancock, 'the indomitable believer in *laissez-faire*',[47] went out of his way to refute the racial and cultural stereotypes about the potato-eating Irish (Hancock, 461). Many British classical economists were firmly of the opinion that the Irish people would have to develop 'a taste for other objects besides mere food',[48] if economic development was to succeed.

Isaac Butt, another former Whately professor, an early member of the Council (though he does not appear to have been an active member) and the founder of the Irish Home Rule movement, rejected the dominant belief among political economists in the benefits of free trade. Butt justified the case for protecting native industry with an argument similar to that advanced by economists who criticised absentee landlords: that unemployed labour and other underused natural resources would be put to work in a protected economy.[49] Butt took issue with Mountifort Longfield's claim that a large export trade was evidence of a nation's prosperity; he claimed that the true test of prosperity was the volume of domestic consumption. In 1848, Hancock read a paper which attacked the views of the eighteenth-century philosopher George Berkeley, and of Isaac Butt, on the merits of protecting native industries (Hancock, 488). Butt's lectures on the Protection of Home Industries had already been reviewed at length in the *Dublin University Magazine* of April 1846, where they attracted unfavourable comment. The fact that Butt never actually read a paper to the Society, and that his Council membership was brief, may indicate that he felt out of step with its prevailing views.

Despite such differences of opinions, R.D.C. Black argued that Longfield, Butt, Lawson and Hancock all dissented from the prevailing Ricardian economic orthodoxies: they ranked in Schumpeter's view with 'the Men who wrote above their Time'. All four rejected the Ricardian labour, or production theory of value, in favour of a theory that came closer to the utility theory adopted by Stanley Jevons in the 1870s. The details of this debate do not directly concern us; our interest lies with their views about the Irish economy. Black's original article was published in 1945; by the time he reconsidered the matter in the early 1980s, Maurice Dobb had dismissed the so-called Irish dissenters as "'harmony theorists" defending the status quo or, in other words, the lackeys of capitalism'. Black concluded that they should be described 'neither as radicals nor as defenders of the status quo but rather as concerned reformers' whose stance on different issues varied from conservative to radical. Both Black and Dobb concur that one of the distinctions between Ricardo and the so-called Irish dissenters was the greater faith which the Irish economists expressed in the possibility of economic progress.[50] Such optimism may have derived from Whately, who was much less gloomy than Ricardo about the possibility of achieving higher wages under capitalism. Whately also rejected nineteenth-century evangelical gloom concerning man's fallen nature and the moral benefits of affliction.[51] As we have seen, Hancock rejected providentialist explanations for the Irish Famine.

The twin themes of optimism and reform appear frequently in papers to the Society, though both messages are not necessarily included on every occasion. Hancock dominated the early proceedings, reading one paper in 1847, six in 1848 and again in 1849, and four in 1850. Between the 1847/48 session and that of 1882/83, Hancock contributed a total of 88 papers. The majority would not be described as statistical by a modern reader. In the early years they often consisted of what Hancock described as an exposition of 'natural laws and the application of them to Ireland'. In addition to refuting economic heresy, and endeavouring to wean the Irish people from their demands for government intervention in the economy, a belief which, Hancock claimed has 'perverted the minds of the people on economic questions' (Hancock, 488), he presented several papers that recommended ways to extend market forces within the Irish economy. Five papers suggested that in order to improve the condition of Irish agriculture, it would be necessary to remove the legal impediments to the transfer of land and to compensating tenants for carrying out improvements. A paper in 1850 on the causes of famine in Skibbereen and Skull [sic], two areas which had attracted considerable publicity during the Famine years, particularly in the pages of the *Illustrated London News*,[52] rebutted the suggestion that the failure of the potato crop was the chief cause of distress in these areas. Hancock blamed the disaster on the reckless improvidence of insolvent landlords, the short-sighted attitude of middlemen, and ultimately, on 'legal impediments to the free transfer and sale of land, whether waste or improved; and the legal impediments to the application of capital to agricultural operations' (Hancock, 414).

Although Hancock's views were very much at variance with those of John Mitchel and James Fintan Lalor, he cannot be seen as an uncritical defender of 'existing socio-economic relations, including landlordism',[53] at least not as experienced in West Cork in the 1840s. Irish landlords had been roundly condemned by many influential voices in Britain during the Famine years; Hancock and many other members of the Society would have concurred with the views of the English Liberal government that the Irish landlord class should be purged, and that tenants should be compensated for improvements, though their legal rights would be narrowly defined.[54] Other papers by Hancock demanded reforms in the laws relating to limited liability, patent law and the operations of the poor law, especially the less generous treatment of women and children in Ireland relative to Britain.

The theme of optimism crops up repeatedly in the Society's *Journal*, both in the widespread expectations that removing impediments to market forces would automatically result in economic progress, and in the generally upbeat reading of the Irish economy in the immediate post-Famine period. Papers on the condition of Ireland, or on the progress which had been achieved, whether in the past twenty years, or since the Society's foundation, became a staple ingredient. The topic was probably inescapable, given that the Society had been founded at the height of the Famine; it also afforded considerable scope for citing long lists of statistics, almost at random. This theme was first aired in November 1851, when Sir Robert Kane, a vice-president, addressing the opening of the fifth session, claimed that 'we may feel confident that the period of social ignorance and economic error has nearly passed away in Ireland, and that we shall soon participate in the worldly prosperity and moral grandeur secured to the sister kingdom, by conduct based upon economic laws, and guided by generous liberality'. Kane's optimism rested on his faith in the ability of political economy to provide a blueprint for progress – the motive behind the Society's foundation. Like Sir Charles Trevelyan, author of *The Irish Crisis*, Kane chose to interpret the Famine as a potential force for good. He believed that the decline in population should be viewed with 'mixed feelings' because it offered the prospect both of higher wages for labourers and an improved agricultural sector. Emigration offered 'our wanderers that certainty of reward for honest industry which has been found so doubtful here' (Kane, 632).

A similar interpretation is found in an 1854 paper by J.A. Lawson. While ostensibly dealing with Irish agricultural statistics, he also cited the trends in Irish population from 1821 in support of a benign, anti-Malthusian interpretation. According to Lawson, the decline in the rate of population growth between 1821-31 and 1831-41 gave grounds for placing 'more confidence in the operations of nature and the prompting of self-interest'.[55] Lawson regarded the rise in emigration in a positive light, because it removed people from areas of labour-surplus to places where labour was in demand. Like some modern scholars, such as Ó Gráda,[56] Lawson gave a relatively optimistic interpretation of the state of the economy on the eve of the Famine: in 1841, the country was 'in a comparatively prosperous condition and seemed to be improving'. By 1854, Irish agriculture was on a 'surer foundation that it has been at any former time', producing more grass and less cereals, a product mix that suited the soil and climate. The prosperous condition of Irish agriculture undermined the fears of those who had opposed the abolition of the corn laws (Lawson, 677). Recent scholarship confirms Lawson's account of the prosperity of Irish agriculture in 1854: prices rose sharply because of the Crimean War, good weather brought record crop yields. By the late 1850s, however, the value of Irish agricultural output had declined from its 1854 peak.[57]

The most wide-ranging analysis of new-found Irish prosperity can be found in the address given by Mountifort Longfield in November 1855. The paper is liberally laced with data on the number of pigs (then above pre-Famine levels), milch cows and horses; the latter had shown a substantial increase, particularly in the province of Connaught. According to Longfield, the continuing decline in the numbers claiming poor relief, and the fact that average wages in many areas were now double pre-Famine levels, indicated that there had been a steady improvement in the condition of the poor. Longfield contrasted the co-operation that the Irish constabulary experienced in carrying out the annual agricultural census, with the opposition that the Ordnance Survey team had encountered, and the difficulty in completing an agricultural census in England, to suggest that the Irish people were adopting a more positive attitude towards the government. He regarded the large sums remitted by emigrants, more than the sum provided by taxation for poor relief, as yet another positive trend, and he was less fearful than many contemporaries that higher wages would automatically result in drunkenness and idleness, arguing that 'There is no natural reason why a well-paid workman should be more prone to vicious indulgence than his wealthier and idler neighbour.'

Longfield extended his discussion from economics to morality, suggesting that economists were probably inclined 'to attach too much weight to the desire which exists among mankind for the accumulation of wealth'. Many sections of the population had little hope or desire of accumulating wealth; finding solutions to their problems would require 'something more than the ordinary principles of political economy'. He was rather vague as to what these solutions might be, though he suggested that it was necessary to consider how far the state could, without coercion, alter the tastes and habits of the labouring classes and assist them 'in the pursuit of innocent enjoyment'. Longfield believed that if hard-working workmen were given access to 'comfortable and cheerful lodgings, dry and airy public walks, innocent recreations', they would be less likely to frequent 'the dram shop' and even more unwilling to end up in either the workhouse or in prison (Longfield, 726).

MORAL STATISTICS

While land reform was the major economic issue that concerned the Society during its early years, the papers relating to social questions concentrated on crime, alcohol and the poor law. Crime

and its causes, whether hereditary or environmental, attracted
immense attention among statisticians in England and on the
Continent,[58] in part because the subject generated lots of figures,
but also because of growing fears at the apparent threat posed by
the urban masses. In Ireland, there was considerable concern
about agrarian violence, which was fuelled by the regular publication of crime statistics.[59] In England, many social scientists
argued that education offered a means of preventing working-
class crime, though this argument came into question when some
researchers produced statistical evidence, which appeared to
prove the contrary.[60] These themes were examined by the Dublin
Society, most notably in the contributions of James Haughton.
Black remarks that Haughton differed from most active members
in having no academic training or professional concern with
statistical or social investigation. A grain merchant and a Quaker,
Haughton's membership was motivated by a concern with moral
reform. Shortly after the Society was established, there were
moves to establish a Dublin branch of the Howard Society, which
would be involved in 'investigating the nature and effects of legal
punishments'. The plan was abandoned at Haughton's instigation;
he claimed that the aims of the Howard Society came within the
remit of the Statistical Society.

Haughton was also active in campaigns against war, capital
punishment, the opium trade and slavery. In 1852, he contributed
a paper, which examined the question of compensating slave-
owners on its abolition (Haughton, 521). He was well known in
temperance circles in both Britain and Ireland. An associate of
Father Mathew, he served as president of the Dublin Total
Abstinence Society, and as a vice-president of the Irish Temperance
League.[61] During the Society's early years he read several papers
on the relationship between education and crime, which generally
gave the topic an ameiliorist spin. He claimed that there was a
close coincidence between crime and ignorance: 'we might not
unreasonably assume, that if care were taken to impart to all our
population the benefits of a superior education, our criminal
calendar would be light indeed' and believed that crime was often
caused by lack of employment, which in turn arose from a lack of
industrial skills and absence of education. Thus far Haughton's
case appears to be not dissimilar to many contemporary liberal

sociological explanations for crime. However he believed that other factors, such as parental neglect and intemperance, contributed to criminality. For education to be effective, it was necessary to 'break down the habits of the people, those habits of self-indulgence which are obstructions in the way of all progress', in particular, 'the growing desire for intoxicating drinks', which weakened the will to acquire knowledge (Haughton, 528).

In 1854, Haughton gave evidence to a Select Committee of the House of Commons on Public Houses, which formed the basis of a paper which he subsequently read to the Society. On this occasion he argued that 'the drinking customs of our country' led to so much property being destroyed, and so much wealth being frittered away, that it was impossible to distribute resources wisely throughout the community, i.e. without temperance there was obviously little point in paying higher wages to workers. However he was optimistic about the possibility of changing the lifestyle of workers; opening Dublin Zoo on Sundays kept many working men out of public houses.[62] (His step-nephew, Samuel Haughton, who wrote a memoir of James Haughton's life, was a life member of the Royal Zoological Society of Ireland; the restaurant complex was named in his memory.)[63] Haughton's papers constitute the most overt instances of statistics being employed to disguise propaganda as fact. It appears that some members of the Society were uneasy about this, because an addendum to Haughton's 1852 paper noted that: 'It has been objected that this paper which purposes to be Statistics of Crime in connection with Ignorance, enlarges too much on the subject of Intemperance'. In defence, Haughton claimed that 'the drinking customs of society are the true source of the greater part of our social evils' (Haughton, 528).

Other papers expressed a moral agenda, though generally in a more covert manner. In 1856, for example, Richard Hussey Walsh (yet another former Whately professor), read a paper to the British Association meeting at Cheltenham, which challenged the view that crime increased in line with greater prosperity. Walsh distinguished between major and minor crime, i.e. between committals and summary convictions. While there was no apparent relationship between convictions for drunkenness and other minor offences, for more serious offences, i.e. committals, he showed that there was a positive relationship between an increased incidence of crime and economic distress, both in England and Wales and in Ireland. Although the number of committals in Ireland rose sharply during the years 1847-49, Walsh asked 'why, according to the theory of want being the parent of crime, was there not much more crime in Ireland in 1847 than in 1849'. He suggested that destitution was so great in 1847 'as to actually disarm the law', i.e. that many crimes went under-recorded during the years of the Famine. After 1850 the number of convictions showed a dramatic fall (Walsh, 1279). In 1857, James Moncrieff Wilson, an actuary employed by the National Assurance Company, concluded that criminality was strongly associated with poverty and ignorance. Educating the ignorant would reduce crime, not only among that class but among the better classes. However it should not be limited to teaching the 3 Rs: pupils should be schooled in industrial habits, cleanliness and morality and made fully aware of the dangers of drink (Wilson, 1304).

Walsh's paper was unusual because it did not present a clear case for legislation. Although members regularly expressed a belief that the Barrington lectures would bring about a change in working-class attitudes, on the whole they preferred to employ legislation to accelerate the pace of social and moral reform. This approach held obvious attractions; the Society included among its members many peers, Members of Parliament and senior government officials. The Lord Lieutenant frequently attended the inaugural lecture at the beginning of each session. Many members held a legal qualification and the Society devoted considerable attention to jurisprudence.[64] At the beginning of the 1862/63 session, the subjects proposed to Council for discussion included the propriety of appointing either a Minister for Justice or a Board which would be responsible for the revision and consolidation of Irish laws; the growing divergence in statute law between England and Ireland; the need for more comprehensive judicial statistics; the procedures of superior courts; the practice of private bills; circuit arrangements; the constabulary; the Landed Estates Court; bankruptcy and insolvency; the law of lunacy; English divorce law; laws relating to marriage; how far judicial functions should be entrusted to stipendiary magistrates, and the organisation of the legal profession, including the exclusion of solicitors from many legal appointments.[65]

At a Council meeting on 23 April 1870, W.N. Hancock proposed the establishment of a commission to examine the revision of statute laws affecting Ireland. On 7 June 1870, he reported that he had asked a friendly Irish MP (the name is illegible) to prepare a draft bill to expunge obsolete statutes; he was also taking steps to explore the possibility of assimilating the bankruptcy laws in Ireland to those in Britain.[66] In 1874, the Council appointed a committee to consider whether the Council should take steps to bring to the government's notice the various recommendations for amendments in the law, which had been made in the papers read before the Society.[67]

Council regularly debated the merits of setting up a committee to conduct a detailed examination into the differences in the laws between England and Ireland. In 1874, however, when Henry Jephson, a civil servant who was private secretary to the Irish undersecretary, pressed the Council to do so, members were apparently unwilling to undertake the enormous volume of work. In his 1876 presidential address, Jonathan Pim repeated the proposal, and suggested that the inquiry be extended to include Scotland. He believed that Irish provisions were defective in matters such as local government, poor relief and education (Pim, 1064). In a paper on Irish Statue Law Reform in November 1878, Jephson remarked on the 'defects in the Union' between Britain and Ireland, and his distaste for Ireland's anomalous position, which was 'somewhere between union and colonial independence'. This paper included a lengthy list of discrepancies between English and Irish legislation, ranging from the parliamentary and municipal franchise, to local government, the legal status of women and the poor law. Jephson believed that legislation should be enacted simultaneously for England and Ireland, and that as far as possible it should be identical. He remarked that the Society had long accepted the principle of legislative assimilation (Jephson, 604). In 1881, a memorandum which examined the Society's achievements emphasised that it fulfilled 'an important function in keeping the progress of Ireland up to the rest of the United Kingdom in the important subjects which fall within its discussions'.[68]

Most speakers who advocated economic or social reform

during the mid-nineteenth century appear to have favoured assimilating Irish laws and administrative practices to those in England and Wales. In 1854, William Harvey Pim advocated the establishment of reformatories in Ireland, similar to those which were already operating in England (Pim, 1073), while a succession of papers from Dr Edward Dillon Mapother, who had been appointed medical officer of health to Dublin Corporation in 1864,[69] emphasised the need to bring Irish public health legislation into line with the laws in England (Mapother, 835, 838, 839). In 1876, Jonathan Pim argued that Mapother's contributions had been influential in achieving the 1866 Sanitary Act, which brought Irish legislation into line with England (Pim, 1064).

This assimilationist model is clearly spelled out in a series of papers by W.N. Hancock on the Irish poor law. In England, 86 per cent of those who were supported by the poor law received outdoor relief, against 6 per cent of Irish recipients. Seven per cent of the population of Scotland was on outdoor relief, 4 per cent of the population of England, but only 1 per cent in Ireland. Hancock was particularly exercised by the fact that many destitute Irish widows with children were forced to enter the workhouse, because outdoor relief was permitted only when a widow had two or more dependent children, and then only at the discretion of the board of guardians, which was rarely exercised. He argued that, as far as possible, children should be raised within a family; widows should be awarded outdoor relief, and orphans should be boarded out. Hancock contrasted the generous approach adopted in England, where not only widows, but mothers with illegitimate children and wives and children with non-resident husbands, including those whose husbands were in jail, were commonly in receipt of outdoor relief. Outdoor relief was regularly provided when a husband was sick and out of work. According to Hancock, a generous attitude towards outdoor relief not only kept the family intact, and reinforced the natural social order, with mothers caring for their children, it protected widows and grown-up daughters from contact with 'the impenitent and depraved of their sex'. Boarding out orphans – the practice favoured by many charities – reduced mortality, ensured better moral training, and left children better equipped to cope with adult life (Hancock, 406, 424, 448, 457, 496).

In concluding that the workhouse was not the appropriate place to raise children, Hancock reiterated the findings of a study presented to the London Statistical Society in the late 1830s by James Phillips Kay, an assistant poor law commissioner.[70] Hancock believed that more extensive use of outdoor relief would make it easier to bring the Irish land system into line with England. English rural labourers were content to be landless, because the 'liberally and charitably administered poor law in England guards them against many of the vicissitudes of their lot', whereas Irish labourers clung to their plots of land, because these appeared to provide protection against the workhouse. Seasonal migration to Britain meant that Irish labourers were fully conscious of the differences in the operation of the poor law on both islands. Hancock's proposals for reforming the poor law were consistent with the Society's attitude towards economic reform. They were also guaranteed to save money – and for that reason we should not overstate the degree to which they subverted prevailing ideas concerning the role of the state.

NOTES TO CHAPTER ONE

[1]   Donal Kerr, *'A Nation of Beggars'? Priests, People and Politics in Famine Ireland 1846-1852* (Oxford, 1995), p. 92.
[2]   Kevin B. Nowlan, 'The political background', in R.D. Edwards and T. D. Williams (eds), *The Great Famine* (Dublin, 1956), pp. 164-74.
[3]   R.D. Collison Black, *The Statistical and Social Inquiry Society of Ireland. Centenary Volume 1847-1947 with a history of the Society.* Hereafter, Black, *Centenary Volume* (Dublin, 1947). p. 1.
[4]   M.J. Cullen, *The Statistical Movement in Early Victorian Britain. The Foundations of Empirical Social Research* (Brighton, 1975), p.10.
[5]   James Meenan and Desmond Clarke, 'The RDS 1731-1981', in Meenan and Clarke (eds), *The Royal Dublin Society 1731-1981* (Dublin, 1981), p. 22. William Tighe, *Statistical Observations Relative to the County of Kilkenny,* (Dublin, 1802); Isaac Weld, *Statistical Survey of County Roscommon,* (Dublin, 1832). Other works published during these years used the term statistical in a similar fashion, such as Edward Wakefield, *An Account of Ireland, Statistical and Political* 2 vols. (London 1812).
[6]   Theodore M. Porter, *The Rise of Statistical Thinking 1820-1900* (Princeton, New Jersey, 1986), pp. 24-25.
[7]   Cullen, *Statistical Movement*, p. 11.
[8]   Porter, *Rise of Statistical Thinking*, pp. 27-31.
[9]   Cullen, *Statistical Movement*, pp. 77-85, 119-124; Philip Abrams, *The*

Origins of British Sociology 1834-1912 (Chicago, 1968), p. 14.

[10] Cullen, *Statistical Movement*, pp. 77-85, 119-124.

[11] Abrams, *Origins of British Sociology*, p. 13.

[12] Silvana Patriarca, *Numbers and Nationhood. Writing Statistics in Nineteenth-Century Italy* (Cambridge, 1996), p. 54; Porter, *Rise of Statistical Thinking*, p. 27.

[13] Black, *Centenary Volume*, pp. 1-2; 48-70. Black's book provides detailed biographical notes on Whately, Larcom, Longfield, Lawson and O'Hagan.

[14] Abrams, *The Origins of British Sociology*, p. 14.

[15] *Dublin University Magazine*, April 1845, pp. 452-56.

[16] Black, *Centenary Volume,* pp. 1-2.

[17] Antoin E. Murphy, 'Mountifort Longfield's appointment to the chair of political economy in Trinity College, Dublin, 1832', in Antoin E. Murphy (ed.), *Economists and the Irish Economy. From the Eighteenth Century to the Present Day* (Dublin, 1984), pp. 13-24.

[18] D.H. Akenson, *The Irish Education Experiment. The National System of Education in the Nineteenth Century* (London,1970) p. 117.

[19] Thomas A. Boylan and Timothy P. Foley, *Political Economy and Colonial Ireland. The Propagation and Ideological Function of Economic Discourse in the Nineteenth Century* (London, 1992).

[20] For details of the Barrington lectures during the early years, see Boylan and Foley, *Political Economy and Colonial Ireland,* pp. 100-115. The minutes of the Council of the Statistical and Society Inquiry Society of Ireland give details of the recruitment of lecturers; Black, *Centenary Volume*, p. 149, lists Barrington lecturers appointed before 1947.

[21] Report of the Council 1854.

[22] Cullen, *Statistical Movement*, p. 84. In the course of some research concerning the poor law, Nassau Senior discovered that on the basis of current life tables, nearly half of those who had reached their twentieth birthday survived until the age of 60. From this Senior concluded that nearly half the adult population was over 60!

[23] Cullen, *Statistical Movement*, p. 84.

[24] Mary E. Daly, *The Famine in Ireland* (Dublin, 1986), p. 32.

[25] Abrams, *The Origins of British Sociology*, pp. 15-16.

[26] Social Inquiry Society: Report of the Council read at the Annual Meeting, 3 November 1851, pp. 7-8.

[27] Cullen, *Statistical Movement*, pp. 111-16, 123-29.

[28] *Journal of the Dublin Statistical Society*, January 1856. Report of the Council, 19 November 1955, pp. 151-52.

[29] Black, *Centenary Volume*, p. 13.

[30] Black, *Centenary Volume*, pp. 19-20.

[31] Black, *Centenary Volume*, pp. 6,14-21. S. Shannon Millin, *Historical Memoirs*, pp. 55-56.

[32] Meenan and Clarke, 'The RDS 1731-1981', pp. 31-34.

[33] Maurice Craig, 'The Society's Buildings', in Meenan and Clarke (eds), *The RDS*, p. 62.

[34] Black, *Centenary Volume*, p. 17.

[35] W.N. Hancock, *Three Lectures on the Question: Should the Principles of*

Political Economy be Disregarded at the Present Crisis?, (Dublin, 1847).

[36] James S. Donnelly, 'The construction of the memory of the Famine in Ireland and the Irish Diaspora, 1850-1900', *Éire-Ireland,* xxxi, 1 & 2, spring/summer 1997, pp. 27-38.

[37] Robert Kane, *The Industrial Resources of Ireland* (Dublin, 1844). Thomas Davis, 'Udalism and Feudalism', in *Prose Writings of Thomas Davis*, ed. T.W. Rolleston, (London n.d.) p. 60. Mary E. Daly, 'The economic ideals of Irish nationalism: frugal comfort or lavish austerity?', *Éire-Ireland,* winter 1994 p. 83.

[38] John Mitchel (ed.), *Irish Political Economy* (Dublin, 1847).

[39] Amartya Sen, *Poverty and Famines, An Essay in Entitlements* (Oxford, 1981).

[40] Jeffrey G. Williamson, 'Economic convergence: placing post-famine Ireland in comparative perspective', *Irish Economic and Social History,* xxi (1994), pp. 5-27. Williamson noted that his argument concerning Ireland had been anticipated by R.C. Geary (358).

[41] Boyd Hilton, *The Age of Atonement. The Influence of Evangelicalism on Social and Economic Thought 1785-1865* (Oxford, 1988); Charles Trevelyan, *The Irish Crisis,* (London 1850); Peter Gray, 'Ideology and the Famine', in Cathal Portéir (ed.), *The Great Irish Famine* (Cork, 1995), pp. 86-103.

[42] Trevelyan, *The Irish Crisis,* p. 4.

[43] Boylan and Foley, *Political Economy and Colonial Ireland*, pp. 2, 9.

[44] Nowlan, 'The Political Background', in Edwards and Williams (eds), *The Great Famine,* pp. 187-200.

[45] Legislation setting a maximum working day of ten hours for women and young persons who were employed in factories. The bill eventually became law in 1850. Ivy Pinchbeck, *Women Workers and the Industrial Revolution, 1750-1850* (London, 1981 edition), p. 190.

[46] R.D. Collison Black, *Economic Thought and the Irish Question, 1817-1870* (Cambridge, 1960), pp. 77-84.

[47] Black, *Economic Thought*, p. 46.

[48] Black, *Economic Thought*, p. 137.

[49] Isaac Butt, *Protection to Home Industry: Some Cases of its Advantages Considered* (Dublin, 1846); Black, *Economic Thought*, p. 141.

[50] R.D. Collison Black, 'The Irish dissenters and nineteenth-century political economy', in Murphy (ed.), *Economists and the Irish Economy*, pp. 120-35.

[51] Boyd Hilton, *Age of Atonement*, pp. 54-55.

[52] Peter Gray, *The Irish Famine. New Horizons* (London, 1995), p. 53.

[53] Boylan and Foley, *Political Economy and Colonial Ireland*, p. 2.

[54] Black, *Economic Thought*, pp. 35-40.

[55] This interpretation depends on the accuracy of the 1821 and 1831 Censuses. See Joseph Lee, 'On the accuracy of pre-Famine censuses', in Max Goldstrom and L.A. Clarkson (eds), *Irish Population, Economy and Society: Essays in Memory of K.H. Connell* (Oxford, 1981), pp. 37-56.

[56] Cormac Ó Gráda, *Ireland: A New Economic History 1780-1939* (Oxford, 1994), part II.

[57] Michael Turner, *After the Famine. Irish Agriculture 1850-1914* (Cambridge,

1996), pp. 104-09.

[58] Porter, *Rise of Statistical Thinking*, p. 31. For a discussion of the relationship between criminal behaviour and material prosperity in nineteenth century France, see Roger Chartier, 'The Saint-Malo—Geneva Line' in Pierre Nora (ed.), *Realms of Memory. The Construction of the French Past. Volume I Conflicts and Divisions* (New York, 1996), pp. 467-496.

[59] For example *Dublin University Magazine*, May 1847, p. 674; W.E. Vaughan, 'Ireland c. 1870', in W.E. Vaughan (ed.), *A New History of Ireland V. Ireland Under the Union. I. 1801-70* (Oxford, 1989), pp. 864-65.

[60] Cullen, S*tatistical Movement*, pp. 138-43.

[61] Elizabeth Malcolm, *'Ireland Sober, Ireland Free'. Drink and Temperance in Nineteenth-Century Ireland* (Dublin, 1986), pp. 128, 134, 168, 194-95; Black, *Centenary Volume*, pp. 66-67 and p. 5.

[62] James Haughton, *Statistics (with some Additions) given in Evidence before a Select Committee of the House of Commons on Public Houses* i, 39 (1855).

[63] W.J.E. Jessop, 'Samuel Haughton: A Victorian polymath', *Hermathena*, vol. xcvi, (winter 1973) pp. 5-26.

[64] Colum Kenny, 'Paradox or pragmatist? 'Honest Tristram Kennedy (1805-85): lawyer, educationalist, land agent and Member of Parliament', *Proceedings of the Royal Irish Academy*, Section C, vol. 92, no. 1 (1992), p. 19.

[65] Council Minutes, 5 November 1862.

[66] Council Minutes, 23 April 1870; 7 June 1870.

[67] Council Minutes 14 April 1874.

[68] 'What the Statistical and Social Inquiry Society of Ireland has effected (1847-1880)', *JSSISI,* viii, Jan 1881 (Appendix to Report of Council), p. 152.

[69] Mary E. Daly, *Dublin: the Deposed Capital. A Social and Economic History, 1860-1914* (Cork, 1984), p. 255.

[70] Abrams, *Origins of British Sociology*, p. 21.

CHAPTER TWO

'Facts and Arguments', 1860-1920

The middle of the nineteenth century proved to be the heyday for social inquiry societies in Britain and in North America. In 1865, the American Social Science Association was founded by 'genteel New England intellectuals and reformers who wanted both to understand and to improve their rapidly changing society'.[1] The Statistical Society's belief that it had a mission, as a mid-Victorian pressure group, to campaign for reforming legislation, was shared by the National Association for the Promotion of Social Science, which was founded in 1857 and was regarded by its first president, the British Liberal peer Lord Brougham, as a lever of legislation.[2] Both societies investigated a similar range of issues. In 1858, the Statistical Society expressed the belief that: 'The prejudice which has hitherto prevailed against any inquiries beyond the strict limits of Political Economy, lest they might be found to trench on politics, will be removed when the leading statesmen of England are found patronising an Association for the Development of Social Science'.[3]

A similar air of triumphalism can be detected in the vice-presidential address by James Anthony Lawson at the opening of the 1858/59 Session. When the Society was founded in 1847, according to Lawson, free trade had been seen as very much a party political issue, 'whereas now no man can be found to stand up in any society to say that these principles are to be disputed; we argue on them as the very alphabet of economic science'. The Society had contributed 'in some degree' to the creation of 'something like a sound public opinion upon economic and social questions', supplying 'the wholesome food of rational discussion, instead of the unwholesome diet of party politics'. Lawson claimed that 'there is hardly a child in the national schools that would not establish the fallacy' of the 'levelling doctrines' of socialism. Meanwhile the Barrington lectures enabled men in many provincial towns to refute the heresies of 'unconvertible paper currency or a project for land banks'. Legislation had been passed implementing many of the reforms, which had been advocated in papers read to the Society. Lawson claimed that 'an enlightened public' increasingly realised that this was the way to bring about both institutional or legislative change, rather than by embarking on 'great political agitation or by the moving of masses'. He expressed satisfaction that the Society's membership included 'all classes and orders – the merchant, the professional man, and the land-holder', though apparently no labourers, small farmers or tradesmen. Meetings had remained immune from sectarian and political bitterness – presumably because of the limited socio-economic background from which the members were drawn. The formation of the National Association in England, and the growing number of communications received from similar bodies in both the US and on the Continent proved that the Society was part of a wider international movement (Lawson, 673).

In the twenty years or so following Lawson's triumphant paper, many of the underlying premises, that had prompted the establishment of the Dublin Statistical Society, came into question. The forces for change were twofold; some were specific to Ireland, others reflected cultural and intellectual influences, which were operating throughout Europe and North America. It was becoming less obvious that Irish interests were automatically best assured by integrating its laws with those in England; the effectiveness of social investigation as an instrument of change, as opposed to 'great political agitation', seemed problematical; the air of optimism that appears to have characterised the years immediately after the Famine was no longer apparent, while the scientific credentials of statistical investigation were being questioned.

The first doubts about the progress being made by the Irish economy came in the early 1860s. Although the agricultural depression of the years 1859-62 has been largely ignored by historians,[4] Black has shown that economists at that time were deeply divided over whether the decline in agricultural output was caused merely by bad weather, or should be seen as a reflection of 'deep-seated defects in social organisation'.[5] During the 1850s several papers interpreted the high level of emigration in a positive light, and suggested that it would be a short-term phenomenon. This argument was thoroughly refuted by D. Caulfield Heron in January 1862. Heron, a barrister and professor of jurisprudence and political economy at Queen's College Galway, was MP for County Tipperary from 1870 to 1874.[6] According to Heron, 'A progressive decrease in population and in the production of wealth is a sign that something is not right in the legal and social conditions of a country'. As evidence that the wealth of Ireland was declining, he presented data showing falling crop acreage and livestock numbers, though the decline in livestock numbers was only of one of two years' duration. Heron claimed that emigration had removed 'the best educated, the most energetic of the peasantry'. As a result of the legal conditions governing land tenure, those remaining were left with little more than turf and potatoes. 'And whenever turf and potatoes fail, famine, eviction, and assassination again become the normal conditions belonging to the tenure of land in Ireland'.

The condition of Ireland in the years since the Famine gave Heron little cause for joy: 'In the ruin represented by starvation, emigration, judicial sales and agrarian murders, the amount of human misery represented by the statistics of Ireland for the last fifteen years I trust will ever retain a melancholy pre-eminence in European history'. Whereas others had spoken favourably about the workings of the Encumbered Estates Court, Heron claimed that its statistics of land sales ranked with statistics of agrarian murder, as 'statistics of ruin'. Sheriffs' sales and bankruptcy sales could never be regarded as signs of a flourishing economy. This paper provided an extremely bleak account of post-Famine Ireland: 'institution after institution is disappearing', the number of peasants had fallen, as has the number of barristers and students attending Trinity College Dublin. Ireland had failed to share in the prosperity experienced by the rest of the United Kingdom. Blame for such misery rested with the land system. Ireland needed 'independent and prosperous peasantry, such as are found among the vine dressers of Vevay, and the hardy mountaineers of Fribourg and Berne'.

Much of Heron's paper reads like a concise summary of what was to become the nationalist interpretation of Irish economic history, epitomised by the writings of George O'Brien (president of the Society 1942-46).[7] Indeed, Heron ranged far beyond economics to produce a paper, which would fully meet Brendan Bradshaw's plea for recognition of the 'catastrophic dimension of Irish history'.[8] Beginning with Edmund Spenser and Sir John Davis, he describes the complete subjugation of the Irish people by the late seventeenth century, the dispossession of the native landowners and the chronic poverty which prevailed.

> Yet the future historian will characterise the three centuries of Irish history ending with 1850 as a period of rebellion, civil war, penal laws, and famine, during which more human misery was suffered upon the number of square miles called Ireland than upon any other geographical district of the same size in the world.
>
> The dominions over which Queen Victoria rules have been for some time at the height of a prosperity unrivalled in the history of mankind. One class of her subjects does not share that prosperity. The Irish peasantry are still the worst clothed, the worst lodged, and the worst fed in Europe. The savage and heathen races in Central Africa have better food and lodging than the civilised and Christian cultivators of land in Ireland. The historical events of the seventeenth and eighteenth centuries are partly the causes of this condition.

History caused Heron to conclude that the causes of Irish poverty lay far beyond economic matters: 'The natural progressive development of a people has been rendered impossible in Ireland by foreign historical causes', in particular the presence of 'the foreign-historical element' which 'is not yet amalgamated with the people' (Heron, 545). We can only regret that the *Journal* did not summarise the discussion following this paper, which brought the Society squarely into the realm of political debate, contrary to its laws. We can however read the counter-arguments put by Randal McDonnell (McDonnell, 788) and W.N. Hancock, whom Black notes was 'now a semi-official advisor on economic questions' to the Irish administration. Both McDonnell and Hancock (whose paper was not read to the Society) regarded the distressed conditions of the early 1860s as a short-term phenomenon; they countered Heron's arguments that the Irish economy was in decline by citing statistics showing a rise in the level of bank deposits, and in customs and excise returns (McDonnell, 788).[9] Black concluded that the parties were arguing at cross purposes:

> But behind these statistics lie two radically different views of social organisation. The official view, as represented by Hancock, envisaged prosperity in terms of increased net returns, considering the means by which these were obtained as relatively unimportant. The nationalist view, moderately represented by Heron, considered security on the land for the existing population more important than increasing productivity.[10]

Heron regarded declining population as an indicator of the poor condition of the Irish economy. The issues raised in this argument – by what criteria should Irish economic well-being be assessed, and what are the causes of Irish economic decline? (are they rooted deep in the Irish past, or merely a reflection of current economic conditions?) – remain at the heart of most debates on the condition of Ireland, which have taken place since the Famine. Most papers read to the Society have been closer to the spirit of Hancock than to that of Heron.

A CRISIS OF CONFIDENCE IN POLITICAL ECONOMY

Although the disagreement between Heron, Hancock and McDonnell related to the condition of Ireland, this uncertainty as to whether the Irish economy was progressing or in decline, and the inability to reconcile conflicting arguments by citing statistics – all protagonists quoted statistics for their own ends – was an indication that statistics could no longer be trusted to provide an objective answer to contentious questions. As a result of the Great Depression, which began in 1873 and lasted until the mid-1890s, the belief that political economy provided the key to prosperity receded (and not only in Ireland). This event appears to have marked a dividing line between the earlier interest shown by classical economists in economic growth, and the preoccupation of their neo-classical successors with equilibrium.[11] This change of direction can be seen in a paper, that the distinguished British economist Stanley Jevons (an honorary member) read to the Society in August 1878, on the causes of recurrent commercial cycles, where Jevons outlined what subsequently came to be known as the sun-spot cycle. The argument that economies were subject to periodic crises at ten-yearly intervals, which appeared to be caused by the weather (Jevons, 607) and were consequently beyond the power of man was a far cry from the optimism, that Whately had expressed at the foundation of the Society. Abrams claims that the centenary celebration in London in 1876 of the publication of Adam Smith's *The Wealth of Nations* 'was from all accounts a dismal affair', despite the fact that the attendance at a special meeting of the Political Economy Club in London included Gladstone, Léon Say, the French Minister for Finance and grandson of the great economist of that name, and the Belgian economist Emile de Lavaelaye.

The centenary of the publication of *The Wealth of Nations* coincided with a serious attempt by a group of natural scientists, led by the geneticist Francis Galton, to disband Section F of the British Association, the section in which papers relating to economics and statistics were presented. They asserted that few of the subjects discussed by Section F fell 'within the meaning of the word "scientific"'. Galton also claimed that many papers in Section F attracted listeners who lacked scientific training; consequently the discussions were apt to become 'even less scientific than they would otherwise have been'.[12] Although Galton is probably best remembered as the founder of eugenics, a discipline with dubious scientific credentials, he has also been described as 'the parent of modern statistical methods'. He played a major role in developing the use of regression, correlation coefficients, probability and frequency curves as analytical techniques.[13] Galton's misgivings, which were shared by some other statisticians, reflected growing dissatisfaction with probability as a predictor of social behaviour, and their efforts to devise a more reliable mechanism.[14]

In 1878, the British Association held its annual meeting in Dublin as a guest of the Statistical Society. When Mr Gordon, secretary elect of the British Association, met the Council of the Statistical Society in November 1877 to discuss arrangements for the meeting, he explained that the Council of the Association had decided to retain the Economic Section, 'notwithstanding the questions which had been raised as to the scientific character of the papers'.[15] At the Dublin meeting of the British Association, the ever-resourceful W.N. Hancock read a paper on the value of *The Wealth of Nations* for the present day. In what was presumably an attempt to counter criticism within the British Association, Hancock argued that Adam Smith was not 'a mere economist' but someone with a breadth of views, whose approach was never 'too exclusively deductive'. This argument appears to concede the rather unscientific nature of economics, while making some concessions towards Galton's strongly empirical line. Hancock referred specifically to Smith's writings on the division of labour, his 'wise, good and humane principles as to human labour' and his opposition to slavery or any form of indentured labour. He also argued against what he termed 'the abuse of the free trade principle – what is called free trade in education' (presumably the narrow application of market forces to this subject) – and his own belief in the value of providing better access to education for gifted people, and resources to support research (Hancock, 405).

This paper does not rank among Hancock's strongest. Ironically these themes were discussed at the same meeting, with infinitely greater effect by Hancock's old friend, John Kells Ingram. Ingram was President of the Statistical Society in 1878, and presumably for that reason he also served as president of battle-scarred Section F of the British Association during its Dublin meeting. Ingram conceded that the debate within the British Association over the scientific status of economics and statistics 'is only the counterpart, in a more limited sphere, of a crisis in the history of economic science, which is apparent on the face of English – and ... not of English only, but of European – thought.' He argued against Galton's allegations that economics was lacking in scientific rigour, maintaining that it 'is the most difficult of all the sciences, because it is that in which the phenomena dealt with are most complex and dependent on the greatest variety of conditions, and in which, accordingly, appearances are most deceitful, and error takes the most plausible forms'. Ingram claimed that the doctrines of political economy were distrusted by the working classes, largely because of the 'not altogether unfounded belief that it has tended to justify too absolutely existing social arrangements, and that its study is often recommended with the real, though disguised, object of repressing popular aspirations after a better order of things'. He cited with approval Auguste Comte's criticism of political economy: that it tended to study economic matters in isolation, was unduly abstract in its reasoning, overly reliant on deduction, and enunciated its conclusions in too absolute a manner (Ingram, 593). In place of a narrow, abstract deductive economics, Ingram posited a scientific sociology, which would be concerned with social phenomena as a whole.[16] Black has rightly described this paper as 'one of the most widely-acclaimed addresses ever given before this Statistical Society' (Black, 71). Ingram was undoubtedly reacting against the limitations of single-cause explanations for social phenomena, which had been a major factor in discrediting statistics as a tool for social analysis, i.e. lack of education was obviously not the sole explanation for criminal behaviour, though it may have played a role. (This shortcoming would be met to some extent by advances in statistical techniques, notably regression analysis). On the occasion of Ingram's death in 1908, C. Litton Faulkiner noted that 'If Ingram has any criticism to pass on the early stages of the Society's activity, it was, perhaps that, as was natural enough in the circumstances of the time, the bent of our work was mainly in the direction of the discussion of purely economic problems, as distinguished from those social questions which appealed so strongly to his own sympathies' (Falkiner, 304).

Ingram's defence of a more holistic approach towards socio-economic investigation, and his opposition to narrow specialisation, reflects what actually happened in Ireland, where the Statistical Society survived as a broadly based institution, though, as Black suggests,[17] it may have fallen into the doldrums during the 1890s. In Britain, however, most provincial statistical societies disappeared, with the notable exception of the Manchester Statistical Society.[18] In 1887, the London Statistical Society evolved into the Royal Statistical Society – a much more specialist organisation which was primarily interested in the technical analysis of statistics. The collapse of the National Association for the Promotion of Social Science in the mid-1880s, at a time when, as Cullen has noted, social research was about to be transformed by men such as Charles Booth,[19] is testimony to the growing tendency to organise intellectual activity on the basis of specialist disciplines. There was no longer a role for the National Association, 'whose discussions betrayed little sense of anxiety about stepping outside one's proper sphere or, apart from frequent wrangles over the practical teachings of political economy, even any acknowledgement of the existence of putatively authoritative academic disciplines'.

The intellectual frustration posed by the need to cram papers covering the gamut of economics, sociology and social policy into the crowded schedules of Section F of the British Association proved intolerable to many trained professionals, who were probably also losing patience with the contributions of amateur members. Specialist bodies such as the Royal Historical Society and the British Economics Association, which was the forerunner to the Royal Economics Society, were established in 1868 and 1890 respectively.[20] In Britain, the year 1903 marked the formal parting of the ways between statistics and sociology, with the founding of the Sociological Society.[21] When the American Social Science Association (ASSA) died in 1909, the initiative in economic and social research passed to the universities and to professional bodies, such as the American Economics Association, the American Historical Association and the American Academy of Political and Social Science. Like the Statistical and Social Inquiry Society of Ireland, the ASSA's membership had included people from all walks of life, including business and political leaders. The newer bodies tended to be dominated by university-based professionals.[22]

Such developments may have left the Statistical and Social Inquiry Society of Ireland in a rather isolated position. No longer the Irish variant of a prevalent international intellectual phenomenon, its survival appeared to reflect the failure of a corresponding growth of professionalisation within the social sciences in Ireland. The small size of the country, the handicaps that sectarian divisions imposed on Irish university development, and the failure to develop a civil service whose elite was dominated by university graduates,[23] meant that the Statistical Society continued to play an important role in Irish intellectual life well into the twentieth century. In this respect a number of factors ensured the survival of a multi-disciplinary Society such as the Statistical: the absence of professional associations of economists, sociologists and social workers, the small numbers of professional social scientists, combined with the fact that many Irish economists held qualifications in disciplines such as law,[24] while most leading Irish lawyers had been educated in the humanities or the social sciences. The historicist approach which was prominent in sections of Irish political economy was also a contributory factor.[25] The lack of specialist Irish academic periodicals also meant that its *Journal* was one of the few outlets available for the publication of academic papers within Ireland. In 1881, a decision was taken to reorganise the Council by appointing sectional secretaries for municipal law, suppression of crime, education, public health, social economy and trade (one section) and art – a list which reflects the wide-ranging, if dilettante interests of members. They shared a common interest in Ireland and its problems – whether these related to trade, taxation, public health, the care of orphaned children or municipal law.

The revolution in statistics, in which several scholars with Irish connections such as George Boole (professor of mathematics at Queen's College Cork), Francis Ysidro Edgeworth, 'the poet of statisticians', and W.S. Gosset (an employee of Guinness's brewery who published his statistical work under the nom-de-plume of Student), played a significant role, had little if any impact on the Society.[26] Although Edgeworth was an honorary member, he never read a paper; neither Boole nor Gosset appear to have had any association. Correlation coefficients and frequency curves, even the use of elementary probability were unknown during the nineteenth century. The first paper to deal with statistics in any technical sense was read in 1889 by Robert E. Matheson (assistant registrar-general and one of the commissioners responsible for the 1881 Census). It described the procedures involved in collecting, tabulating and summarising large quantities of official statistics and it contains a fascinating description and illustrations of primitive calculating aids, such as arithmometers, racks for cross-totting and extended slide-rules, but says little about the intellectual potential of the discipline (Matheson, 842). The first paper to discuss statistical methods was one in 1924 by R.C. Geary on sampling techniques (Geary, 360).

The Society showed intermittent interest in the compilation of statistical series, though lack of resources meant that its intentions were not always realised. The Transactions of the First Session of the Dublin Society included a 'Notice of a Plan for the Systematic Collection of Irish Economic Statistics', which would be drawn by a Committee, but nothing further is heard of this proposal, or of the suggestion that the Society should collect data on regional wage rates.

The campaign to extend the civil registration of births, marriages and deaths to Ireland proved more fruitful, because this entailed lobbying, rather than an actual research project. Given that most continental pioneers of the statistics such as Adolphe Quetelet, regarded the compilation of accurate data on demography as the cornerstone of the new statistical science, the Society's interest in this subject is unsurprising. Civil registration was introduced in England in 1837. Although an Act passed in 1844 provided for the introduction of vital registration in Ireland, it was regarded as offensive by the catholic clergy, because it deemed all marriages of a catholic and a protestant, performed by catholic clergymen, to be illegal. A bill introduced in 1857 to rectify this problem was lost with the collapse of the Aberdeen government. In 1858, the Council of the Statistical Society set up a committee to examine the matter. As an indication of the Society's perceived influence, Arthur Moore, who had submitted a registration Bill in 1856, joined the Society in order to further his campaign (Moore, 890). In December 1862, the National Association for the Promotion of Social Science asked the Statistical Society to co-operate in preparing a Bill for the registration of births, deaths and marriages in Ireland, and Jonathan Pim and W.N. Hancock were part of a joint deputation.[27] Vital registration began in 1864.

Given that Sir William Wilde and Thomas Larcom were among the founding members, the Society's apparent lack of interest in the compilation of the early Censuses of Population is puzzling In 1871, the occupational tables of the Irish Census were altered to bring them into line with the English Census, a practice to which the officials responsible for the Irish Census objected.[28] Neither the Council minutes nor the Journal refer to the matter, and there is no evidence that they were consulted about the changes. In 1874, however, the Lord Lieutenant asked for the Council's response to a proposal from the Registrar General to introduce changes in the form in which agricultural statistics were published.[29] In 1877, Baron Emly, formerly William Monsell, who served as president of the Society during the years 1872-75, drew the attention of Council to the lack of uniformity in the compilation of the Irish, English and Scottish Censuses of Population. Although the Council proposed the establishment of a Census Committee, consisting of Baron Emly, Dr Abraham – a member of the Irish Census Commission from 1861 to 1881 – and other interested members, it is unclear whether they compiled a report.[30]

The year 1880 marked the first occasion when a paper to the Society contained informal suggestions for items to be included in the forthcoming Census. The proposal to collect data on the occupation of land in every townland – a kind of Irish Domesday Book which would be used in the formulation of agrarian policies – was successful (Jephson, 605).[31] In 1888, the Council considered a memorandum on census returns prepared by the distinguished economist Alfred Marshall and 'Mr Booth' (presumably Charles Booth) and concluded that the report contained useful and practical suggestions which 'would considerably increase the value of public censuses' if they were adopted.[32] Since the contents of the memorandum are unknown, it is not clear whether it was implemented.

From 1882-83, when the registrar-general, Sir Thomas Grimshaw, read a paper, which drew on data collected in the 1881 Census, the Society generally either heard a paper which anticipated the holding of a Census of Population, or received a report on the preliminary conclusions from a member of the Society who was actively involved in the process (Grimshaw, 395; Matheson, 844). Black noted that the papers presented to the Society in the 1890s and the early 1900 indicate a growing interest in more statistical subjects.[33]

In May 1911, shortly before Census night, the registrar-general, Sir William Thompson, read a paper which emphasised the importance of the Census as a tool of public policy: 'The inquiries of a Census should lead to improvements being effected for the population under each of the various headings, such as education, house accommodation, industrial occupations, etc.' (Thompson, 1247). Such contributions reflected a continuing faith in the value of statistical information to provide a rational basis for policy, which was reminiscent of the founding fathers of the Society. However, neither Thompson nor the earlier papers relating to the Census of Population showed any interest in the potential offered by more discriminating statistical techniques. The Society's *Journal* contains nothing comparable to Charles Booth's paper to the Royal Statistical Society, which attempted to standardise the occupational data in the English Census for the years 1841-81. When Booth provided a comparable reclassification for the Irish Census data at the request of the Royal Commission on Financial Relation, it was published by the Department of Agriculture.[34]

THE SOCIETY AND THE LAND QUESTION

Although the Statistical Society escaped the centrifugal forces that were ravaging similar bodies in Britain and in the United States, it had to confront the problems of diminishing enthusiasm for statistical inquiry and the impact of changes in Irish politics. The Society seems to have relied unduly on a small coterie of active members, who had been involved from its early years. W.N. Hancock, for example, presented seven papers in 1860 – including one on a 'Plan for Obviating the Identification of Luggage at Kingstown and Holyhead, and so accelerating the Through Traffic between London and Dublin' (Hancock, 467) – which suggests diminishing intellectual returns. By the late 1870s, there was less scope for optimism about the prospects for economic progress. Although Jonathan Pim's presidential address in 1876/77 presented an encyclopaedic list of favourable changes that had taken place in Ireland in recent years, there was an apologetic tone to his paper, as Pim defended himself against accusations that he had painted the condition of Ireland in 'roseate hues'.

Between the year 1847 and the passing of the 1870 Land Act, the Society presented almost forty papers on the Irish land question (Pim, 1064). Until 1860, British government policy on this issue is best summarised by the phrase 'free trade in land', i.e. the application of market forces, and the extension of signed legal contracts to cover all aspects of tenurial relations.[35] This process culminated in the passage of the Cardwell and Deasy Acts in 1860.[36] In 1870, however, the attempt to place landlord-tenant relations on a contractual basis, and to bring Irish land law into conformity with English practices, was swept aside by Gladstone's Land Act, which gave legal recognition to custom as a mechanism for regulating tenure. This was a response to the agricultural depression of the early 1860s, coupled with the aftermath of the Fenian uprising, the growing attack on landlordism within the ranks of English liberalism, and the impact of John Stuart Mill's public advocacy of fixity of tenure for Irish tenant farmers in 1868.[37] Several members of the Society played a major role, both in the evolution of land policy up to 1860, and in its subsequent change of direction. In 1848, the Society established a committee to examine legal impediments to the transfer of land, and three members of this committee, Lawson, Hancock and Longfield, gave evidence before the parliamentary committee whose report ultimately led to the enactment of the 1848 Encumbered Estates Act.[38]

In a pioneering article on the evolution of official attitudes towards landlord-tenant relations, published in 1974, Clive Dewey claimed that Hancock shifted from being 'a passionate critic of tenant-right before 1865' to become 'an equally passionate advocate of tenant-right thereafter'. This statement needs some qualification. Hancock was obviously familiar with the Ulster Custom, (the implicit tolerance by Ulster landlords of an outgoing tenant's right to sell the interest in his holding), because his older brother John, who also presented several papers to the Society (Hancock, 399-401), was estate agent to the Earl of Lurgan, and the custom applied on this estate. W.N. Hancock had never opposed a tenant's right to compensation for improvement, provided the matter was regulated by prior agreement with the landlord. In later years, however, he began to advocate the recognition of tenurial arrangements that were based on customs and whose roots were believed to lie deep in the Irish past.[39] According to Black, Hancock and Larcom, (undersecretary for

Ireland, i.e. the most senior civil servant in Dublin Castle), who were both active in the Society, 'were probably the most influential people in the framing of economic policy for Ireland' in the early 1860s. The two land acts passed in 1860, follow closely on 'suggestions for Legislation', which Hancock presented to Cardwell, the Irish Chief Secretary, in October 1859.

Black suggests that there is evidence that by 1863 both Hancock and Larcom were showing greater sympathy with tenant right, as a result of the problems which tenants faced in meeting their rents during the harsh years of the early 1860s. Black also refers to the influence of Mountifort Longfield's presidential address at the opening of the 1864 session of the Society, when, in the presence of the Lord Lieutenant, the Earl of Carlisle, he expressed the opinion that, although fixity of tenure was 'wild and impracticable … the claim for compensation for improvements is one that ought not lightly to be passed over' (Longfield, 727).[40] The fact that Longfield was a judge attached to the Landed Estates Court – the court responsible for the sale of encumbered estates – lent greater significance to this address. In 1860, Hancock read a paper to the Society concerning the case of O'Fay versus Burke, a dispute between Canon O'Fay, parish priest of Craughwell, Co. Galway, and his landlord concerning compensation for improvements. The contents suggest that Hancock was becoming aware of the disadvantages of regulating landlord-tenant relations by purely contractual arrangements (Hancock, 469).

Although tenant right had been an issue in Irish politics since the 1840s, successive British governments appear to have shown little interest until the 1860s when the combined impact of the radical Fenian movement and the moderate constitutional movement, the National Association, forced Lord Palmerston, the British prime minister, to establish a select committee in 1865 to examine the working of Irish land legislation. Palmerston was an Irish landlord, who showed little interest in social reform; however his agent John Kincaid was a member of the Society.[41]

Some months later in February 1866, Randal William McDonnell, a barrister, presented a 'Report on the Impediments to Express Contracts as to the Occupation of Land in Ireland'. The report had been commissioned by the Council, on the initiative of Jonathan Pim, and advance copies were circulated to Council members. McDonnell was paid a fee for carrying out this research. On 30 January 1866, shortly before the paper was due to be read to the Society, Lord Rosse, a vice-president, wrote to the Council resigning his membership, because the Society was 'about to take up the Land Question', and he wished to guard himself 'from being supposed in any way to be a party to the agitation of that question within the rules of the Society'. The Earl objected to the Society 'entering at all upon the Land Question', because it was a political issue and therefore precluded by its rules. In reply, the Council claimed that

> ... by the rules and practice of the Society its proceedings have never been limited to the mere collection of facts, without applying the principles of Political Economy and the facts of statistics to disputed social questions. The only restriction recognised by the rules of the Society is that discussion should not involve *party* [underlined in original] politics or religious polemic.

The Council noted that the Society had first discussed the land question in response to the Report of the Devon Commission. Because successive governments had introduced legislation relating to land, it determined – rather disingenuously – 'that the land question has never been considered by the Council as one of party politics'. During the course of the 1848/49 Session, when the Earl of Rosse was already a member, the Society heard eight papers on the Irish land question, including papers on tenant right and on compensation for improvements. The papers read to the Society on the land question contained diverse views. A variety of opinions and freedom of discussion were essential if social questions were to be treated in a scientific manner; the Council did not consider itself to be responsible for these views. Nevertheless, the Council appears to have gone to considerable lengths to mollify the Earl of Rosse and the proofs of McDonnell's paper were modified to take account of the Earl's objections. The Council claimed that other members had objected to the same passages – which regrettably it failed to identify. Although the Earl withdrew his resignation, he noted that 'No doubt the Land Question is not a " Party Question" between Whigs and Tories; but I fear it is a very exciting party question as between those who have no land and those who have'.[42]

The Earl's parting shot serves only to confuse the issue, because the offending report was a technical document, which examined the difficulties that had arisen in compensating tenants for improvements carried out to their holdings. It said nothing about the distribution of land, or about landless labourers. Using as its starting point an earlier report by Robert Longfield to the Social Inquiry Society (Longfield, 732), McDonnell indicated the impact of recent changes in legislation and drew attention to some matters which had been 'less prominent' in Longfield's report. Reading through this detailed and rather arid analysis of impediments to contracts between landlords and tenants, where the owner is either an infant, a lunatic or a married woman, it is impossible to detect any whiff of political controversy, though the report suggests that considerable obstacles existed to compensating tenants for improvements. McDonnell reached the conclusion that the 1860 Landed Property (Improvement) Ireland Act, (the Cardwell Act), 'has, in practice, proved a dead letter' (McDonnell, 787).[43] It may have been this suggestion that the contractual approach to landlord-tenant relations was not working, which triggered a protest from the Earl of Rosse.

This incident took place at a time when the Council was concerned about falling attendance at meetings. The controversy over McDonnell's report also led the Council to re-examine its procedures, to ensure that future publications would distinguish between the relative responsibility of the author and the Council.[44] Before 1866, each volume of the Journal contained the sentence 'No communication is read unless the Secretaries, or two of them certify that they consider it in accordance with the rules and objects of the Society'. Subsequent volumes carried an additional sentence, 'The Council thus sanction only the general scope of the papers; but for any particular opinion, representation of facts, or train of reasoning in a paper or report the author is alone responsible'.

This was not the only occasion when politics intruded on the Society. On 4 December 1866, the Council rejected an application from Alderman John Gregg to read a paper on the more equitable adjustment of the municipal franchise, because 'in the present position of the franchise question (a reference to the 1867 Reform

Act which was then being drafted) the subject involved topics likely to produce discussion connected with party politics'. Although Alderman Gregg countered that his paper was in no way connected with party politics, the Council persisted in its decision.[45] In 1873 a paper by Henry L. Jephson, a civil servant, on the Irish railway question was read before the matter was discussed in Parliament (Jephson, 603), but another paper on the railway question was rejected in favour of a paper on higher education for women, which was judged to be 'more interesting at present'.[46]

Higher education for women was an acceptable subject, presumably because it was not a matter of great political controversy. Despite the Society's original intention of investigating education, the subject was rarely discussed, with the exception of peripheral aspects such as reformatories and workhouse schools, though education was a major preoccupation for comparable English societies. Matters such as the quality of Irish national schooling, school attendance, teacher training, and access to secondary or superior schooling were ignored, because they crossed the denominational fault-lines of Irish society. The university question, one of the long-standing preoccupations of these years, was also ignored, with the exception of a brief reference in Lord O'Hagan's address to the Social Science Congress in Dublin in 1881 (O'Hagan, 998). However, the Society continued to discuss the Irish land question. Yet the concluding remarks of D.C. Heron's paper on the 1870 Land Act suggest that he was venturing into sensitive territory:

> The Land Act has disappointed many, and great expectations have not been realised. A further development of tenant-right is hoped for; and I purpose to consider in another paper the further claims of the tenants of Ireland. But the tenants of Ireland understand that Gladstone's bill is worth to them forty millions of money. The Statistical Society has a right to pronounce an opinion upon the act which embodies many of the principles year after year promulgated within these walls; and we trust that recent legislation will tend to the tranquillity of our country, and that in every county in Ireland there may be a wealthy resident gentry, living in peace and happiness amongst a prosperous and independent tenantry' (Heron, 547).

It is not surprising that Heron gave a guarded welcome to the 1870 Act, because in a paper to the Society in 1852 he had anticipated its key provisions. Heron approached the subject from the perspective of natural law, without referring directly to the Ulster custom. Most of the citations in this article refer to legal commentaries and to case law. Heron adopted a historical approach, charting the evolution in property rights from early times, as in ancient Germany where property belonged in common to the tribe to the feudal system. Whereas current legal practice guaranteed a tenant's ownership of improvements carried out to non-agricultural properties, such as a soap-boiling plant or a colliery, the residual influence of feudal law left landlords as absolute owners in the case of improvements to agricultural property. Heron regarded this position as 'injurious to society at large'; removing this power would be akin to the abolition of slavery, or ending a monopoly. He proposed that 'in the absence of agreement to the contrary, the property in the improvement should be vested in the tenant, and that no such tenant should be evicted without being reimbursed the full value of his improvements at the time of his eviction'. Heron contrasted the condition of a man who rented land without security: 'his cabin is only half thatched; his field are slovenly; whatever money he has is hid … he is clothed in rags', with the secure peasant: an 'indefatigable worker [who] waters the earth with the sweat of his brow … takes from the hours of the day all that human strength can give to industry.' Heron's argument did not depend on drawing a distinction between England and Ireland. The principle could apply equally to England, indeed he suggests that 'enlightened judges' in England have favoured tenants in exceptional cases (Heron, 549). It is no coincidence that Heron's argument was based on legal precedent, given that Heron held the chair of jurisprudence and political economy at Queen's College Galway.[47]

Peasant proprietorship was first discussed by the Society in 1862, in a paper by Henry Dix Hutton, a lawyer and a former honorary secretary. Hutton was very much in favour of peasant proprietorship; he travelled to Prussia to investigate how the reforms introduced earlier in the century by Hardenberg and Stein had fared (Hutton, 580, 581). The subject came to prominence during the 1877/78 session. G. Shaw Lefevre MP and President of the Statistical Society of London, who had been responsible for the appointment of a parliamentary committee that had inquired into the comparative failure of the so-called Bright Clauses of the 1870 Land Act (the clauses which enabled peasants to buy their farms, with state-assisted loans),[48] published in the *Journal* some highly favourable descriptions of visits to farms, that had recently been purchased by former tenants of the Church of Ireland. He subsequently addressed the Society on the merits of peasant proprietorship, as did Hugh Law MP another members of this parliamentary committee. Both MPs referred to the experience in continental countries, and to the Channel Island of Guernsey – an analogy which Parnell was also to use as a role model for Ireland[49] – where Law argued that there was an almost complete absence of pauperism because farmers owned their land (Hancock, 454, 480; Shaw Lefevre, 1135, 1136).

Although such papers were influential, and some members of the Society gave evidence to the Bessborough Commission, which was established in 1880 to inquire into the relations between landlords and tenants, it would be naive to assume that the Society or its members exerted a formative influence on Gladstone's 1881 Land Act, in marked contrast to the position that had previously prevailed. While the influence of an intellectual and professional elite over legislation was by no means dead, it was most evident in technical matters, such as the problems which peasant proprietorship might pose for the registration of land (Hancock, 445). The timing and direction of land reform were dictated by the fear of crime and the political leverage exercised by Parnell and his party.[50]

The unsettled conditions of the 1880s impinged directly on the Society's activities. The winter of 1879/80 was a time of considerable hardship, both in the countryside and in Dublin.[51] On 22 June 1880, the Council tentatively decided that, 'in case there was a favourable harvest', the president and secretaries might join the Town Council of Dublin in inviting the Social Science Congress to hold its 1881 meeting in that city. On 9 May 1882, three days after the assassination of Irish Chief Secretary Lord Frederick Cavendish and under-secretary T.H. Burke in Dublin's Phoenix Park, the Council decided to postpone a paper on 'The Reconstruction of the Education Department' (Graves,

384) until later in the session, 'owing to events which have just occurred'.[52]

The rise of mass politics and the highly polarised atmosphere of the 1880s were singularly uncongenial towards the (theoretically) apolitical technical consensus, which was at the heart of the Statistical Society. The fact that political economy was excluded from the syllabus of the new intermediate certificate examinations (Moylan, 901), whereas Whately had succeeded in having the subject included in the National School curriculum, is further evidence of the subject's loss of status. If, as Ingram had noted, political economy had lost influence, in part because the working-class were unsympathetic to its views, the activists in the Irish Land League showed no greater enthusiasm. Abrams suggests that the British Association, which had prided itself on its involvement in the process of reforming social legislation, collapsed during the 1880s because the major political parties were divided on such issues, and the debates at its annual congresses became increasingly rancorous.[53] In the United States, Haskell attributed the founding of the American Social Science Association in 1865 to a 'Tocquevillean impulse to defend authority, to erect institutional barriers against the corrosive consequences of unlimited competition in ideas and moral values in an interdependent mass society'.[54]

By the 1880s, 'mass society' had taken control of many aspects of the debate over social and economic policy in Ireland, leaving an elite group such as the Statistical Society to fight a losing battle in its efforts to retain influence. In vain did Hancock present a paper to the Society in January 1880 (at the height of the land war), which argued that, 'in the present crisis', education and access to cheap law for smallholders were of equal importance to the land question (Hancock, 437). Hancock no longer determined the agenda for the Irish administration. At the next meeting in February 1880, he read an interesting paper about Irish migratory labourers, which attempted to account for the outbreak of unrest in County Mayo during the months April-June 1879, which had led to the formation of the Land League. He exposed the fallacy of the widely-held belief that the agitation had been 'artificially created for some purpose', suggesting that it was caused by rising debt among Mayo smallholders, who were unable to earn sufficient money as seasonal labourers in England, because of agricultural depression. While Hancock provided a rational explanation for unrest in rural Ireland, there is no evidence that it carried any influence in the feverish conditions of 1880 (Hancock, 479).

In November 1880, the Council published a memorandum listing the Society's achievements since its foundation in 1847, with the aim of attracting new members, who would be interested in preparing papers and carrying out research, thus enabling the Society to offer an extensive programme of papers to the 1881 meeting of the Social Science Association . Among the measures which had allegedly resulted from papers presented to the Society, or from research carried out by its members, it listed the establishment of the Encumbered Estates Court, the passage of the Reformatory Schools Act (1858), the establishment of the Probate Court (1856-57) and the Post Office Savings Bank (1861). It also mentioned Cardwell's Land Act of 1860 and the 1870 Land Act. No subsequent list, however exaggerated, would have added the 1881 Land Act. The memorandum emphasised that the Society believed 'in keeping the progress of Ireland up to the rest of the United Kingdom' in matters of social reform.[55]

During the 1870s, when presidents included Lord Justice O'Hagan (afterwards Baron O'Hagan, who had served as Lord Chancellor of Ireland) and William Monsell MP (Baron Emly, who had held office in various Liberal administrations),[56] the Society seemed to be in the process of becoming a kind of nineteenth-century pressure group cum think-tank for government, a role successfully achieved in Britain by the Social Science Association. O'Hagan's interests included local government reform, the care of lunatics, and education; he was involved in devising the 1878 Intermediate Education Act, though this legislation was never discussed by the Society, presumably because of its denominational connotations. Both Monsell and O'Hagan were instrumental in having the Society's views aired at Westminster, and occasionally at Whitehall, as well as Dublin Castle.[57] O'Hagan spoke in the House of Lords about the treatment of idiot and imbecile children.[58] Both men were successful Catholics who had assimilated to British politics and to the Union. By the 1880s, however, the polarisation of Irish politics between unionism and nationalism made it more difficult for their successors to occupy the middle ground. That decade also saw the effective extinction of Irish liberalism, the political philosophy that appears to have been most compatible with the Society's ethos.[59]

There is some evidence that the Society was conscious of this loss of influence. In a presidential address in August 1883, Lord Monteagle admitted that he could not entirely 'avoid misgivings that we are regarded by the public as a strange body, living on blue books and dry bones of knowledge, with a tendency to political monomania'. He noted that 'in the present state of Ireland every social question of any importance – I fear I might almost say any public question of any kind – inevitably becomes political'. Yet there were limits to Monteagle's grasp of such issues. Although his paper contained the well-worn refrain that it was the Society's 'privilege and our pride to meet without distinction of party, class, or creed', it offered an uncompromising defence of the landlord class. It was, and remains, an acutely political document, which had undoubtedly been prompted by the fact that the 1881 Land Act, which conceded the 3 Fs (fair rent, fixity of tenure and freedom to sell a tenant's interest), had failed to bring peace to rural Ireland. According to Monteagle, the most vital question facing Irish society in the 1880s was 'whether [or not] an upper class is to continue to exist, especially in country districts?' His paper showed the extent to which judicial rents were eroding landlord incomes and raising tenants' expectations.

Monteagle, who obviously believed that the survival of the landlord class was in Ireland's interests, sketched out a survival plan that would, if Paul Bew is correct,[60] have been sympathetically received by Parnell. He argued that landlords must no longer be seen as an English garrison; there was an urgent need to promote peasant proprietorship, grand jury reform[61] and greater co-operation between resident landlords, farmers and tradesmen at local level, together with the involvement of the farming community and the middle class in public administration, preferably as magistrates. He warned that the alternative would mean either placing Ireland under military control, or the 'Canadianization of the country', in other words Ireland as a Dominion, though he feared that the latter would only result in the annihilation of the upper class and the emergence of a violent labour movement (Monteagle, 888). The presidential address given by James McDonnell in December 1884 reinforced the sense that members were ill at ease with the political and social changes that were taking place. McDonnell suggested that political economists had a duty to stand out against prevailing trends. He speculated on the implications of transferring power

> ... to the people at large ... as when power was vested in the aristocracy we find that there was a tendency to legislate in favour of that class, so now one may anticipate a tendency to legislate in favour of the class in which political power is now or will very shortly be vested, and it will be the duty of political economists to point out the folly and injustice of class legislation in the supposed interest of the multitude, just as they did in the case of the aristocracy.

McDonnell took little pleasure in the burgeoning state involvement in economic life, though he admitted that his views might not necessarily please fellow members, since he believed that feeling within the Society had for some time been 'running counter to the principle of laissez-faire'. Although McDonnell's address referred to compulsory state education, state regulation of housing for the poor, measures to combat contagious diseases and controls on the liquor traffic, his strictures were primarily directed against the 1881 Land Act, which had, in his opinion, brought an end to freedom of contract with regard to land (a touchstone of the Society's founding years, though he does not make this point). He claimed that the speech (presumably by Gladstone) introducing the Bill at Westminster, had 'relegated political economy to Saturn or the Moon', because the measure could not be defended on economic grounds.

McDonnell regarded the 1885 Bill, (subsequently known as the Ashbourne Act)[62] which provided £5m. to enable tenant farmers to purchase their holdings, as equally objectionable, because, in contrast to the Bright clauses in the 1870 Act, prospective purchasers were not required to provide a deposit. Whereas the Bright clauses would 'strengthen the conservative element, and form a small but powerful and growing party in favour of property and order', giving 100 per cent mortgages to tenant farmers left them with the delusion that they could now do less work, because their circumstances had improved. Far from bringing peace to rural Ireland, McDonnell believed that the first bad harvest would result in demands for lower repayments. He favoured the much more limited step of reducing the cost of selling land, with the aim of perpetuating 'a mixture of large, small, and middle sized estates' (McDonnell, 783). The defensive tone of this address contrasts with the demands for reform found in the earlier journals of the Society, though his views appear mild when compared with the strident tones of some Irish landlords.

It would be incorrect however to regard the Society merely as a mouthpiece for a beleaguered landlord class. Some members were actively involved in implementing the revolution which McDonnell decried. In April 1885, a paper by Stanislaus Lynch, a Land Commissioner, examined the provisions of the future Asbhourne Act (Lynch, 740). Further support for the concept of peasant proprietorship emerged during the 1888/89 session when Murrough O'Brien, another Land Commissioner, argued that despite the depressed state of agricultural markets and the ravages of pyllhoxera (a devastating disease) which had attacked their vineyards: 'the small French peasant proprietor working for himself by increased exertion and economy, both lives and thrives'. Under a system of peasant proprietorship, O'Brien claimed that the economic well-being of the French peasantry was 'immeasurably greater than that of the Irish peasant'; moreover the rate of emigration from rural areas was extremely low (O'Brien, 961).

In 1913, Stanislaus Lynch re-examined the land question. By this stage over 222,000 holdings had been transferred from landlord to tenant, and the process of redistributing land to smallholders in the Congested Districts was underway. However the growth in peasant proprietorship had slackened, because the bonds offered to landlords under the 1909 Land Purchase Act had depreciated in value. As had been the case in his 1885 paper, Lynch was concerned to break the logjam of land sales. He urged that the Society 'should intervene and give some light and leading to our legislators'; he recalled that it had been described as '"the cradle of land law reform in Ireland"'. On the apparent eve of Home Rule, and the unforeseen brink of World War I, Lynch appeared to believe that the Society's members could still exert influence 'by counsel and suggestion to further the peaceful solution of this problem'. His appeal appears to have been designed to reverse the political process of the previous 30-40 years; he wished to see the question 'lifted out of the slough of party strife and political conflict', committing into the Society's hands 'the cause of those who are still waiting to be enfranchised' (Lynch, 739). By 1913, however, aspiring peasant proprietors were more likely to appeal to the Irish Parliamentary Party than to rely on the intervention of the Statistical Society.

FREE TRADE AND PROTECTION

Another topic which preoccupied the Society from the 1880s was the debate over tariff protection, further evidence that the mid-nineteenth triumph of liberalism was under attack. The Anglo-French Cobden Chevalier Treaty of 1860 had appeared to signal the dominance of free trade in continental Europe. By the late 1870s, however, with the collapse of agricultural prices, protection was again in vogue. The threatened competition from American agricultural imports and their impact on European farming were intimately connected with the debate on the Irish land question. In 1883, in a paper dealing with competition from American agriculture, William F. Bailey, a barrister and a future Estates Commissioner, suggested that the impact of American agricultural imports on British food prices had been exaggerated. Bailey claimed that free trade in agricultural produce would best promote the prosperity of the overall population and consequently the interests of the Irish farmers (Bailey, 22).

The merits of free trade and protection were also relevant to the debate over the decline of Irish manufacturing industry. In 1881, Parnell expressed regret that Ireland lacked a parliament with power to protect the nation's industries.[63] In 1884 the Select Committee on Industries (Ireland) collected extensive evidence from firms and other witnesses on the merits of protection. Although almost half the firms that were questioned blamed foreign competition for their difficulties, relatively few saw tariff protection as the solution; they called instead for measures which could have been accommodated within the Union, such as government subsidies or adjustments to railway tariffs.[64]

This discussion became a contest between rival schools of political economy: the neo-classical and the historical. In February 1883 Richard R. Cherry, (a barrister and a future judge) drew a clear distinction between pure or abstract political economy, where the deductive method was valid, and the applied science, 'where the only safe method to follow is that called the historical, according to which, before applying any theory, the whole of the surrounding circumstances must first be inductively investigated'. Cherry rejected the argument that the principle of free trade had universal application, like the law of gravity. His case for protection rested on a belief that the fragile condition of modern Irish industry was not due to a lack of natural resources, but to historical factors, such as the disturbed state of Ireland, and England's hostile commercial policy. At the end of his paper, however, Cherry abandoned the call for protection, in favour of a demand for government subsidies to develop industry, following the precedent created by government assistance to landlords and tenants. He believed that such measures would demonstrate that the English people had 'put aside the selfish jealousy of the last century' (Cherry, 150).

There was a certain lack of rigour in Cherry's reasoning, which was fully exploited by C.F. Bastable in a paper some months later. Black rightly regards Bastable and Cairnes as the two most distinguished economists to be associated with the Society during its first hundred years. Bastable, Whately Professor of Economics from 1882 to 1932, was a leading authority on international trade.[65] Like Cherry, he accepted that past events, such as commercial restrictions, had retarded 'industrial progress'. However he contended that, by the 1880s, the major handicaps facing Irish industry were the inferior quality of labour and natural resources relative to those available in England. Bastable asserted that Irish economic growth should be based on agriculture. He ruled out using artificial means to stimulate industrial development and dismissed the arguments advanced by those who favoured such incentives as a reflection of either economic ignorance or national prejudice, though he admitted that neither vice was 'Exclusively of Irish manufacture' (Bastable, 54).

When George Coffey read a paper on tariff protection in November 1885, he suggested that the topic might soon become 'of more than academic interest' because Home Rule seemed a distinct possibility. Coffey argued that 'under Free Trade population must flow from the poorer parts of the earth to the more productive'. Accordingly, 'countries, such as Ireland, of limited productive powers, must suffer when brought in contact with those more richly endowed by nature' unless some means were found of remedying these disadvantages. He believed that both Irish agriculture and industry were in decay. This paper ended, not with a firm endorsement of protection, but with a more qualified statement

> ... that if the people of Ireland are persuaded that the country possesses facilities in certain directions for manufactures, which want of private capital, skilled labour, and industrial organization preclude them from developing, and which, if started under present conditions, would, owing to the competition of established industries in other countries, have to be carried on for years at a loss, they would be economically justified in submitting to a general tax for the purpose of so developing the resources of the country (Coffey, 158).

Following the publication of the report of the Select Committee on Industries (Ireland) – which failed to come down either for or against tariff protection – interest in tariff protection appears to have receded until the early years of the twentieth century, when Arthur Griffith began to advocate economic self-sufficiency for Ireland, and the British Conservative Party adopted protectionist policies. In 1905 Hanbury S. Geoghegan read a paper attacking the protectionist case put forward by Joseph Chamberlain's Tariff Commission (Geoghegan, 369). Although the issue lost ground in Britain following the Conservative débâcle at the 1906 election, it remained very much alive in Ireland. While many members were undoubtedly familiar with the views of Arthur Griffith, his name is never mentioned. The most regular advocate of free trade was Charles Oldham, the first principal of the College of Commerce in Rathmines and subsequently Professor of Commerce and Professor of National Economics at University College Dublin. Although Oldham believed that Irish industry was in decline, he dismissed efforts to stem this tendency by means such as the 'buy Irish' campaign as 'idiotic', though he later apologised for using this term. He believed that an educational system that favoured manual and scientific training (as in Rathmines College of Commerce) offered a more valid mechanism for halting industrial decline (Oldham, 1010).

In 1908, Oldham launched an attack on efforts by the Dublin Industrial Development Association to promote the sales of Irish-produced goods (Oldham, 1017). A paper on Belfast shipbuilding, which he presented in November 1910, complete with lantern slides,[66] reiterated the case for free trade (Oldham, 1020). Oldham's most outspoken statement on this subject came in 1917, when he launched a strong attack on Alice Murray's book *A History of the Commercial Relations between England and Ireland from the Period of the Restoration*.[67] Murray blamed the decline of Irish industry on the introduction of free trade consequent on the Act of Union. While Oldham admitted that Irish industries had decayed in the early nineteenth century, he saw the technological changes associated with the industrial revolution and the transport revolution as the primary causes. Free trade had provided a 'prodigious stimulus' to Irish commerce and trade; among the beneficiaries were the modern linen trade, Belfast shipbuilding and the export trade in porter, biscuits and livestock. Oldham claimed that

> ... modern Ireland is a terra incognita to most of the Irish people. It is the creation of free trade conditions, and thrives by free trade – yet most Irish people blandly believe that it is free trade that has 'ruined' Ireland, although, in truth, there never was a period in the whole history of Ireland when the country was so prosperous; and especially so its manufacturing industries, which many of us sarcastically compare with the Irish snakes in being conspicuous only by their absence.

By 1917, the partition of Ireland seemed highly probable, yet Oldham, a Protestant Home Ruler,[68] appears to have been thinking in terms of an unpartitioned island, because he emphasised that Ireland was 'a country that enjoys the good fortune of having mixed employments, both industrial and agricultural', adding that 'the industries of Ireland ... are probably producing more wealth than the land of Ireland produces under the present system of usage'. In what must be seen as a rebuttal of the views of the unmentioned Arthur Griffith, Oldham pointed out that 'a system of protection' becomes endurable only when the area enclosed is sufficient to be nearly self-supporting, as in the case of the United States of America. By contrast a country as small as Ireland, 'cannot afford to be self-contained' (Oldham, 1022).

The statistics relating to Irish external trade, which were compiled by the Department of Agriculture and Technical Instruction from 1904, appeared to furnish considerable ammunition for supporters of free trade, and Oldham drew heavily on this source in a paper to the Society in 1919 (Oldham, 1013). In 1909, Arthur W. Samuels (a liberal unionist and MP for Dublin University)[69] who was president of the Society, used them to argue against the protectionist case, by demonstrating the 'immense volume of Irish trade' and the high level of mutual dependence between the British and the Irish economies. Samuels also cited data on the volume and price of agricultural exports as evidence of the economic benefits accruing from the co-operative creamery system and the work of the Department of Agriculture. Yet despite the impeccable unionist credentials of this paper, it was laced with frequent references to the ruinous commercial policy which England had adopted towards Ireland in the past, and to the damage resulting from contemporary British fiscal policy towards Ireland. Samuels asserted that the development of Irish agriculture, industry and commerce constituted a 'common ground for all of us in Ireland' (Samuels, 1107), which was undeniably true, though it ignored the extent to which protagonists disagreed on the appropriate remedy.

ANGLO-IRISH FISCAL RELATIONS AND THE ACT OF UNION: THE QUESTION OF OVER-TAXATION

One of the most widely debated economic topics around the turn of the century was the alleged over-taxation of Ireland. In many ways it replaced the long-standing obsession with absentee landlords as a scapegoat for economic retardation. Taxation came to the fore during the 1880s with the introduction of Gladstone's first Home Rule Bill, and the need to determine future fiscal relations between Britain and Ireland. The topic was analysed at length by a royal commission which was established in 1894 Although it failed to reach a unanimous conclusion, the evidence collected and the multiple reports fuelled an already volatile debate. That the majority report began with the assumption that Britain and Ireland should be considered as two separate entities was in itself a political judgment. Discussion of Anglo-Irish fiscal relations focused on two issues. Firstly, the fact that between 1817 (when the two Exchequers were united) and 1890, revenue collected in Ireland appears to have exceeded government expenditure on the island. Secondly, that taxation, which was heavily weighted towards indirect taxes, bore more heavily on the poorer population of Ireland than on the more affluent population of England.[70] Several papers on this topic steered a middle course: expressing some sympathy with the nationalist case, while recasting it in a more acceptable form. In 1886, W.F. Bailey took issue with the claims of the English economist Robert Giffen that Ireland was heavily over-taxed relative to Britain, yet in the same paper he expressed support for a major scheme of state-funded land purchase. However, Bailey justified land purchase, not as a means of rectifying past wrongs, but by arguing that it would prove cost-effective to the British Exchequer, resulting in a significant reduction in the cost of law enforcement (Bailey, 20).

In 1907, A.W. Samuels presented a highly technical paper on Irish public finances, (an instance of the rising intellectual standard of papers to the Society), which offered considerable support to the Home Rule case. Side-stepping the heated and extremely politicised arguments concerning the over-taxation of Ireland, Samuels examined whether recent changes in public finances, notably the use of grants in aid from the Exchequer to relieve ratepayers throughout the United Kingdom, and the provision of an agricultural grant, which was introduced to compensate for partial derating of agricultural land, were compatible with the financial principles which had been laid down under the Act of Union.[71] He concluded that they were not, and that 'the present system of taxation, with its narrow basis and peculiar incidences, presses, and has long pressed, unduly upon Ireland'. In particular, he criticised the system of subvention for local needs, which was first introduced in 1888, as 'neither constitutional nor financially sound', a criticism that also applied to the practice of segregating expenditure into '"Imperial", "English", "Scotch" and Irish"' (Samuels, 1114).

Although the Society never directly debated the economic benefits and/or losses consequent on the union of Great Britain and Ireland, the issue was implicit in many papers. Some speakers expressed impatience that the apparently inescapable evidence of statistics was frequently rejected by the masses, who tended to resort to arguments which were not amenable to analysis within the parameters favoured by the Society. Members often contrasted the apparent objectivity of economics and statistics with the 'lamentations of historians and the denunciations of poets'.[72] In 1908, Charles Oldham agreed with the view expressed by Professor Stanley Jevons that '"there is a kind of ignorant dislike and impatience of political economy"' (Oldham, 1017). In 1888, the Registrar General, Sir Thomas Grimshaw, devoted his presidential address to reviewing the changes that had taken place in Ireland since the Society's foundation. Grimshaw indicated that he had refrained from speaking about conditions in Ireland before 1841 (an omission which would have been fully justified by the lack of statistical data) because of his wish 'to avoid as much as possible all disturbing elements of a historical, and therefore, in Ireland, of a political nature'. He argued that there was a need 'to accept facts as we have them, and deal with the results of the recent past, not with the Church of Patrick, or the Norman invasion', though St Patrick was not a politically divisive subject.

One of the most contentious topics was emigration. Although Grimshaw acknowledged that the level of emigration was high in the 1880s, he countered that Ireland had 'advanced in the arts of civilisation and in material prosperity', though he hedged his bets somewhat by remaining undecided about whether or not 'she has done so at an equal rate with other countries'. This paper was very much in the tradition of earlier contributions by members such as Hancock, who wrote about the progress which Ireland had made since the Famine (Grimshaw, 396). In 1903, in yet another paper reviewing the changes that had taken place in Ireland since the Famine, W.F. Bailey concluded that any further decline in the population of Ireland would result in a 'real loss of the well-being of the country'. Anticipating later arguments about a brain-drain,

Bailey suggested that emigration removed 'the best, the most active and the most enterprising of its people'. This comment may reflect some awareness of contemporary interest in eugenics, i.e. the quality of a nation's population. In an argument that was later employed by Éamon de Valera when asked to account for the record level of emigration during the 1950s, Bailey suggested that the solution to emigration did not necessarily lie in 'mere material prosperity'; rather it lay in discouraging 'the tendency to introspection and mobid brooding' and the practice of 'living on the memory of former wrongs and past grievances' in favour of greater self-reliance.

In the ensuing discussion, Rev T. Finlay, SJ – a pioneer of the co-operative movement and Professor of Political Economy at University College Dublin – argued that 'Ireland was a separate entity, and economic legislation for it must be specific in character, and specially adapted to the peculiar needs of the country' (Bailey, 24). In a 1907 paper Finlay blended elements of what could be described as nationalist economics with catholic social teaching. He regarded government provisions for the indigent as an essential consequence of both the growing complexity of modern society and the protestant Reformation, when the 'confiscation of ecclesiastical property … took out of the hands of the Church the patrimony of the poor'.[73] He suggested that the solution to unemployment in Ireland lay in a programme of land reclamation, which would provide work for the unemployed, though he was deliberately vague on the extent to which the state should finance such a programme (Finlay, 316). His comments anticipated the Irish report to the Royal Commission on the Poor Laws, which was written by the Bishop of Rosse, Dr Denis Kelly.[74]

Other echoes of what may be termed Sinn Féin economics, particularly the belief in the potential offered by Ireland's natural resources, can be found in three papers relating to forestry, one by a member of the Indian forestry service (Muriel, 906; Falkiner, 303; Stanuell, 1178). A paper by Hanbury Geoghegan, pleading for the establishment of a board to develop Irish mines and minerals, under the control of the Department of Agriculture and Technical Instruction, could have been taken from the pages of Arthur Griffith's newspaper, the *United Irishman* (Geoghegan,

368). Similar comments apply to the paper by Charles Dawson, 'Industrial Progress of Belgium: a Lesson for Ireland', which argued that Ireland should follow Belgium's example in promoting intensive agriculture and afforestation (Dawson, 215). Belgium was more commonly cited than Denmark as a role model for Ireland during these years. In November 1915, Charles Stanuell gave his presidential address on 'The Example of Belgium. A Possible Effect of the War upon Ireland'. Stanuell was not alone in contrasting Belgium's population density of 589 people per square mile with Ireland's 135 people.[75] He linked his account of the Irish economy with emotional references to 'the gallant resistance of the Belgians against the overwhelming forces of Germany' and suggested that Belgian's successful economy indicated that a troubled history did not necessarily preclude economic prosperity. If Ireland followed the Belgian example, it should increase the tilled acreage, export processed meat rather than live cattle, make greater use of co-operation and 'agricultural county councils', provide more state-funded education in agriculture; carry out forestry development under state control and construct many more miles of narrow-gauge light railways. (Stanuell, 1166) Papers such as Stanuell's are interesting less for their intellectual content, than for the insights that they provide into the then current discourse on the Irish economy. They suggest that, whereas leading nationalist economic commentators such as Arthur Griffith, D.P. Moran and Patrick D. Kenny were not involved in the Society, some members sympathised with their views.

MORAL AND SOCIAL STATISTICS: CHILD WELFARE

Economics was never the sole preoccupation of the Statistical Society; indeed the Council minutes suggest that legal and social reforms were often regarded as more important. From its foundation the Society showed a keen interest in the welfare of children. The Society regarded the successful campaign by members for the establishment of industrial schools in Ireland in 1868 as one of its greatest achievements. On 7 December 1875, the Council decided to establish a Charitable Organisation Committee to collect information about the major causes of pauperism in Dublin and the working of charities in the city; the committee would also make recommendations for improvements in the organisation of charitable services and would inform itself about the activities of similar bodies in London, New York and elsewhere.[76] This committee was established in response to a paper by the Society's president, John Kells Ingram, on 'The Organisation of Charity, and the Education of the Children of the State'. Ingram queried 'whether the wealthy, and influential, though never deficient in liberality when their aid is invoked for cases of distress, have not been too supine and passive with respect to the administration of our charities, and too willing to devolve on others – on the officials of societies, or on the clergy, often overburdened with their strictly spiritual duties – the management and control of our agencies for the relief of the poor.' He highlighted the efforts of the London Charity Organisation Society (COS) to ensure that relief was distributed as efficiently as possible, and suggested that a similar body should be established in Ireland (Ingram, 592).

Founded in 1869, the COS set out to organise the distribution of charitable relief in an orderly manner. One of the most active members was the leading civil servant Sir Charles Trevelyan, who was notorious in Ireland for his unsympathetic management of government relief programmes during the Famine. The COS was utterly opposed to indiscriminate charity. It gave preference to families, who would best profit from assistance and those known as the 'deserving poor', though the COS eventually discarded this term, preferring to describe those it deemed ineligible for relief as 'not likely to benefit' or 'not assisted'. The COS established a register of charities, which it subjected to inspection. Its most important innovation lay in the practice of visiting those families that had applied for assistance, in order to determine their needs, and how they would best be met. Although this was very much in line with old-style philanthropic visiting of the poor, this is generally seen as the beginnings of the case-history approach to social work, which has remained integral to that profession ever since. Visitors were expected to observe professional standards in collecting information and in their treatment of the poor.[77] The Statistical Society's Charitable Organisation Committee attempted, though with less success, to introduce similar procedures to Dublin charities.

By 1880, the Charitable Organisation Committee had produced a total of eight papers, mostly concerned with the reform of social legislation, such as the laws relating to lunatics, the blind, deaf and dumb, the houseless poor, workhouse relief, drunkenness and derelict housing in urban areas (Millin, 867; 166-68). In 1876, the Council decided that copies of all reports completed by the Charitable Organisation Committee should be sent to Peers and Members of Parliament, who were members of the Society, and to interested senior civil servants. When the Committee's report on the laws relating to ruinous houses in towns was completed in February 1876, the Council sent copies to all town authorities in Ireland.[78] The Charitable Organisation Committee began work at a rapid pace. By April 1876, four reports had been completed, including one recommending that the cost of poor relief in the Dublin area should be borne by all local authorities in the metropolitan area, a practice that applied in London. This reform, which was not introduced until 1900, would have remedied a major grievance for Dublin Corporation, which claimed that the suburban areas did not meet their fair share.[79]

On the advice of Sir Charles Trevelyan, the Charitable Organisation Committee devoted considerable attention to investigating the laws relating to imbeciles and lunatics, with a view to making proposals for new legislation. In May 1877, three members of the Council, including Lord O'Hagan, took part in a delegation, which met the secretary of the English Local Government Board. The purpose of this meeting is puzzling, because the English Local Government Board had no control over practices or legislation in Ireland. We can only assume that the Society believed that if certain reforms were introduced in England, they would soon be replicated in Ireland.

The reports of the committee followed in the tradition of the investigations that had been commissioned by the Social Reform Committee during the 1850s, though the COC, whose reports were written by members as opposed to paid investigators, tended to analyse existing data, rather than collect new information. Most reports recommended that Irish laws and practices should be brought into line with those applying either in England or in

Scotland. There is no evidence that the committee attempted to fulfil its original aim of investigating the causes of pauperism in Ireland, or collecting information on the operations of Dublin charities, despite the fact that acute distress in Dublin city in the late 1870s provided ample scope for such efforts. The Sick and Indigent Roomkeepers' Society, one of Dublin's most prominent charities, was undergoing a major crisis, and a Mansion House Committee was established in 1879 to relieve emergency distress.[80] The failure to intervene more strongly in the field of charitable organisation is scarcely surprising: while the Society occasionally strayed into politically contentious areas, it appears to have done its utmost to avoid sectarian divisions, and most charities in Ireland were organised on denominational lines. Efforts to investigate charitable organisations, or recommendations that the number of existing institutions should be reduced in the interests of efficiency, would have come up against this problem. It proved safer to recommend changes in the treatment of prisoners and lunatics, which was the responsibility of government.

Despite such limitations, the Society played an important role in the development of professional social work, by alerting members to changes in social policy which were taking place elsewhere. With a membership which included peers, members of parliament, members of the legal and medical professions, prominent civil servants, members of Dublin Corporation and the city engineer and medical officer of health, the Society provided a valuable platform for those wishing to publicise various causes. It proved especially valuable to women, who were eligible for associate membership and were consequently in a position to present papers (though in the early years they were often read by a male member). Indeed the Society was one of the few institutions in Ireland where women could present their views to a mixed audience. The first paper by a woman was given in 1863 by Charlotte Stoker, wife of a member, Abraham Stoker, a civil servant, and mother of the writer Bram Stoker. Mrs Stoker spoke about the need for state provisions for the education of the deaf and dumb (Stoker, 1191). No women followed Charlotte Stoker's lead until 1878, when several women presented papers to the Dublin meeting of the British Association, which was hosted by the Society. An appendix to the Journal for 1878 reproduced a paper by Isabella Tod, one of the pioneers of women's education in Ireland,[81] on the boarding-out of pauper children (Tod, 1255). This may have prompted other women to offer papers, because during the 1879/80 session, Anna Haslam, an early suffragist,[82] read a paper which had been written by Mrs Morgan John O'Connell on the treatment of women and children within the workhouse (O'Connell, 978), and John Kells Ingram, presented a paper, prepared by the late Miss Menella Smedley, on the relative merits of caring for children in the workhouse or providing foster homes (Smedley, 1157). Miss Emily Foote read a paper on the same subject, which she had previously presented at the Dublin Meeting of the British Association, though this was not printed in the *Journal*. Since these papers dealt with themes that had been previously examined by luminaries of the Society such as Ingram and Hancock, they cannot be seen as in any way subversive or revolutionary. However they illustrate the important role, that middle-class women played in Victorian philanthropy.[83] All these papers, whether written by men or by women, share common values: the importance of the family as a social organism, the assumption that families are part of the natural order, and the duties of parents, particularly mothers. The concept of 'separate spheres' for women and men is implicit throughout, irrespective of the gender of the presenter.

Women who read papers to the Society were concerned to bring about changes in social policy. Isabella Tod was active in efforts to have pauper children boarded-out, as opposed to being kept in the workhouse. This marked an extension to Ireland of a campaign that had achieved widespread support among women in England; it was also a cause which Hancock had upheld. Tod believed that finding foster-parents was 'the proper work of the ladies who undertake to assist in boarding-out'. She reminded her audience that 'The state is composed of men and women and has both masculine and feminine duties', and she welcomed the fact that a women's committee had recently been formed in Dublin to look after children who had been boarded out by the city's unions. Tod noted that the 'ladies' on this committee faced a dual responsibility – to the children and to the state – but she argued that this was typical of the type of work 'which ought eventually to reach their hands'.

Mrs Morgan John O'Connell examined similar issues from the perspective of 'a country lady, widow and daughter of energetic ex-officio guardians, and who, as a land-owner, employer of labour, and signer of red tickets [which entitled people to free treatment in the dispensary] has an intimate knowledge of her poor neighbours'. O'Connell claimed that women were better suited to determining how women and children should be cared for within the workhouse, because men 'did not meddle with these questions within their own homes'. She was less hostile to institutional care for children than Tod (who was the principal of a girls' boarding-school) because she believed that in rural areas children would have to be boarded with farm labourers, who would provide them with little if any training; though 'matters were otherwise in the suburbs'. O'Connell also assumed the existence of denominational 'separate spheres'. She spoke of 'kind Protestant ladies who have cripples' homes, convalescent homes and incurable homes' and 'the Orders of Charity and Mercy, specially trained, skilled, and devoted to the person of Jesus, in the members of his suffering poor'.

Mrs O'Connell's more sympathetic approach towards institutional care was not shared by Menella Smedley, which leads to the question of whether or not there was a distinction between catholic and protestant attitudes on this issue. 'Kind Protestant ladies' were presumably better suited to monitoring and organising foster homes, whereas 'Orders of Charity and Mercy' preferred to care for children in an institutional setting. However we should not push this distinction too far. Protestant women did not rule out institutional care for orphaned and destitute children. Rosa Barrett, who read two papers to the Society during the 1890s, founded an orphanage, the Creche and the Cottage Home for Little Children, in Kingstown (now Dun Laoghaire) in 1879.

Barrett, who deserves to be remembered as a pioneering figure among Irish social workers, was typical of many middle-class Victorian philanthropic ladies. A member of the Philanthropic Reform Association, an organisation founded in 1896 whose ideology was reminiscent of the COS,[84] Barrett was the driving force behind the establishment of the National Society for the Prevention of Cruelty to Children, a founding member of the Women's National Health Association, and a member of Lady

Aberdeen's Irish Home Industries Association.[85] In 1884, she produced a guide to Dublin charities,[86] which was organised in the manner recommended by the Charity Organisation Society; she also wrote several pamphlets on child-care. In 1892 and in 1896, she presented two substantial papers to the Society, outlining legislation relating to neglected children in various states of the United States, the Australian states and several European countries. The space allotted to Barrett – at over seventy pages, her second paper far exceeded the specified maximum length – indicates a sympathetic Council. She argued that voluntary child-care should be supplemented by a far greater degree of state intervention than actually applied in either Britain or Ireland. Most of the countries examined possessed a much more extensive legal code governing child welfare. In many instances the state could override the authority of fathers if children were being neglected; this could include the authority to remove children from the parental home and to place them either in institutions or with families. Barrett employed a combination of moral and economic arguments in support of her campaign for greater state intervention. 'To lessen pauperism and crime – both of which are largely the result of heredity and association – it is necessary to go to the source of the evil, and prevent children, if possible, from being brought up in injurious surroundings.' (She does not attempt to evaluate the relative weight of heredity and environment.) Barrett believed that 'Humanity and political economy are not in opposition – they are identical' (Barrett, 34, 35).

Barrett played a key role in the establishment of the NSPCC in Dublin in 1889, five years after a comparable society was founded in Britain. Its first president was Dr Thomas Grimshaw, the registrar-general and president of the Statistical Society. The NSPCC publicised the provisions of the Prevention of Cruelty and Protection of Children Act 1889, which made it possible to punish persons who mistreated or neglected children, or forced them to beg or perform in the street.[87] The NSPCC sought to keep children in their own homes by helping 'those worthless parents who make children wanderers, homeless and destitute, and to render other provisions than their own home less necessary'.[88] It attributed most cases of child neglect to poverty, unemployment, and most particularly to drunkenness.[89] The two papers that Rosa

Barrett read to the Society reflected many of the views of the NSPCC. A footnote to her 1896 paper referred to the 'terrible Coombe Case', where a Dublin jury had acquitted parents of neglect. The parents in question had 'enjoyed several nights of drunkenness' from the money raised for the funeral of their dead infant, who was left unburied (Barrett, 34).

Throughout the 1890s a succession of papers from Edward Daly, chief clerk of the police courts, examined issues such as crime, drink, parental neglect and how best to cope with the children who were the casualties of such problems (Daly, 205-08). The views expressed in these papers are remarkably similar to those found in papers read to the Society during the 1850s. The relationship between drunkenness, crime and the need for licensing reform was a recurrent theme, though by the turn of the century, as Malcolm notes, the campaign to introduce tighter legal controls over the drink industry appeared to have failed.[90] Child welfare remained a long-term interest of the Society. In January 1953, the Council received a letter from E.W. McCabe, of the Adoption Society of Ireland, thanking it for having granted him the facility of reading a paper to the Statistical Society in 1949 on the subject of adoption (McCabe, 758). He claimed that the Adoption Society believed that this presentation had 'played no small part in the Society's efforts in bringing about the legislation represented by the Adoption Act of 1952'.[91] Rosa Barrett, who had emphasised the importance of legislation permitting adoption, in papers to the Society during the 1890s, would have been pleased.

PUBLIC HEALTH

Public health also engaged the Society's interest over many years. The first volume of the journal contained a paper by Richard Dowden, which explored the relationship between disease and overcrowding (Dowden, 244). This was a typical exposition of the then-fashionable miasmic theory of disease. It contained no specific reference to conditions in Dublin, though a paper by William Hogan in 1849 employed data collected by the Rev. Thomas Willis concerning the level of infant mortality among the Dublin labouring population[92] (Hogan, 559). Although the Society devoted much less attention to urban social problems and to public health than comparable English societies, one paper examined the high incidence of smallpox in Ireland and suggested that many cases were caused by itinerant inoculators – untrained men who inoculated people with smallpox, not with cowpox (McDonnell, 792).

Many of the early papers relating to public health were given by Edward Dillon Mapother, the first medical officer of health appointed by Dublin Corporation, who used the Society as a forum for his campaigns to have Irish public health legislation brought into line with Britain (Mapother, 833-38). However, public health was not a major preoccupation in Ireland. Voluntary bodies that campaigned for public health causes attracted much less support from middle-class philanthropists than in Britain, and such organisations were slower to emerge. The Dublin Sanitary Association, the most prominent pressure group advocating sanitary reform, was dominated by medical men[93] and there was some overlap of membership between the Statistical Society, the Dublin Sanitary Association and the Dublin Artisans Dwellings Company. Yet although Sir Charles Cameron, the Dublin City analyst and subsequently medical officer of health – a man who made extensive use of statistics in his reports to Dublin Corporation – was a member of the Statistical Society for many years and served on its committees, he never presented a paper. Another key figure in Irish public health, Surgeon Colonel D. Edgar Flinn, chief medical inspector of the Local Government Board, contributed two papers on the slightly eccentric topic of the geographical distribution of Irish intellectual talent, but nothing relating to his work in public health (Flinn, 327, 328). The Registrar General, Sir Thomas Grimshaw, served as president for the sessions 1888-90 and presented six papers, including one dealing with child mortality in Dublin (Grimshaw, 392). Otherwise his contributions seem to have deliberately avoided Irish vital statistics.

Many members of the Society were active in organisations, that were involved in either the treatment or the prevention of tuberculosis. Sir William Thompson, the Registrar-General, who was president from 1918 to 1920, was honorary treasurer of the Women's National Health Association, an organisation founded by the Vicereine Lady Aberdeen. Thompson also sat on the committees of other medical charities that were concerned with tuberculosis. In 1907, Professor E.J. McWeeney read a paper on the comparative epidemiology of tuberculosis in Ireland and Britain, which suggested that whereas mortality was steadily declining in England and Scotland, it was on the increase in Ireland. McWeeney, professor of pathology and bacteriology at University College Dublin, pressed the case for making tuberculosis a notifiable disease. He also advocated the establishment of sanitoria and isolation hospitals and suggested that all schoolchildren should be subject to medical examination in order to identify those at risk from tuberculosis (McWeeney, 818). The proposal to make tuberculosis a notifiable disease had been under discussion for several years. McWeeney's recommendations reflected advanced thinking on the treatment and prevention of tuberculosis. Although his recommendations were endorsed by the Women's National Health Association, they failed to command popular support. In 1901, provision had been made for the voluntary notification of all cases of tuberculosis, but this was not successful; the majority of Dublin doctors regarded it as a breach of the confidential doctor-patient relationship. In 1905, Dublin Corporation rejected a proposal to erect a municipal TB sanitorium. It was widely believed that susceptibility to TB reflected racial or moral failings. Consequently, some nationalist members of Dublin Corporation and Sinn Féin's Arthur Griffith claimed that publicity about the high incidence of TB in Ireland, coming from a predominantly Anglo-Irish elite, 'has conveyed the impression abroad that we dwell in an island reeking with TB, whose inhabitants are foredoomed to a lingering and hopeless disease'. Nevertheless, in 1909 tuberculosis was declared a notifiable disease.[94]

Dr Edmund McWeeney used the Society to press for other reforms in public health, though his efforts were not always welcome. When, in 1915, he presented a paper on immunity to infectious disease, with special reference to anti-typhoid inoculation, he requested that the paper should be circulated to all clerks of Poor Law Unions and county secretaries in the hope that the local authorities would introduce an inoculation programme. Although he was supported by Sir William Thompson and

Dr Ninian Falkiner (both medical men), two members of the Council, David Chart and Herbert Wood, dissented. The Council eventually agreed to print 200 copies of McWeeney's pamphlet for distribution (McWeeney, 817).[95] The next paper that McWeeney proposed to the Society, a discussion of the findings of the Committee on Venereal Disease,[96] proved even more controversial. A special meeting of the Council was called to determine whether this was a suitable topic. Council gave its approval and the paper, complete with lantern slides showing the results of bacteriological research and the prevalence of the disease, was read in 1918 and reprinted in pamphlet form (McWeeney, 819).[97]

HOUSING

Between 1900 and 1920, the Society devoted more attention to housing than to any other social problem: three papers in volume XI, covering the sessions, 1900-06; four in volume XII (1906-11), and no less than six – the majority relating to Dublin – over the period 1912-19. Housing had been a recurrent theme in papers presented to the Society; the standard presidential address summarising changes over the previous twenty, thirty, forty or fifty years, invariably referred to improvements in housing standards as indicated by data in the Population Census. A paper by the Dublin city engineer, Spencer Harty, contains the best factual account of the Coombe Housing scheme – which became Dublin Corporation's flagship effort to rehouse the city's working-class (Harty, 507). Two papers by Nicholas Synnott examined the costs and benefits of the rural labourers' housing scheme (Synnott, 1230,1232). In 1914, the aftermath of the 1913 lock-out and the establishment of a Local Government Board inquiry into Dublin housing, prompted a flurry of interest in the city's slums and their inhabitants.

On 2 February 1914, a motion proposed by Sir William Thompson and Charles Oldham led to the establishment of a committee to examine the Dublin housing question. At the same meeting, the Council decided that David Chart would present a paper on casual labourers 'on a date which will suit the convenience of Lady Aberdeen'; the Council also agreed that the following two meetings would deal with housing or cognate subjects, with a further session devoted to a report from the committee established to consider the housing question. The committee's report was approved by Council on 24 March 1914, and read to the Society three days later.[98] It relied heavily on the Report of the Local Government Board Inquiry into the housing conditions of the Dublin working class;[99] there is no evidence that the committee conducted independent research. It recommended more stringent regulation of tenement housing, including a system of licences; resident caretakers in cases where a landlord was not resident; provisions requiring better washing and cooking facilities, and the enforcement of existing bye-laws. The report, which was highly moralistic in tone, and almost devoid of statistics, failed to consider the cost of implementing these recommendations (171). By comparison, David Chart's paper on unskilled labour in Dublin, which was read on 6 March 1914, emphasised the association between low wages and tenement housing. Chart provided data on the income of families living in tenement housing, which he had obtained from the Housing and Town Planning Association of Ireland. While acknowledging the need to enforce existing bye-laws and to educate tenement dwellers in hygiene, he believed that the solution rested with higher wages (Chart, 146). This factor was ignored, both by the Society's Committee and in the report of the LGB inquiry.

The Society's interest in the Dublin housing problem peaked in the spring of 1914. After the outbreak of war in August 1914, the British government froze all capital expenditure on housing. However the Society did not entirely ignore the subject during the war years: the somewhat rambling presidential address of William Lawson, entitled 'Social Problems and the War', at the opening of the 1916/17 session devoted considerable space to housing. Whereas Chart had emphasised that Dublin's housing conditions were a consequence of the city's employment structure, in particular the high proportion of casual labourers, Lawson echoed a long-standing preoccupation of the Society when he claimed that 'it is too often found that drink is the cause of the poverty of the occupiers of tenements'. He called for legislation to reduce the number of public houses in the city, echoing the views of the attorney general Richard Cherry in his 1911 presidential address, which dealt with juvenile crime (Lawson, 700; Cherry 151).

MEMBERSHIP

During the 1880s, the growing divisions within Irish society over matters such as Home Rule and the survival of the landlord class shattered the liberal consensus which had been the Society's bedrock. By the 1890s, these passions had receded somewhat. There was little immediate prospect of Home Rule; the British Conservative Party had embarked on a programme of socio-economic improvement, with the apparent aim of converting the masses to unionism; the Anglo-Irish ascendancy, shorn of its role as landlords and political leaders, was busily seeking other outlets, whether in the co-operative movement or in cultural revival. The report of the Recess Committee saw unionist and nationalist politicians coming together to recommend measures to revive the Irish economy.[100] Such a climate appeared to open up new opportunities for the Society. As Mr Serjeant Dodd, the president, noted in his opening address to the 1896 session, its membership included

> ... men fresh from the universities, who have knowledge of the most recent teachings of economists on such matters. We have men of most diverse views in practical politics. We have relations as corresponding societies with the Trades' Council and the University Societies, whose delegates can take part in debates. It is subjects upon which men differ in opinion that we desire to discuss, though we do not reject non-contentious matter.

Dodd's list of suggested topics included compulsory purchase of land; protection of native manufactures; monopolies and combinations; the establishment of a Catholic University; and 'even such a burning topic as the establishment of Local Self-Government in Ireland'. He continued:

> We do not encourage or invite discussion on matters in the acute stage of political controversy. There is a time in the

discussion of such social matters as spring out of politics, when the platform is the more fitting place for promulgating opinions. But there is a time when the discussion of arguments for or against a measure with something of the philosophic calm which we affect in this society may tend to allay asperities. What we mainly desire is facts and arguments (Dodd, 235).

However, the Society's menu of 'facts and arguments' does not appear to have captured the Irish imagination. In 1898/99, the Society had only 74 members, compared with 120 ten years earlier, and a record 164 members in 1849. As Black notes, the Society's golden jubilee in 1897 was not celebrated; at times it proved difficult to attract sufficient papers; 'Special committees became few and far between, prize essays quite unheard of'.

Black has suggested that the growing reliance on state aid to resolve socio-economic problems, as opposed to voluntary effort, might be one factor explaining this loss of interest.[101] Although there was some overlap in membership between the co-operative movement and the Society (both Sir Horace Plunkett and George Russell were members), the former was much more successful at engaging the interest and energy of constructive unionists. Despite the fact that the Society examined matters that were central to the economic and fiscal aspects of Irish self-government, it apparently failed to broaden its membership to include many of the newer voices. The overwhelming majority of members continued to belong to the higher professions and the senior ranks of the Irish administration.

In 1912/13, Tom Kettle, Professor of National Economics at UCD and a former MP, was the Society's only obvious link with the Irish Parliamentary Party, which was expected to form the government of a Home Rule state. In 1913, he was elected to the Council, a gesture which suggests some attempt to establish links with a forthcoming Irish administration. However, Kettle seems to have been an inactive member and although his name appeared on the ballot for Council in June 1914, he was not re-elected. Both Sinn Féin and the Labour movement were conspicuously absent. Leading businessmen were also under-represented. Four members of the Council of the Dublin Chamber of Commerce were members of the Society in 1912/13: Sir Horace Plunkett, solicitor

William Fry, Frederick W. Pim, owner of the Greenmount Spinning Co., whose family had long been associated with the Society, and barrister R.K. Gamble. Two directors of the Bank of Ireland were members: Joseph Todhunter Pim, governor of the Bank of Ireland, and Nicholas Joseph Synnott. No MPs or members of Dublin Corporation were listed. The membership was overwhelmingly Dublin-based; *no* member listed a Belfast address, which may explain the lack of attention given to Ulster.

Nevertheless, politics intruded into the relatively closed ranks of the Society. In January 1910, Nicholas Synnott drew the Council's attention to a letter which Shannon Millin – another member of the Council – had written to *The Irish Times*, claiming that Synnott's recent paper on the revaluation of land in Ireland 'was written from party motives' and that, consequently, he would object to it being published in the Journal.[102] This paper, which was presented on 17 December 1909, criticised the proposal in the 1909 Finance Bill – the famous Lloyd George budget, which had been rejected by the House of Lords, precipitating a major political crisis – to revalue agricultural land in Britain and Ireland at five-yearly intervals. Synnott claimed that the process would be vexatious to Irish landowners, and suggested that land purchase had given the state 'a new and larger thing to tax' (Synnott, 1238). Synnott informed the Council that he rejected Millin's allegations; he also read them a letter he had received from Millin (this is neither summarised nor included in the minutes). The Council deferred discussion to a special meeting, at which both the aggrieved parties would be present. Although the two men attended a Council meeting on 25 February, Millin protested that notice had not been given of a special meeting, so the Council decided that the matter should be discussed on an informal basis. This meeting reached no conclusion and the matter was not discussed on any subsequent occasion. Although the Society published Synnott's paper, he withdrew from the Council, whereas Millin remained a member.[103]

The only paper to touch, however obliquely, on the question of self-government, 'The Foundations of Colonial Self-Government', which was read in April 1917, carried a special disclaimer that 'The Author, while thanking the Society for leave to publish the paper, wishes it to be understood that for the statements and conclusions in it he alone is responsible'. In the introduction, Sir John Robert O'Connell spoke of the 'amazing progress in population and in material prosperity which had been achieved by Canada, Australia and South Africa'. Although he asserted that the topic was 'eminently within the province of this Society', since it had repeatedly considered the Irish fiscal system, at no stage does he imply that a similar constitutional status would be appropriate for Ireland. Rather, O'Connell appeared to view the subject from the perspective of the 'Mother Country', as if Ireland were part of that entity (O'Connell, 974).

Others papers also assumed that Ireland would remain an integral part of the United Kingdom, despite indications to the contrary. In 1919, R.J. Kelly read a paper on 'The Recent British Bank Amalgamations and Ireland', which referred to 'the denationalisation of the Irish Banks', that had been purchased or absorbed by British banks, as 'a matter for Irish public consideration, and [is] a matter of particular concern for Irishmen'. Kelly feared that the amalgamations would lead to capital being removed from Ireland, making it more difficult for Irish businesses to acquire the necessary funds (Kelly, 643). During the same session, Dr Michael Cox, a consultant physician at St. Vincent's Hospital, called for the establishment of a Ministry of Health for Ireland, with a Minister responsible to the Crown or to Parliament (Cox, 192). Cox not only failed to acknowledge the existence of Dáil Éireann, he also appears to have discounted the possibility of a Home Rule Parliament, which would have been given responsibility for health. In January 1920, Charles Oldham read a paper on public finance, which does not contain any reference to the possibility of Home Rule This indicated, that from 1915/16, revenue from taxation levied in Ireland substantially exceeded expenditure, reversing the deficit which had existed since the introduction of old age pensions in 1909 (Oldham, 1024).

The Society continued to meet after the outbreak of war, because the Council was of the opinion that it should examine the impact of war on the Irish economy and society, and this was duly done, with sessions devoted to the impact of the war on Irish agriculture and the difficulties involved in financing the war (Stanuell, 1169; Oldham, 1011). Although the number of meetings was reduced, the Society functioned more or less as normal, though the membership fell from 76 in 1914 to 54 by 1916. In November 1914, the Society decided in the interests of economy to dispense with the annual general meeting and not to appoint a new assistant secretary.[104] According to Black its survival rested on a small number of committed members: Charles Oldham, Dr William Lawson (son of a founding member), Sir Thomas Molony and Sir William Thompson, the Registrar General and his assistant, Daniel S. Doyle. [105] Several meetings were cancelled because no papers were forthcoming.

In 1910, the longstanding practice of holding meetings in the Friends' Hall in Molesworth Street ended, and after a brief peripatetic existence, the Society moved in 1912 to the premises of the Institute of Bankers in Ireland at 93 St Stephens Green. A meeting was scheduled for 28 April 1916, the fifth day of the 1916 Rising. Although the president, Charles Stanuell, braved the battle to reach the meeting place, the scheduled paper, 'Post-war functions of commercial education' by Professor Arthur Williamson, was postponed until the June meeting (Williamson, 1301). Professor Williamson's paper proved to be a double casualty of the Rising: the galleys were destroyed by a fire in Thoms' printing works in Abbey Street and the Council decided not to supply a replacement copy for the June meeting.[106]

By December 1918 the Council appears to have become worried about the threat of fire (whether or not this was due to political unrest is not clear) and it decided to transfer the collection of books, which had been bequeathed by Sir Thomas Larcom, to the National Library. In January 1919, 'on account of the difficulty of late travelling', meetings were scheduled for 8 p.m. rather than 8.15.[107] However the landmark dates of Irish political history, such as the opening of a Northern Ireland parliament in June 1921; the Truce in the Anglo-Irish war on 12 July 1921; the signing of the Anglo-Irish Treaty on 6 December 1921; its ratification by Dáil Éireann in January 1922 and the establishment of the Irish Free State in December 1922, all went unnoticed.

NOTES TO CHAPTER TWO

[1] Thomas L. Haskell, *The Emergence of Professional Social Science. The American Social Science Association and the Nineteenth-Century Crisis of Authority* (Urbana, Illinois, 1977), p. vi.

[2] Abrams, *The Origins of British Sociology*, pp. 45-47.

[3] *Report of the Council at the Opening of the Twelfth Session of the Society* (26 November 1858), p. 235.

[4] An exception is James S. Donnelly, 'The Irish agricultural depression of 1859-64', *Irish Economic and Social History*, 3 (1976), pp. 33-54.

[5] R.D.C. Black, *Economic Thought and the Irish Question*, p. 47.

[6] Boylan and Foley, *Political Economy and Colonial Ireland*, p. 103.

[7] George O'Brien, introduction to E.J. Riordan, *Modern Irish Trade and Industry* (London, 1920).

[8] Brendan Bradshaw, "Nationalism and historical scholarship in Modern Ireland", *Irish Historical Studies*, xxvi (1988/89), pp. 329-51. For a critical examination of this approach to Irish history see Liam Kennedy, 'Out of history: that "most distressful country"', in Liam Kennedy (ed.), *Colonialism, Religion and Nationalism in Ireland* (Belfast, 1996), pp. 182-223.

[9] W.N. Hancock, *Report on the Supposed Progressive Decline of Irish Prosperity* (Dublin, 1863).

[10] Black, *Economic Thought*, pp. 47-48.

[11] Black, 'The Irish dissenters', p. 123.

[12] Abrams, *The Origins of British Sociology*, pp. 77-79

[13] Abrams, *The Origins of British Sociology*, p. 125.

[14] Porter, *Rise of Statistical Thinking*; Theodore M. Porter, 'Lawless society: social science and the reinterpretation of statistics in Germany, 1850-1880' in Lorenz Kruger, (ed.), *The Probabilistic Revolution* (Cambridge, Mass., 1987), pp. 351-70.

[15] Council Minutes, 6 November 1877.

[16] Abrams, *The Origins of Sociology*, p. 54.

[17] Black, *Centenary Volume*, p. 35.

[18] T.S. Ashton, *Economic and Social Investigations in Manchester 1832-1933* (London, 1934).

[19] Cullen, *Statistical Movement*, pp. 146-47.

[20] Stefan Collini, *Public Moralists. Political Thought and Intellectual Life in Britain 1850-1930*, (Oxford, 1991), pp. 210-18.

[21] Cullen, *Statistical Movement*, pp. 146-47.

[22] Haskell, *Emergence of Professional Social Science*, pp. 24, 164-207.

[23] Mary E. Daly, 'The formation of an Irish nationalist elite? recruitment to the Irish civil service in the decades prior to independence, 1870-1920', *Paedagogica Historica. International Journal of the History of Education*, xxx (1994), no. 1, pp. 381-401. Haskell, p. 121, citing Bernard Crick, *American Science of Politics*, vol. 32, on the relationship between civil service reform and the rise of the university.

[24] Nineteenth-century names are numerous; nearly all the early Whately professors had legal training, as had many of the early professors of

economics at Queen's Colleges. In more recent times names such as George O'Brien and James Meenan come to mind.

[25] Ian Hacking, 'Prussian Numbers, 1860-1882', in Kruger, *Probabilistic Revolution*, p. 383.

[26] Porter, *Rise of Statistical Thinking*, pp. 79-82, 255-69, 315-17.

[27] Council Minutes, 9 January 1863.

[28] *Census of Ireland for the Year 1871. General Report*, pp. 62-74.

[29] Council Minutes 17 November 1874.

[30] Council Minutes, 6 November 1877.

[31] *Census of Ireland for the Year 1881.General Report*, p. 11 mentions that the Irish Government gave the Census Commmissioners a direction to collect this information 'at the suggestion of the Statistical and Social Inquiry Society of Ireland'.

[32] Council Minutes, 5 January 1888.

[33] Black, *Centenary Volume*, p. 39.

[34] Charles Booth,'The economic distribution of population', in William P. Coyne (ed.), *Ireland: Industrial and Agricultural* (Dublin, 1902), pp 64-72. The data were originally presented in a paper to the Royal Statistical Society.

[35] W.L. Burn, 'Free trade in land, an aspect of the Irish euestion', *Transactions, of the Royal Historical Society,* xxxi (1949), pp. 61-74.

[36] Cardwell's Act ensured that tenants would be compensated for improvements, provided that they had obtained prior approval from their landlord. Deasy's Act sought to place the relationship between landlord and tenant on a contractual basis. For details see J.C. Brady, 'Legal developments, 1801-79', in Vaughan (ed.), *A New History of Ireland. V*, pp. 457-63.

[37] David Steele, *Irish Land and British Politics. Tenant-Right and Nationality 1865-1870* (Cambridge 1974), pp. 43-70.

[38] Black, *Centenary Volume*, p. 8.

[39] Clive Dewey, 'Celtic agrarian legislation and the Celtic revival: historicist implications of Gladstone's Irish and Scottish Land Acts 1870-1886', *Past and Present,* no. 64 (1974), pp. 30-70.

[40] Black, *Economic Thought*, pp. 46-49.

[41] Steele, *Irish Land*, pp. 68-73.

[42] Council Minutes, 13 March 1866, Appendix B.

[43] Brady, 'Legal Developments, 1801-79' in Vaughan (ed.), *A New History of Ireland V*, p. 457.

[44] Council Minutes, 13 March 1866, appendix B 2.

[45] Council Minutes 4 December 1866; 10 January 1867.

[46] Council Minutes, 3 June 1873.

[47] Boylan and Foley, *Political Economy and Colonial Ireland,* pp. 57-62.

[48] *Report from the select committee on the Irish land act, 1870; together with the proceedings of the committee, minutes of evidence and appendix,* 1877 (328), xii; *Report from the select committee on the Irish land act, 1870; together with the proceedings of the committee, minutes of evidence, and appendix,* 1878 (249), xv.

[49] Daly 'Frugal comfort', p. 82.

[50] Margaret O'Callaghan, *British High Politics and a Nationalist Ireland Criminality, Land and the Law under Forster and Balfour* (Cork, 1994).

[51] Daly, *Dublin: The Deposed Capital*, pp. 57-58.

[52] Council Minutes, 22 June 1880, 9 May 1882.

[53] Abrams, *Origins of British Sociology*, pp. 49-51.

[54] Haskell, *Emergence of Professional Social Science*, p. 63.

[55] Report of Council at Opening of Thirty-fourth Session, read 30 November 1880 , *JSSISI,* vol. viii, pp. 142-53.

[56] For biographies of both O'Hagan and Monsell, see Black, *Centenary Volume*, pp. 68-70, 79-80.

[57] There did not appear to be any direct evidence of the Society exerting influence on the chief secretary, the undersecretary or senior Dublin Castle officials in the Registered Papers of the chief secretary's Office. If such influence was brought to bear, and I firmly believe that it was, it was done by individual members acting on a personal basis and not by the Society as a whole.

[58] Lentaigne, 705. 1877, p. 7.

[59] For Ulster, see B.M. Walker, *Ulster Politics. The Formative Years, 1868-86* (Belfast, 1989).

[60] Paul Bew, *C.S. Parnell* (Dublin, 1980), pp. 137-38.

[61] Grand juries were unelected bodies, consisting of landlords, who were responsible for many aspects of local government, including road repair and courts and jails in each county. Despite several attempts to transform them into elective bodies, they continued unaltered until 1898 when they were replaced by elected county councils.

[62] Lord Ashbourne, formerly Edward Gibson, served as honorary secretary of the Statistical Society, 1862-66.

[63] Liam Kennedy, 'The economic thought of the nation's lost leader', in Kennedy (ed) *Colonialism*, p. 91.

[64] Liam Kennedy and David S. Johnson, 'The Union of Ireland and Britain', in D.G. Boyce and Alan O' Day (eds), *The Making of Modern Irish History. Revision and the Revisionist Controversy* (London,1996), p. 49.

[65] James Meenan, *George O'Brien, A Biographical Memoir* (Dublin, 1980), p. 129.

[66] Council Minutes, 5 November 1910.

[67] (London, 1903). This book was based on Murray's D.Sc. Econ, which was awarded by the London School of Economics in 1902/03, the first such degree awarded to a woman recorded on the LSE register. See Maxine Berg, 'The first women economic historians', *Economic History Review*, xlv, no 2 (May 1992), p. 317.

[68] R.F. Foster, *W.B. Yeats. A Life. I: The Apprentice Mage* (Oxford, 1997), p. 39.

[69] Andrew Gailey, *Ireland and the Death of Kindness. The Experience of Constructive Unionism 1890-1905* (Cork, 1987), pp. 82-83; Lawrence W. McBride, *The Greening of Dublin Castle. The Transformation of Bureaucratic and Judicial Personnel in Ireland, 1892-1922* (Washington, 1991), p. 229.

[70] Kennedy and Johnson, 'The Union of Ireland and Britain, 1801-1921' in Boyce and O' Day, *The Making of Modern Irish History*, pp. 48-54; Pauric Travers,'The financial relations question,1800-1914', in F.B. Smith (ed.), *Ireland, England and Australia. Essays in Honour of Oliver MacDonagh*

(Cork, 1990), pp. 50-56.

[71] On grants in aid and de-rating of agricultural land see Mary E. Daly, *The Buffer State. The Historical Roots of the Department of the Environment* (Dublin, 1997), pp. 25, 35-37.

[72] A phrase used in the course of a similar argument by the nineteenth century Italian statistican Cesare Correnti, quoted in Patriarca, *Numbers and Nationhood*, p. 43.

[73] A similar argument is presented at much greater length by Finlay's successor as professor of political economy at UCD. George O'Brien, *An Essay on the Economic Effects of the Reformation* (London, 1923).

[74] Daly, *The Buffer State*, p. 40.

[75] Daly 'Frugal Comfort', p. 82.

[76] Council Minutes, 7 December 1875.

[77] Gertrude Himmelfarb, *Poverty and Compassion. The Moral Imagination of the Late Victorians* (New York, 1991), pp. 5-6, 12, 185-94.

[78] Council Minutes, 11 January 1876; 8 February 1876.

[79] Daly, *The Deposed Capital*, pp. 230-32, 237-39.

[80] Daly, *Deposed Capital*, pp. 97-98.

[81] Maria Luddy, 'Isabella M.S. Tod', in Mary Cullen and Maria Luddy (eds), *Women, Power and Consciousness in Nineteenth-Century Ireland* (Dublin, 1995), pp. 197-230.

[82] Mary Cullen, 'Anna Maria Haslam', in Cullen and Luddy, *Women, Power and Consciousness*, pp. 161-97.

[83] The topic was first explored in F.K. Prochaska, *Women and Philanthropy in Nineteenth-Century England* (Oxford, 1980). For Ireland see, Maria Luddy, *Women and Philanthropy in Nineteenth-Century Ireland* (Cork, 1995).

[84] Daly, *Deposed Capital*, pp. 104, 114.

[85] Luddy, *Women and Philanthropy*, pp. 86-93.

[86] Rosa M. Barrett, *Guide to Dublin Charities* (Dublin, 1884).

[87] Joseph Robins, *The Lost Children. A Study of Charity Children in Ireland 1700-1900* (Dublin, 1980), pp. 307-08.

[88] NSPCC first report 1889-90, as cited in Daly, *The Deposed Capital*, p. 96.

[89] Luddy, *Women and Philanthropy*, p. 94.

[90] Malcolm, *'Ireland Sober, Ireland Free'*, p. 274.

[91] Council Minutes, 13 January 1953.

[92] Thomas Willis, *Facts Connected with the Social and Sanitary Conditions of the Working Classes of Dublin* (Dublin, 1845).

[93] Daly, *The Deposed Capital*, pp. 247, 272-75.

[94] Daly, *The Deposed Capital*, pp. 266-67.

[95] Council Minutes, 1 February 1915 and 30 April 1915.

[96] *Report of the Inter-Departmental Committee on Infectious Diseases in Connection with Demobilisation* 1919 Cmd. 322, xxx.

[97] Council Minutes 21 November 1917; 24 January 1918.

[98] Council Minutes, 2 February 1914; 24 March 1914.

[99] *Report of the Departmental Committee appointed to inquire into the Housing Conditions of the Working Class in Dublin* 1914 (cd. 7317), xix, 61.

[100] *Report of the Recess Committee on the Establishment of a Department of*

Agriculture and Industries (Dublin, 1896); Gailey, *Ireland and the Death of Kindness.*

[101] Black, *Centenary Volume*, p. 35.

[102] It would seem that the *Irish Times* did not publish Millin's letter; I have failed to find it.

[103] Council Minutes, 15 January 1910; 25 February 1910.

[104] Council Minutes, November 1914

[105] Black, *Centenary Volume*, p. 41.

[106] Council Minutes, 22 May 1916.

[107] Council Minutes, 6 December 1918, 14 January 1919.

CHAPTER THREE

The Society and the Irish Free State 1922-49

During the early 1920s the Society had to establish a rapport with the Irish Free State and confront a number of internal difficulties. In December 1919, the Council took steps to revive the Barrington lecture series, which had lapsed in 1912.[1] This appears to have prompted Shannon Millin, the Society's honorary librarian, and a member of Council, to write to the Commissioners of Charitable Bequests and Donations, informing them of the conditions and terms associated with the Barrington bequest, without first consulting the Council. Having read the correspondence – which apparently does not survive – the Council decided 'that, although Mr Millin had explicitly disclaimed in his letter any intention of involving the Society in his action, nevertheless by his repeated reference to the proceedings of the Society and extensive quotations from the Minutes of the Council, he has practically associated the Council with his application to the Commissioners.' Millin declined the Council's request that he withdraw his letter and he resigned from the Council and from the Society.[2] He had compiled an index of the Society's transactions, which he used as the basis of a brief history. Millin was also responsible for the decision to transfer the Larcom Collection to the National Library.[3]

The Society was also forced to vacate its rooms in the Bankers' Institute. Plunkett House in Merrion Square, the headquarters of the Irish Agricultural Organisation Society, offered accommodation, but while this was welcome, it meant that meetings had to take place at 5 pm. By November 1921, the Society was also facing a financial crisis, the outcome of wartime inflation and a declining membership.

Relations with the new administration cannot have been easy.

In July 1920, Sir James Molony, Lord Chief Justice, became President; he held the position until 1924. The Irish Free State inherited two antagonistic court systems: the Dáil Courts, which sided with the anti-Treaty camp, and the British court system, of which Molony was Lord Chief Justice. In the end it largely dispensed with both.[4] During the summer of 1922, Molony travelled to London to confer with senior British officials about the future of the old judiciary. He also reluctantly agreed, on the urging of the Attorney General, Hugh Kennedy, to allow the words 'Rialtas Sealadach na hÉireann' (Provisional Government of Ireland) to be superimposed at the head of future High Court proceedings.[5] Such actions were unlikely to have endeared Molony to the government of the Irish Free State, and it seems probable that the Society would have been better served if the president, during these difficult transitional years, had been a leading academic, a medical man, or a public servant holding an uncontroversial position, such as the Registrar General, Sir William Thompson. In October 1947, during the course of the Society's centenary celebrations, Molony, then aged 82, recalled these years as a time when he was 'sometimes under police protection, sometimes under military protection'. Shortly after stepping down as president he retired to England, owing to 'circumstances'.[6]

A quick glance at the list of papers presented to the Society suggests that it steered clear of controversy. Topics such as 'The Nurse and the State' (Falkiner, 310); 'Irish Intellect: Its Geographical Distribution' (Flinn, 328); 'Some American Views of Penology' (Buchanan, 113); and 'Clean Milk' (Bigger, 67) had little to say about partition, the Anglo-Irish Treaty, civil war, or the teething problems associated with a new state.

The first formal acknowledgement of the existence of the Irish Free State came in the spring of 1924, when the Council announced that Charles Oldham would read a paper on the Fiscal Inquiry Commission. The Commission had been established by the new government, in June 1923, to report on the effect of the existing fiscal system (which had been inherited virtually unchanged from the British administration) on industry and agriculture, and on any changes intended to foster industrial and agricultural development.[7] Although this paper does not seem to have materialised, it was an augury of a new era. In July 1924, i.e. before the beginning of the

1924/25 session, Oldham succeeded Molony as president, and the Society experienced the largest single increase in membership since 1847. All the new candidates were proposed by Oldham and seconded by Sir William Thompson. They included Professor William Magennis, professor of philosophy at UCD, and a pro-government Dáil deputy; William Leet, lecturer in banking and finance at TCD, the German consul in Dublin, and the librarian of Plunkett House. The most important accessions were the eight new members from the Department of Industry and Commerce, including John Hooper, Stanley Lyon, Thomas Barrington, and Callaghan McCarthy from the Statistics Department of the Ministry of Local Government.[8] As a special concession the Council decided that their subscriptions would apply until the end of the 1924/25 session. On 14 November 1924, the Council approved the membership of two secretaries of government departments: Gordon Campbell of Industry and Commerce, and E.P. McCarron of Local Government and Public Health. Other new members elected on this occasion included TCD economist Joseph Johnston and Osborn Bergin, professor of Early and Medieval Irish at UCD.

Further evidence of *rapprochement* with the new state came at the first general meeting of the 1924/25 session, when the Society received a letter from President W.T. Cosgrave, conveying his interest in the subject of that night's paper – 'The Interpretation of Irish Statistics' by Charles Oldham – and regretting his inability to be present because of illness. It was an astute move for the Society to invite Cosgrave, the head of government, rather than the Governor General Tim Healy (the Viceroy had tradition-ally been invited to attend the opening meeting of each session). The 1924/25 session saw a continuing stream of new members, mostly drawn from the civil service, with the largest contingent drawn from the Department of Industry and Commerce. At a council meeting on 22 January 1925, Oldham suggested that the Society respond to the upsurge in membership by introducing additional activities, though there is no evidence that this happened.[9]

Most accounts of the formation of the Irish Free State emphasise the degree of continuity between the membership of the new Irish civil service and the former British administration. While it is true that 21,000 civil servants transferred from the British civil service,

whereas only 131 had been employed by Dáil Éireann, independence brought the resignation or retirement of most of the senior
officials who had been associated with the British administration.[10]
Although men such as Thomas Barrington, John Hooper and E.P.
McCarron had been employed by the British administration in
Ireland – Barrington and Hooper in the Department of Agriculture
and Technical Instruction, McCarron in the Local Government
Board – the change of government ensured their promotion to
more senior ranks. While some new members, such as Joseph
Brennan (secretary of the Department of Finance), John Hooper
and Roy Geary, were university graduates, others, like Thomas
Barrington had received little formal education.[11] At a time when
there were no provisions for in-service training for public servants,
the Society offered an informal medium of further education, and
provided a mechanism for contact between the civil service and
the universities. The latter was potentially important (whether
or not it was fully exploited we cannot say) because the close
relationship which existed between Oxbridge and Whitehall,
with the First Division men of the civil service overwhelmingly
recruited from these universities, was not replicated in Ireland.[12]

Membership of the Society almost doubled between 1921 and
1925, and the new recruits soon began to play a prominent role.
In 1926, R.C. Geary became an honorary secretary; John Hooper,
director of statistics in the Department of Industry and Commerce, was elected president in 1929/30. By 1931/32, the Council
included Joseph Brennan, who was now chairman of the Currency
Commission, J.P. Colbert, head of the Agricultural Credit
Corporation, Stanley Lyon, who succeeded Hooper as director of
statistics in the Department of Industry and Commerce, and
Bridget Stafford of the Department of Industry and Commerce.
Lord Glenavy, governor of the Bank of Ireland and former
secretary of Industry and Commerce, and three secretaries of
departments of state: John Leydon (Industry and Commerce), J.J.
McElligott (Finance) and E.P. McCarron, (Local Government
and Public Health) were members. Although Industry and
Commerce accounted for the strongest representation, the Society
also drew members from the Departments of Agriculture and
Lands, Finance, the Revenue Commissioners, Local Government
and Public Health, Education, and External Affairs. The medical

profession was strongly represented, particularly those who were active in the field of public health, but the number of legal members declined, as did the number of papers devoted to jurisprudence and legal reform. Mr Justice J.C. Meredith, a former King's Counsel who had served as president of the Supreme Court of the First Dáil, and as a member of the High Court of the Irish Free State, was the last senior legal figure to serve as president.[13]

Businessmen were also conspicuous by their absence: Louis Cullen has described J.C.M. Eason, managing director of the Dublin bookseller and the country's leading distributor of published material, as 'the only twentieth-century Dublin businessman who played a prominent role in the Society'. Eason was also active in the Dublin Chamber of Commerce and the Civics Institute – an organisation that interested itself in projects to improve the quality of life for the urban working class.[14] He was president from 1930 to 1934. By the 1920s membership appears to have been almost mandatory for academic economists, though they remained a minority presence. Another new member was R.J. Mortished, assistant secretary to the Irish Labour Party and Trade Union Congress, whose election marks the first links between the Society and the trade unions. Ministers and deputies began to attend on an occasional basis. In February 1927, the Minister for Fisheries, Fionán Lynch, heard TCD economist George Duncan deliver a paper on rural industry in North Carolina, and contributed to the discussion (Duncan, 255). In April 1927, General Richard Mulcahy TD attended as a visitor and replied to a paper by Thomas Barrington on the clash between individualist and social concepts of value (Barrington, 41). A paper on national economic councils in France and Germany in March 1929 attracted comments from both Éamon de Valera and Tom Johnston of the Labour Party (Mortished, 898). Seán MacEntee replied to a paper on the currency problems in the Irish Free State in December 1931, three months before he became Minister for Finance (Brennan, 95). When the leading British economist and statistician Sir Josiah Stamp visited Dublin in 1930, the Council hosted a lunch to which Ernest Blythe (Minister for Finance) and Patrick McGilligan (Industry and Commerce and External Affairs) were invited. In 1931, as part of a membership drive, the Council sent a circular outlining the Society's objectives to selected members of the Dáil and Seanad.

As a consequence of the influx of new members, positions on the Council were keenly contested for the first time in many years. There were 21 nominations for 12 places at the beginning of the 1925/26 session.[15] In 1925, the Society balloted members to ascertain the most suitable time for meetings: most expressed a preference for 8 p.m., which ruled out Plunkett House. In June 1925, the Royal Irish Academy, which had hosted the first meeting of the Society came to the rescue,[16] and meetings took place in Academy House, Dawson Street until 1982 when they were moved to the Economic and Social Research Institute premises at Burlington Road.

The economic dislocation which followed the ending of World War I, and the birth pangs of the new state both provided ample material. In January 1925, the Council invited a number of experts on housing to attend a paper which examined housing policy in Britain and Ireland, including T.J. Byrne of the Office of Public Works, a former housing inspector with the Local Government Board, the town clerks of Dublin and Pembroke and an alderman from Wexford town. The speaker, J. Maguire, formerly chief clerk at the Registry of Deeds, favoured self-help, co-operative housing ventures, the establishment of public utility societies and the encouragement of owner-occupied housing, proposals that were very much in keeping with the thrust of the government's 1924 Housing Act (Maguire, 821).[17] After what appears to have been an unusually successful meeting, the Council set up a committee to evaluate various solutions to the housing problem – an activity which was reminiscent of the Society's earlier years.[18] There is no evidence that the committee reported

While the growing number of public servants invigorated the Society and offered fertile scope for papers, it also restricted its ability to establish independent committees. It was both acceptable and appropriate for the scholars and private citizens who founded the Society to offer recommendations on policy to a government, but not for public servants. The involvement of civil servants would also have strengthened the traditional veto on political discussion. Given the divisions which existed within Irish society during the 1920s, this may have been a good thing.

IRISH OFFICIAL STATISTICS

The Society's interest in the formation of the new state focused primarily on the collection and interpretation of official statistics. R.D.C. Black dates to these years the close connection between the Statistical Society and the Statistics Branch of the Department of Industry and Commerce (the forerunner of the Central Statistics Office). [19] Although this may be true in a formal sense, a careful scanning of earlier volumes of the Journal reveals a growing interest in the collection and interpretation of Irish official statistics, which was extended after 1922. The critical date seems to be 1899, when the Department of Agriculture and Technical Instruction (DATI) was founded. Many of the key figures, who were responsible for establishing the statistical service of the Irish Free State, such as John Hooper, Stanley Lyon and Thomas Barrington, had previously worked in the statistics section of the DATI.[20] With the holding of the first Census of Production in 1907 (by the UK Board of Trade), and the appearance in 1904 of the first official Irish trade statistics to be produced since 1825,[21] the range of economic statistics had already expanded significantly before 1922. Moreover, according to Sir William Thompson, official statistics were increasingly regarded as essential tools in determining economic and social policy (Thompson, 1249), although whether or not there was much scope for implementing such policies before 1922 remains a moot point.

One of the key figures in the development of Irish official statistics was W.G.S. Adams, an economist, who was educated at Balliol College, and who was the head of the statistics section of the DATI from 1906 until 1910, when he returned to Oxford where he had been appointed Gladstone Professor of Political Economy. Adams was responsible for producing the first estimate of Irish agricultural output, which related to the year 1908.[22] In 1909, he explained that 'the inquisitorial faculty of the State has become very much more highly developed, and one nation cannot afford to be behind another in its knowledge and scrutiny of social and economic conditions'. Adams argued that statistics were an essential instrument in the development and evaluation of public policy, and that they were equally essential to private enterprise. This was the first paper to examine the inadequacies of the existing statistical data, and it suggested how they might be overcome. Speaking about the trade returns prepared under his direction by the statistics branch of the Department of Agriculture,[23] Adams highlighted the deficiencies that resulted from valuing trade on the basis of official values, rather than on the basis of values as declared by traders. He also argued that there was a need to introduce a more precise classification of articles traded. Adams believed that the greatest shortcoming was the absence of a declaration as to the country of origin of goods imported into Ireland, and the country of destination of goods exported. Most goods were shipped via Britain; consequently the ultimate origin and destination was unknown (Adams, 1). Until 1935, data on goods imported into Ireland related to the country of consignment, not the country of origin.[24]

The number of papers devoted to the collection and interpretation of national statistics rose sharply after 1922. This is scarcely surprising given the background of many new members, and the fact that these years saw the further development of an Irish statistical service. Further stimulus came from the comparative statistics collected by international organisations such as the League of Nations and the International Labour Organisation. The fledgling Irish Free State played an active role in both the League of Nations and the ILO, using the opportunity to assert Irish independence. C.H. Oldham, who served as president from 1924 until his death in 1926, read five papers on statistical topics between 1922 and 1925. Oldham had an almost missionary belief in the importance of statistics. In December 1925, he noted that

> To-day Irish statisticians are proudly conscious that they are the interpreters to other nations of the social and economic character of an independent Member of the League of Nations. Hence we may expect to find in the statistical publications of the Irish Free State an habitual use of comparison of Irish figures with the corresponding figures for other European or Dominion countries, which are of the type most suitable for comparison with our own type. This will be an absolutely new departure in Irish Statistics; it will carry the minds of the Irish people into regions of thought hitherto unknown to them. I do not mean that their knowledge of Ireland itself will dawn for the

first time upon their intelligence with a quite novel significance. Nobody can know Ireland who only Ireland knows. The statistical purpose of such international comparisons is to provide the human mind with a norm or standard by which the character of the Irish fact (when reduced to measurement by statistics) can be judged and assigned its peculiar (often very peculiar!) place among the facts of the contemporary world. The outstanding hitherto-unseen truth which Irish Statistics will now reveal to ourselves is that Ireland is amazingly unlike any other country. Her statistics will become the most quoted of all countries because in most statistical generalisations Ireland will be found to be an exceptional case. But nobody in Ireland is yet aware how anomalous we Irish are, unless he has been at the trouble (and it is a very great trouble) to compare Irish Statistics with the comparable statistics of other countries.

Oldham ended by reiterating that 'The People that is [*sic*] unable to properly use statistics is not yet capable of self-government' (Oldham, 1025). Such comments suggest that he may have harboured doubts about Ireland's readiness for self-government. In an article for the *Manchester Guardian Commercial* in 1923, which he quoted in a paper to the Society, Oldham claimed that 'The Celt had no use for statistics hitherto' and that 'Irish facts are not what they are commonly thought and said to be'. This comment can be linked with a statement in the same paper, that 'the capacity of a people for self-government can be pretty well measured by their capacity to handle statistical evidence as to the economic position of their country'; a capacity, which 'hardly exists among our responsible public representatives' and was 'very rare among our irresponsible private citizens'. Oldham decried the fact that the last census of production dated from 1908, the last population census from 1911; no report had been compiled on agricultural statistics since 1917, and the most recent external trade statistics related to 1921. He blamed this state of affairs on the government of the Irish Free State, because he remarked that 'under the old Dublin Castle government Irish economic statistics were, as a rule, well done'. This comment was intemperate and inaccurate: the lacunae in statistical series was due to the effects of World War I, the Anglo-Irish War and the

Irish civil war, and Dublin Castle was at least partly responsible.

Oldham urged the Society to play a more active role in improving Irish official statistics. He expressed the belief that there was an 'immense job waiting to be done by the present generation of Irishmen in the construction of our statistical records, the interpretation of the figures, and their presentation to our legislators and journalists in a form that is capable of being understood by ordinary people.' This task afforded the Society an opportunity to attract 'a number of workers who would patriotically co-operate together for the improvement of Irish Statistics'. He also suggested that the Society adopt as a new objective: 'the better interpretation of Irish Statistics'. Oldham expressed the hope that 'It might be possible, after some ten years of carefully planned spade work, for us to bring out a Statistical Abstract for the Irish Free State (Oldham, 1023). Oldham's penchant for drawing intellectual links between statistics and self-government echoed attitudes found in other newly independent states. In Italy, for example, according to one recent historian, members of the 'new state elite' – a term that could apply to the Statistical Society – regarded statistics 'as the midwife of a healthy "national body"'.[25]

Oldham was particularly concerned that the 1926 Census was being conducted by the Department of Local Government and Public Health, and not by an independent Commission; he feared that this would mean that tables found in earlier Censuses would be discontinued. He was particularly concerned to maintain comparability between the Population Census of the Irish Free State and that in Northern Ireland and confessed to having a 'Day Dream: to see the formation of a Central Statistics Office, or a Central Statistics Board, which would assume responsibility for all official statistics' (Oldham, 1023). His fears were exaggerated. Indeed, the Minister for Local Government and Public Health, Séamus de Búrca, sought the advice of the Society, and of relevant professors in Irish universities, as to how the Census should be carried out and the data classified. The Society established a sub-committee to consider this matter.

Some of Oldham's strictures against the statistical services indicate a rather old-fashioned attitude towards statistics and a lack of awareness of the potential offered by sampling techniques. Until 1918 the Agricultural Statistics had been collected by members of the Royal Irish Constabulary, who called to each farm holding and laboriously recorded data on crop acreage and livestock numbers; from 1919 the outbreak of the Anglo-Irish war meant that they were based on sample returns obtained through the post. Oldham was concerned that data collected in this manner might not be comparable with the earlier returns. He also spoke at considerable length about the lack of comparability of earlier Censuses of Population, because those taken before 1861 had omitted British military personnel serving in Ireland. Such comments suggested undue concern with statistical minutiae, and no concept of margins of error.

When Oldham's 1924 presidential address was published, it was followed by an addendum which contained the comments of John Hooper, Director of Statistics at the Department of Industry and Commerce. Although this appears to have been the first occasion when the discussion following a paper was published along with the paper, it rapidly became one of the most valuable aspects of the Journal. While Hooper's remarks included an element of self-defence, he made several valid points. He regarded Oldham's comment that 'The interpretation of Irish statistics is specially troublesome, because the statistical material here is so fragmentary, so blotted all over with inaccuracies, public in such an undigested and unintelligible form', as 'a very serious statement', which would shake public confidence. Hooper claimed that Ireland had 'the finest body of agricultural statistics of any country in the world', a claim supported by many modern economic historians.[26] He also indicated that the Department of Industry and Commerce was preparing to compile a census of industrial production, and that a Statistical Yearbook would appear in a much shorter period than ten years. The first Statistical Abstract published related to 1931 (Lyon, 746). A paper read during the 1924/25 session by R.C. Geary, his first to the Society, also contained oblique criticism of Oldham. Geary examined the possibility of applying sampling methods to Irish statistics, and showed that collecting agricultural statistics from a sample of farm holdings, as opposed to the traditional practice of a universal census, would give rise to a low error rate (Geary, 360).

The 1924 trade statistics, one of the first publications from the new statistical section of the Department of Industry and Commerce and the first to be based on customs documents relating to Anglo-Irish trade,[27] were analysed in detail by the Society in the course of a symposium that stretched over two evenings, on 1 and 15 May 1925 (Eason, 285; Leet, 705; Lyon, 751; Manley, 833; Oldham, 1026; Shields, 1145). Speaking on 15 May, Oldham suggested that while the trade statistics, taken in isolation, indicated an excess of imports over exports of £16m, approximately one-third the value of exports, this deficit was fully covered by sources such as foreign pensions and dividends accruing to residents of the Irish Free State, and that consequently the economy was in a relatively healthy condition. In support of this line of argument, both Oldham and Francis Leet (a banker) cited the balance sheets of Irish commercial banks and data on income tax receipts. The two speakers emphasised the merits of using a range of statistical series, as opposed to viewing the trade statistics in isolation. John Busteed, professor of economics at University College Cork, further advanced the Society's discussion of economic statistics in November 1926, when he explored the possibility of devising an elementary economic barometer to monitor cyclical fluctuations, as had been done in other countries by agencies such as the United States National Bureau for Economic Research. Busteed shared Oldham's faith that statistics could promote a more rational attitude towards economic questions. He claimed that 'In Ireland we are not very interested in the cyclical fluctuations in trade; we probably do not believe in them. We are more anxious to prove that the country is going to the dogs'. Busteed expressed the hope that this meeting would make 'a positive contribution to quantitative economics' (Busteed, 114). Quantitative economics is unlikely to have featured much in the curriculum of Irish universities at this stage. Nevertheless Busteed succeeded in persuading the Cork Chamber of Commerce to help him establish a bureau of economic research at UCC.[28]

ECONOMIC AND SOCIAL POLICIES IN THE IRISH FREE STATE

Irish nationalist ideology tended to be highly critical of neo-classical economics, preferring an amalgam of catholic social teaching and romanticised ideas about quasi communal property, which it derived from a sympathetic interpretation of the Brehon Law. The establishment of Dáil Eireann gave renewed life to unorthodox economic ideas, because it opened up the possibility of putting them into practice. In the 1920s, however, interest in alternative socio-economic models was not limited to Ireland. When World War I ended, the pre-1914 economic order was not restored, and the problems posed by rampant inflation, unemployment and frustrated expectations among workers led to a vogue for proposals that seemed to offer a painless alternative to the extremes of capitalism or socialism. Throughout the 1920s the Irish government devoted considerable energy to damping down unrealistic expectations, and to restoring the primacy of economic orthodoxy. Although most papers read to the Society defended economic orthodoxy, some favoured a more radical approach.

In a paper entitled 'Poverty Problems for a Patriot Parliament', presented in April 1922, John Dunne, who described himself as secretary of the Irish Mothers' Pension Society, offered an amalgam of the Sinn Féin assumption that Ireland possessed inexhaustible resources which were ripe for development, with catholic social teaching. Laced with references to 'the Divine Master', 'Christian and patriotic principles', 'those whom Christ loved best', it echoed the philosophy of the Democratic Programme presented to the First Dáil in 1919. The Democratic Programme suggested that it would be the first duty of the government 'to secure that no child shall suffer hunger or cold from lack of food, clothing or shelter' and promised 'a sympathetic native scheme for the care of the Nation's aged and infirm'. Dunne ignored the financial constraints facing the Irish Free State (these became more apparent in 1923 because of the security costs and damage to property consequent on the civil war) and the economy drive that was already evident in Irish social services, with the abolition of the workhouse. He demanded a vigorous government campaign to end unemployment, including a plan to develop all vacant lands, underused waterways and mineral resources, and an investigation of the possibility of developing various industries. Dunne suggested that state grants and loans should be provided to all companies, co-operative societies and individuals who were prepared to develop indigenous resources. Grants should be proportionate to the number of manual workers employed. In all cases where public funds were provided, the state should be given the right to acquire sole ownership of the asset. Additional money should be provided to enable local authorities to carry out public works, while the state should initiate its own series of development projects. Dunne also proposed that a Ministry of Labour should exercise stringent controls over employment, wages and strikes; labour exchanges would be abolished; workers would be required to join a trade union; and workers and employers' conciliation councils would be established. Short-term unemployment benefit would be provided by trade unions, though the state would support necessitous women and children by means of a capital levy on the 'idle wealth' and 'buried millions' in the Irish banks. Dunne's utopia included a national health service and cottage homes for the aged and infirm, 'where freedom, flowers, and human friendship would brighten their declining years', with meals provided by 'a co-operative canteen where profiteering was unknown' (Dunne, 261).

It would be interesting to know whether this paper was vetted in advance by the honorary secretaries. Regrettably the Journal does not record the discussion which followed either this paper, or a paper read in December 1924 on the Social Credit scheme devised by the American Major Douglas (Leet, 704). Douglas, who viewed economic conditions in Doomsday terms several years before the 1929 Crash, was determined to end unemployment, and to raise living standards for the masses by replacing the competitive market system with a society which was organised, on what Douglas believed to be a basis similar to the medieval Guild movement.[29] He argued that 'industry should serve the individual', as opposed to the individual becoming the servant of industry. Banks should be brought under democratic control and required to provide sufficient credit to enable consumers to buy all that society could produce, without worrying about formalities such as security for loans. Higher spending power would raise living standards without the danger of inflation; this would enable borrowers to repay their loans, and everybody would be a winner.

Such ideas were popular in Ireland because they confirmed the belief that the country had considerable unexploited natural resources, and Social Credit appeared to offer a mechanism for ending emigration. The prioritising of social needs over individual wants echoed catholic social teaching, and Social Credit formed the basis of the Third Minority Report to the 1934-38 Banking Commission, written by Bulmer Hobson, a founding member of Sinn Féin, and Mrs Bertram Waters, wife of the president of the Guild of Catholic Doctors. These ideas formed a vital ingredient in the economic policy of the Clann na Poblachta party, founded in 1946. Social Credit marked a direct attack on the commercial banking system. Francis Leet, who read this paper on Social Credit, was a senior official of the Bank of Ireland. He demolished Douglas's ideas in a relatively light-hearted manner, comparing him to 'the strong angel of the *Apocalypse*' and the Pied Piper of Hamelin. He also drew attention to the similarity between Douglas's ideas and those of Bishop Berkeley – an interesting analogy because Berkeley's views were popular with the early Fianna Fáil party.[30]

At first sight, the paper on rural industries in North Carolina, which George Duncan, a future Whately professor of Political Economy at Trinity College Dublin, read in 1926/27 seems an exotic offering. Like Leet, Duncan was attempting to refute popular arguments in favour of dispersing manufacturing industry. He claimed that most enthusiasts for rural industries[31] had 'an emotional repugnance to certain features of industrial economy'. They approached the subject 'from the sentimental or cultural point of view which was attracted by decentralised organisation and small units as a means of "uplift" in character, in the fullness and happiness of life, and in democratic government'. Duncan linked the vogue for decentralised industry with economic nationalism, self-sufficiency, a desire to secure the benefits of industry without the horrors of mass industrialisation, and opposition to mass production. In North Carolina, however, the expansion of rural industries had taken place not as a result of government policy, but as a consequence of socio-economic conditions, such as the dispersed sources of raw materials and water power, over which its promoter had little control. Far from being socially advantageous, the wages in North Carolina textiles mills were much lower and the working hours longer than in comparable mills in New England. As a result, it was often necessary for both husbands and wives to seek employment, and for young children to enter the mills. Geographic isolation gave employers a monopoly of the labour market and consequently control over the labour force (Duncan, 255). Despite Duncan's assault on the concept, decentralisation of industry became a core element of Fianna Fáil's economic policy after 1932, and remained an integral part of Irish industrial policy until at least the 1970s, although a strong Irish trade union movement ensured that national wage rates prevailed.[32]

Thomas Barrington's paper on 'Individualistic and Social Concept of Value' is noteworthy because, although his argument was couched in abstract terms, it contained an implicit criticism of current government policy towards industry, and Barrington was a senior civil servant in the Department of Industry and Commerce. An obituary, published on Barrington's tragic death in March 1930, described this paper as 'profoundly interesting and original'.[33] Barrington was wrestling with a concept that was similar to Pigou's distinction between private and social costs, though the paper, which is liberally sprinkled with footnotes, contains no reference to Pigou's writings. He asserted that 'economic society is, and must remain, predominantly socialistic' and condemned theoretical economics for doing 'a real disservice to mankind by excessively stressing the importance of exchange value in relation to social wealth', and for setting labour 'at the throat of capital'. The penultimate paragraph claimed:

> One of the lessons which the facts adduced in this paper inculcate is that no country can afford to consent to the export, indefinitely of its natural products in return for manufactured goods and for services. Even new or comparatively new countries with enormous natural resources have learned the truth of this lesson, and are everywhere developing internally consuming capacity for the fruits of such resources. There exists abundant evidence in the economic policies of the various countries that their governments are keenly conscious of the national importance of the distinctions between food and raw materials on the one hand and manufactured goods and services on the other. Broadly, it will be found that the production and importation of food and raw materials is encouraged and their export discouraged, whilst the importation

of manufactured goods and services is discouraged and their production and export discouraged (Barrington, 41).

During 1930 and 1931 the international depression deepened, unemployment rose sharply, and Britain abandoned its long-standing commitments to free trade and to the gold standard. The Society responded with papers on the currency problem of the Irish Free State and Separate Markets for the Unemployed (Colbert, 161; Meredith, 864). The former, by John P. Colbert, chairman of the state-controlled Agricultural Credit Corporation, suggested that the Irish Free State had no alternative other than to peg its currency to sterling, and consequently to abandon the gold standard. The second paper, by Mr Justice Meredith, gave rise to such a lengthy discussion that the Society ran an additional session on 4 March 1932, one week after the paper had been read. Meredith's paper, which had been prompted by the simultaneous existence of huge surpluses of food and manufactured goods, and large numbers of unemployed people in need, contained a highly fantasised scheme for establishing barter arrangements between the unemployed, beginning with essentials such as food and clothing, and extending to the construction of housing, and to international barter agreements for commodities such as coal.

1932: A NEW ECONOMIC ORDER

The Fianna Fáil government, which took office (with the support of Labour deputies) in February 1932, rapidly embarked on a programme of self-sufficiency for both agriculture and industry. This was to be achieved by a combination of tariffs, import quotas and guaranteed prices for crops such as wheat and tobacco. Public expenditure rose from 24 per cent of GNP in 1931 to 30.3 per cent in 1933 in order to finance subsidies for agriculture and housing, together with more generous social welfare benefits.[34] In July 1932, a trade war broke out between the Irish Free State and Britain, consequent on Ireland's refusal to pay the money owed to Britain on foot of land annuities – the money advanced by the British government to enable Irish tenant farmers to buy their land holdings. The export market for Irish agricultural produce was seriously damaged, both by the Economic War, and as a result of the measures that Britain had introduced to protect domestic agriculture. Cattle prices fell sharply. The economic policies adopted by the Fianna Fáil government attracted little support from Irish economists, or from senior officials in the Department of Finance. Both groups continued to advocate the merits of free trade and low taxation, and to subscribe to the belief that higher government expenditure was inherently wrong.

Although the Council Minutes conceal more than they reveal, it is obvious that some members were uncomfortable about the change of government. On 7 April 1932, the president, J.C.M. Eason, informed the Council that 'on account of the political implications of the subjects of their proposed papers, Messrs McMillan and Brennan wished to be released from undertakings to read papers during the current session.'[35] Joseph Brennan, an uncompromising critic of Fianna Fáil policies, served as president during the years 1934-38. He made an unsuccessful attempt to have the Society registered as a nominating body under the Seanad Éireann Act of 1937 – which would have enabled it to nominate candidates for election to the Seanad.[36] This suggests a desire to use the Society as a quasi political platform.

Between 1932 and 1939 the overwhelming majority of papers on current economic problems were supportive of neo-classical economics and highly critical of less conventional solutions. In October 1933, George O'Brien examined the role of monetary policy both as the cause, and as a possible solution to the Depression. He acknowledged that the Depression had been caused by an unhealthy economic expansion, which the monetary system had failed to prevent, but O'Brien rejected many of the remedies that had been recommended for achieving economic recovery, such as cheap money, public works or raising the price level of primary commodities. He believed that a reduction in wage rates offered the only possible remedy. This would lead to a fall in the cost of living, bringing about a recovery in demand, and an increase in the prices of primary products. In the ensuing discussion, all speakers, with the exception of Labour Senator Thomas Johnson, endorsed O'Brien's views. George Duncan congratulated him for producing a paper that was 'wholesomely discouraging to a number of beliefs presently much in vogue' (O'Brien, 948) – a phrase which encapsulates a recurring attitude in the Society during these years.

Although O'Brien made no specific reference to Ireland, Joseph Johnston, a Barrington lecturer in economics for 1935, was less reticent. In December 1935, the *Drogheda Independent* reported that Johnston gave 'a most interesting and instructive lecture on the Curse of Cromwellian economics to a large representative and intelligent audience at the beautiful home of Mrs Vera Lentaigne, County Councillor, Newtown, Termonfeckin.' The audience included local representatives, clergy, local solicitors and members of the public. Johnston drew a direct analogy between the curse of Cromwell on seventeenth-century Ireland and the curse of self-sufficiency. This was a potent analogy, because the meeting took place a short distance from the town of Drogheda, which had been sacked by Cromwell in 1649. Johnston claimed that Ireland 'has flourished only during those periods in which we had both a Government that fostered native industries and freedom of commerce with the external world'. He appears to have received an enthusiastic reception. A Major Barrow, proposing the vote of thanks, announced that 'England was only too willing to settle' the trade dispute with the Irish Free State. Fr Doris, seconding the vote of thanks, mused that it had been 'a very interesting lecture to most of us who study history from another angle altogether: from the angle of wars instead of economics.' According to Fr Doris, the economic war had started 'centuries ago. This country seems to have been fighting an economic war all the time'.

When this press-cutting reached the Barrington family, they expressed doubts about the suitability of the lecture. Johnston had already served as Barrington lecturer for several years, and his appointment was not renewed.[37] He had already criticised the government's agricultural policy in a paper during the 1934/35 session. On that occasion, however, he was more measured in his comments, to the extent of also criticising the British government's policy of protecting agriculture as 'the moral and economic equivalent of the Stamp Duty and the Navigation Acts which caused the revolt of the American colonies' (Johnston, 613).

Some of the themes that Johnston raised resurfaced in a paper by Lieutenant-Colonel K.E. Edgeworth, 'Bargaining Power as an

Economic Force'. Edgeworth argued that price theory tended to lay undue stress on what he termed 'the doctrine of satisfaction', while giving insufficient attention to the question of bargaining power. He suggested that independence had deprived Irish farmers of the right to equality of treatment in the British market. Ireland's bargaining powers as an exporter of agricultural produce were further weakened by the low level of world agricultural prices, and by Britain's decision to protect its agricultural sector. The only bargaining counters remaining to Ireland were the prospect of being able to offer Britain a guaranteed supply of food in time of war and more secure sites for aircraft factories; he suggested that efforts to foster a closer friendship with Britain might pay dividends.

This was a highly political contribution, given the delicate state of Anglo-Irish relations at this time,[38] and is not surprising that it provoked a lengthy and apparently heated discussion, which occupies six pages in the Journal, compared with the more usual one or two pages. Most speakers were highly critical of Edgeworth's thesis. T.J. Kiernan, director of broadcasting at Radio Éireann, suggested that the paper was not appropriate for the Society because it dealt with practical politics rather than with statistics or pure economics. Michael Colbert dismissed it as 'purely and simply political', and consequently unsuitable for presentation to a learned society. However, Brennan countered that Edgeworth's paper had been read in advance and approved as suitable for the Society. Edgeworth replied that he was concerned to make the point 'that there were questions in this country that had both political and economic aspects. Economic thought could not be stifled merely because it had also sometimes a political aspect.' The apparent powerlessness of economics in the face of politically determined decisions, such as the drive for self-sufficiency, is best illustrated by Professor George Duncan's comments. He pointed out that Edgeworth's paper suggested that 'if the Government of the Irish Free State were to make certain advances to the British Government they could secure entry for their goods on more advantageous terms'. He continued:

> But that led up to the question of choice. On the one side was
> the advantage that could possibly be obtained by the Irish Free

State, and on the other the fact – call it insanity or higher idealism – that the present Government and probably any future Government, held the view that such an approach would be bending the knee to force. The people making the choice were well aware of the price that had to be paid, and they chose deliberately to move one way rather than the other. The two things could not be weighed against one another.

Duncan's remarks regarding the trade-off between closer trading links with Britain and non-material objectives is reminiscent of de Valera's 1927 speech about the choice between comfortable servitude in a big house or frugal independence in a cottage.[39] Most accounts of Irish economic policy during the 1930s have made a similar point, though it now appears that this trade-off has been overemphasised.[40] Duncan's remarks conjure up a picture of economists at odds with the government and a majority of the electorate; a beleaguered elite, battling in vain against 'insanity or higher idealism' (Edgeworth, 293). Similar sentiments were expressed by A.I. Quresha, an Indian economist, who attended Johnston's paper on the agricultural crisis, when he remarked that 'where politicians are exploiting the ignorance of the people, I think it is the moral duty of economists to come forward and expose their fallacies' (Johnston, 613). Although former Cumann na nGaedheal Ministers Richard Mulcahy and Ernest Blythe replied to papers during the 1930s, and both men joined the Society, as did another Fine Gael deputy, James Dillon, no member of the Fianna Fáil government attended until 1940, when Hugo Flinn, parliamentary secretary to the Minister for Finance, became a member. Ernest Blythe became a member of the Council in 1940. Gerard Sweetman, a future Fine Gael Minister for Finance, joined the Society in 1944. In 1973, Garret FitzGerald continued as a member of Council after his appointment as Minister for Foreign Affairs.

THE COMMISSION ON BANKING, CURRENCY, AND CREDIT

One of the landmarks of Irish political economy during the 1930s was the establishment of the Commission on Banking Currency and Credit in 1934. A majority of the Commission were members of the Society. They included the chairman Joseph Brennan, who was the current president of the Society and his immediate predecessor, J.C.M. Eason. In January 1935, Brennan presented a paper that charted the composition of the national debt and the growth in outstanding dead-weight debt from £10.2m in 1925 to £37.4m by 31 March 1934. Brennan said little about the significance of his findings, but this paper anticipated the more overtly critical attitude towards the increase in government debt, which was adopted by the Commission's majority report (Brennan, 98).

The decision to appoint a Commission on Banking, Currency and Credit prompted widespread criticism of some aspects of the Irish banking system in particular the extent of its investments in Britain at a time when Irish agriculture and industry were perceived to be short of capital. During the 1935/36 session, Professor T. A. Smiddy rebutted these arguments, suggesting that the high proportion of bank assets invested in Britain reflected a shortage of investment outlets within the state. Smiddy was more sanguine than Brennan or the majority membership of the Banking Commission about the current condition of the Irish banking system, an attitude that might reflect his role as economic advisor to de Valera. He deduced that the Irish banking system was in good health; unlike Brennan he believed that recent changes in Irish economic policy had little impact on the composition of bank assets. In the discussion which followed, Bulmer Hobson – a co-founder of Sinn Féin with Arthur Griffith, and a co-author of the third minority report to the Banking Commission, which was actually signed by Peadar O'Loghlen[41] – described the humiliation suffered by Dublin Corporation in its efforts to raise money from a foreign insurance company, at a time when Irish banks had large sums invested overseas. Although Charles Eason and George O'Brien endorsed the policies pursued by the Irish commercial banks, Hobson was not alone in advocating that external assets should be reinvested in Ireland in order to provide work for the unemployed (Smiddy, 1158).

The debate on bank lending policy intensified following the publication of the Commission's report in 1938, perhaps because the majority report had endorsed the policies pursued by the commercial banks, and had directed its strongest criticism at the government. During World War II, Ireland's inability to obtain adequate supplies of imported goods led to a rise in the monetary value (though not necessarily in the real value) of external assets, prompting further discussion as to how this nest egg might be exploited once the war had ended. This debate should also be seen in the context of a continuing discussion in Britain over the functions of the banking system, and the growing interest in economic and social planning. Joseph Brennan's paper to the 1942/43 session on the 'Monetary Functions of Commercial Banks' opened with a statement that the Council believed that the paper and the discussion that would follow 'might help to clarify some of the confusion which has been evident in much of the popular discussion which has been taking place in this country on these topics for some time past'. Brennan gave a rather low-key description of the workings of the banking system, which was carefully designed to deal with the 'snares' involved in phrases such as 'every banker creates his own deposits' and 'every loan creates a deposit' – concepts that had become more widely known in Ireland with the publication of the third minority report to the Banking Commission. In the discussion George Duncan referred to 'the immense army of cranks and theorists' who cited 'unguarded remarks' by the economist Lord Keynes and Reginald McKenna, chairman of the Midland Bank and a former Chancellor of the Exchequer, to the effect that '"every loan creates its deposit, and ... the volume of money is something that is independent of the volume of activity"'.

However, Brennan did not succeed in stamping out such heresies. Professor T.W. Dillon, a distinguished Dublin medical figure, queried how the banks allocated credit between users; in similar vein, Lieutenant-Colonel Edgeworth suggested that the paper 'leaves unanswered most of the fundamental questions which are perplexing men's minds at the present time', while Rev E.J. Coyne S.J. suggested that many 'serious, intelligent and responsible men' were 'extremely anxious, not in their own interests, but in the interest of the community, that some agreement or understanding should be found between their difficulties and what I might call the orthodox system described by Mr. Brennan.' Coyne referred to the belief expressed by 'these men' [who are not identified in a more specific form] 'that the community has a right to a say in the use of private property in the form of savings.' In support of this argument, he noted that in 'a famous Encyclical it was clearly stated that it was the official opinion of a number of intelligent advisers of a certain highly placed person [presumably the pope] that there was too much saving on one side and too little on the other.' Coyne queried whether it would be possible for a central authority to influence the volume and allocation of savings and investment, by exercising some control over the banking system. George O'Brien dismissed his wishes as socialist, and referred Coyne to chapter 5 and appendix 15 of the report of the Banking Commission; the sections had examined the relationship between economics and catholic social teaching and determined that there was no inconsistency between papal encyclicals and neo-classical economics (Brennan, 96).

POPULATION AND PUBLIC HEALTH

The late 1930s and the Emergency years were a time of considerable debate, indeed soul-searching, over the future of the Irish Free State. This was prompted by a realisation that the Fianna Fáil economic experiment had not succeeded, and that it was impossible to recreate the pre-1932 economic order. The 1936 Population Census revealed that the Irish population had continued to decline, despite the attainment of self-government. Moreover, migration from rural to urban Ireland had accelerated, contrary to the stated objectives of government policy. Although Ireland was unique in experiencing a continuous fall in population since the middle of the previous century, demography was a subject of concern to economists and social scientists throughout the world during the 1930s, as successive countries reported a collapse in the birth-rate, and it appeared that Europe was entering a phase of declining population. This prompted several government to introduce measures that were designed to promote population growth.[42] When Stanley Lyon reported to the Society on the 1933 meeting of the International Institute of Statistics, he gave priority to describing the sessions which dealt with demography, including marriage fertility, stillbirths and the epidemiology of cancer

(Lyon, 748). At a meeting of the International Institute of Statistics in Athens in September 1936, a special committee was established to study the world population problem, with special reference to the falling birth rate. The countries chosen for study were the USA, Czechoslovakia, Germany, France, Austria, Italy and Ireland, which was represented by Stanley Lyon. Lyon, the director of the Statistics Branch, Department of Industry and Commerce was President of the Society from 1938 until 1942 (Lyon, 749).

Several papers read during the 1930s reflected the contemporary concern with a low birth-rate; previously, papers on the population of Ireland had concentrated on emigration. In November 1935, Roy Geary presented a remarkable paper on 'The Future Population of Saorstat Éireann'. Geary's forecast was based on deliberately simple assumptions: zero net migration, and unchanged birth and death rates. He predicted that by 1996 the population of the Irish Free State would lie in the range of 3.3 to 3.6m. One of Geary's two forecasts for the population in 1986 was within one per cent of the actual Census count (Black, 70). By demonstrating that, even on such 'artificial' (Geary's word) assumptions, the population of the Irish Free State would rise by only a modest 700,000 over the next 80 years, Geary set out to refute the widely held belief that Ireland could regain its pre-Famine population, and perhaps even reach a figure of 12m or 16m (Geary, 358).

When Joseph Busteed presented another paper on population in March 1937, the president, Joseph Brennan, justified the decision to schedule two papers on this topic within eighteen months by noting that the subject was of current importance, because of the sharp decline in the birth-rate which had occurred in many parts of Europe. Busteed argued that the low rate of marriage in the Irish Free State could be explained by economic factors, an argument that had already been advanced by James Meenan in 1933.

Meenan had examined Ireland's low marriage rate without reference to emigration. Whereas Meenan spoke of the absence of opportunities for employment, and suggested that 'the lack of female employment here has the effect of postponing the time at which marriage becomes financially possible' (Meenan, 854), Busteed, who was an advocate of catholic social teaching, argued that 'additional economic privileges given to the family would strength the institution of the family'. Busteed's paper provoked a lively discussion. Dr N.G. Nolan, an economist, pondered whether access to contraception had been responsible for the falling birth-rate in countries other than Ireland and referred to the pioneers of contraception, Charles Bradlaugh and Annie Besant. Another contributor, a Miss Donnelly, spoke about women's liberty to work, access to divorce and 'the attainment of families of a few properly spaced children'. The discussion also touched on the questions of eugenics: whether 'weaklings' had larger families than more intelligent people (Busteed, 115). This was heady stuff in the 1930s, when publications that mentioned any form of birth control were liable to be banned by the Censorship Board. Both this session and Geary's paper anticipated themes which came to the fore after World War II, most notably in the work of the Commission on Emigration and other Population Problems.

Busteed's paper was followed by James Meenan's preliminary report on the 1937 Northern Ireland Census. Meenan added the 1936 population for the Irish Free State to the 1937 figures for Northern Ireland (a practice which was contested by George Duncan) and suggested that the population of Ireland had actually increased for the first time since 1841, with a marginal fall of population in the Irish Free State being offset by an increase in the population of Northern Ireland. Per Jacobsen, an economic advisor to the Bank for International Settlements and one of the outside experts who served on the Banking Commission, who was in attendance, tried to interpret these data as evidence of the baleful effects of the Economic War on the Irish Free State, when compared with the more open economy of Northern Ireland. However Meenan suggested that the explanation should be sought in a long-term pattern of migration from east to west, and from rural to urban areas, which was common to both parts of Ireland (Meenan, 852).

In 1938, 'The Population Problem' was chosen for the Society's first venture into broadcasting. The idea came from T.J. Kiernan, an active member of the Society, who was the director of broadcasting at Radio Éireann. Joseph Brennan, who chaired the discussion, used the occasion to carry out some free advertising;

he informed listeners that membership was not restricted to experts (Brennan, 97). One participant, George O'Brien, attempted to arouse public interest in the problems posed by a falling population (O'Brien, 949). Roy Geary and George Duncan shared O'Brien's pessimism concerning the future size of the Irish population, whereas the final contributor, Stanley Lyon contented himself with pointing out that the population problem was common to most civilised countries (Geary, 362; Duncan, 254; Lyon, 747). Among the topics raised in the broadcast were the relationship between demography and economic prosperity; the decline in the number of children born in Ireland during the past decade; the fact that the Irish death-rate was high and stable by comparison with other European countries. Contributors pointed out that emigration could be reduced, either by imposing a ban, or by achieving greater economic efficiency, but not by 'making' or 'providing work'. Roy Geary revisited some of these themes in 1941, when he used the 1936 Census as a basis for revising his 1935 projections. On this occasion, however, he argued that the Irish population problem stemmed from emigration, not from a low birth-rate: the Irish net reproduction rate was one of the highest in the world. He also suggested that freedom to migrate should not be an absolute right: 'The State must also "have its say".' Geary recommended the establishment of a government department which would regulate emigration and provide for the care of emigrants (Geary, 359). Such proposals reflect a changing attitude towards emigration during the Emergency. The British authorities imposed restrictions on immigration from Ireland, and the Irish government tried, though with little apparent success, to limit emigration from rural areas in order to maintain a sufficient supply of labour for agriculture and turf-cutting. In 1942, Seán Lemass actually toyed with imposing more stringent controls that would be retained after the ending of the Emergency.[43]

In the 1937 broadcast, Stanley Lyon referred to the importance of collecting detailed statistics on marital fertility and maternal age; he also emphasised the need to bring Irish practices for recording stillbirths into line with international norms, in order to ensure that fertility data were comparable between different countries. Lyon's concern was prompted by his involvement with the Commission on the World Population Problem, established by the International Institute of Statistics. Although the project ceased with the onset of World War II, Lyon continued to carry out independent research, using data on births that took place in the city of Dublin. The findings contain invaluable information on the relationship between the age of the mother on marriage and family size; the interval between marriage and first maternity; and differences in marital fertility by social class. Of the children born to fathers holding professional, clerical and commercial occupations, 83.5 per cent were first to fourth children, against 57.4 per cent in the case of children of unskilled workers; 25.2 per cent of births to families whose father was unskilled were seventh or higher order births, against 6.8 per cent in the case of families whose father had a professional, clerical or commercial occupation. Lyon showed that the net reproduction rate for Dublin city was 1.01, just sufficient to maintain a stable population. The gross reproduction rate at 1.27 had fallen by almost 19 per cent over a five-year period (Lyon, 749). Lyon's data on birth order and age of mother highlighted the shortcomings of the Irish Census. The 1911 Census had collected similar statistics on women's fertility, as had a special inquiry carried out as part of the 1926 Census, though the data were never published. In November 1945, when Stanley Lyon, in his capacity as Director of the Statistics Branch, asked the Society for its recommendations concerning the 1946 Census, it suggested that the Census form include additional questions relating to fertility of marriage, date of marriage and the age of respondents, precisely the information that was of interest to Lyon. Most of these recommendations were included in the 1946 Census (Lyon, 742).

Whether or not Lyon was responsible for the proliferation of papers relating to public health is unclear. During the late 1930s and 1940s, the Society attracted several Irish doctors with an interest in epidemiology and public health, notably Professor T.W. Dillon, Dr Robert Rowlette and Dr James Deeny, who became chief medical officer in the Department of Local Government and Public Health in 1944.[44] The papers which they presented emphasised the relationship between socio-economic conditions and ill-health. In May 1940, Deeny, then in general practice in Lurgan, County Armagh, presented the findings of his research on the medical histories of 205 women – all mothers.

Deeny concluded that malnutrition resulting from poverty was the main cause of ill-health among lower-income women; for those in more prosperous circumstances, he determined that ill-health resulted from the stress of achieving high earnings, while simultaneously coping with the extra household duties which were characteristic 'of the more elaborate home' (Deeny, 221). While aspects of Deeny's argument are open to criticism – many of his inferences concerning the medical condition of these women appear rather subjective – the paper was judged of sufficient value to be published also in the *British Medical Journal*. Roy Geary and Miss D. Lynd (Department of Industry and Commerce) assisted Deeny with his statistical analysis.

In December 1943, Deeny and Dr Eric Murdock presented a paper, which showed that 'low income was the dominant social factor associated with infant mortality' in Belfast (Deeny, 223). At its next meeting, the Society heard a paper by Charles Clancy Gore, the medical officer attached to Guinness's brewery, on nutritional standards in Dublin working-class families. For the overwhelming majority of the families studied, income was either insufficient or borderline. While Clancy Gore acknowledged that living standards had fallen as a result of wartime shortages and inflation, he concluded that, whereas the wages on offer were adequate to provide for small families in peacetime (on the assumption that prices would fall), they would remain insufficient to provide adequate nutrition for larger families (Clancy Gore, 155). Such research provided valuable empirical data at a time when the merits of introducing children's allowances were under discussion.[45]

The Emergency years saw the Society devote considerable attention to the medical and social problems of the Dublin working class. A paper by Colm Barry in October 1941 showed that life expectancy was almost ten years higher for a new-born male in Connacht than for a baby boy born in Dublin city; for women the gap was almost seven years. In recent decades, life expectancy had risen much more rapidly in England and Wales, including London, than in any part of Ireland. Barry drew particular attention to the low rate of decline in Ireland's infant mortality (Barry, 45). Similar conclusions applied to mortality from tuberculosis. When Roy Geary presented a statistical study of that disease in 1930, he came to the conclusion that the decline in mortality in the Irish Free State was well up to average (Geary, 361). By 1943, however, Ireland's position on the international table of tuberculosis death rates had disimproved markedly, apparently due to the rise in the urban population (Counihan and Dillon, 191). Having fallen for many years, deaths from tuberculosis began to increase in 1937.[46] In February 1947, Dr William Kidney presented the results of a survey into the socio-conditions experienced by Dubliners, who had died of tuberculosis. This showed a strong positive association between tuberculosis and poverty, overcrowded housing and poor living conditions, though T.K. Whitaker cautioned against drawing inferences as to causation, unless a comparison of the distribution of deaths from tuberculosis by socio-economic group and the distribution of all deaths suggested that there was significantly greater excess mortality from tuberculosis among the poor (Kidney, 656). However flawed the study, it appeared to carry a political message: the need to raise the living standards of the urban poor.

PLANNING FOR THE POST-WAR YEARS

During the Emergency years, Irish politicians and civil servants engaged in a far-reaching, if intermittent, debate over the future shape of Irish medical and welfare services.[47] This culminated in the establishment of separate Departments of Health and Social Welfare in 1947, and in proposals for an expansion of state medical services. It is not yet entirely clear what prompted this period of change: among the possible factors were the deterioration in living standards consequent on the Emergency, awareness of plans for a welfare state in Britain, and perhaps the impact of the evidence reproduced in the Society's Journal and in publications such as the *Journal of the Medical Association of Éire*. The debate over Irish social services was part of a wider discussion concerning the future direction of the Irish economy. When war broke out in 1939, the Department of Industry and Commerce predicted that up to 50 per cent of the non-agricultural workforce might become unemployed.[48] Such fears may have prompted the Society to make unemployment the subject of its second broadcast symposium in May 1940. The conflicting views that were expressed reflected the diverse backgrounds of the contributors – Lord Glenavy, director of the Bank of Ireland, Labour politician Tom Johnson, UCG economist Senator Liam Ó Buachalla, Fr Edward Coyne SJ and statistician Stanley Lyon – the session probably left listeners more confused than enlightened. Glenavy defended capitalism (Glenavy, 380) whereas Johnson called for its abolition (Johnson, 610). Liam Ó Buachalla claimed that the solution to unemployment rested with creating jobs in intensive agriculture (Ó Buachalla, 967), while Fr Coyne recommended establishing a corporate committee to allocate all the unemployed to specific industries, with the cost being met by a combination of higher taxes and government borrowing. Stanley Lyon simply commented on unemployment statistics (Lyon, 752). Fr Coyne justified his proposals by claiming that the figure of 100,000 unemployed constituted 'an utterly abnormal emergency' (Coyne, 195).

Although other members of the Society were more restrained, several shared Coyne's pessimism about the state of the Irish economy. In January 1940, a short paper by James Meenan on 'The impact of the war on the Irish economy' prompted a lengthy discussion. Meenan referred to 'uncertainty' about the future. He emphasised that the fate of the Irish economy depended heavily on decisions taken in Britain on matters such as Irish access to raw materials; the Irish inflation rate was also largely influenced by the effectiveness of British measures to control prices. Henry Kennedy of the IAOS and Joseph Johnston were sceptical about the potential to expand agricultural output. They pointed out that in the past Irish farmers failed to respond positively to higher prices; they feared that shortages of fertiliser and of imported feeding stuffs would lead to a reduction in wartime output (Meenan, 850). When war broke out in 1939, it can be argued that the future direction of the Irish economy was in the balance. The publication in 1938 of the report of the Banking Commission, which was highly critical of government policy, and the partial reversal of the self-sufficiency crusade by the 1938 Anglo-Irish Trade Agreement, seemed to open up the possibility of a compromise between uncompromising self-sufficiency and unremitting free trade.

The interest aroused by a 1943 paper from J.P. Beddy (chief

executive of the Industrial Credit Company), which compared the economies of Ireland and Denmark, is one indication of this search for a new direction in economic policy. In January 1944, at a time when paper supplies were extremely scarce, the Council agreed to print a further 300 copies of Beddy's paper, in addition to the 200 on order 'in view of the wide public demand'. The periodical *Irish Industry* had begun to reproduce the paper in instalments, without the Society's permission, and the Council had received a request from the editor of the National Planning Handbook to reproduce the paper in full.[49] Beddy concluded that, 'paradoxically', Ireland's 'relative economic and social disadvantages' were a consequence of the country's climatic advantage, which enabled it to adopt a system of extensive tillage farming, resulting in high emigration, low productivity in agriculture and a lack of opportunities to expand industry and trade. The key to economic advancement lay in a more intensive agricultural system, though Beddy acknowledged that it would be difficult to find a profitable market for the additional output (Beddy, 60). Many of the issues raised in Beddy's paper surfaced some months later during the course of a symposium on the future of Irish external trade. Although several speakers emphasised that potential existed for expanding agricultural output, others such as Joseph Johnston and R.J.P. Mortished predicted that Ireland would face difficulties in finding markets for its exports in the post-war years (Johnston, 616; Mortished, 895).

Such pessimism concerning the prospects for the Irish economy must be taken into consideration when we examine the views expressed at various meetings of the Society on Britain's plans to introduce a comprehensive welfare state. Any improvements in British social services would apply to Northern Ireland and this had obvious implications for aspirations towards Irish unity. Moreover, with numerous Irish emigrants working in England, it was inevitable that the Irish public would become aware of the provisions available in Britain, and compare them with the more modest social services available in the Irish state.

The blueprint for a British welfare state was outlined in a succession of publications that appeared from 1942, beginning with Social Insurance and Allied Services (1942), drafted by Sir William Beveridge. The Beveridge Report on Social Services, and two subsequent reports on full employment, were discussed in the course of two symposia organised by the Society, on 5 March 1943 and on 27 April 1945. The symposium on social services was dominated by contributions from officials who were responsible for administering the existing services: John Collins, assistant secretary of the Department of Local Government and Public Health, William Honohan, Stanley Lyon and R. Ó Brolcháin (National Health Insurance) all provided factual accounts of existing provisions and criteria for eligibility (Collins, 165; Honohan, 563; Lyon, 744; Ó Brolcháin, 968).

The symposium began with a brief discussion by Fr Coyne – a staunch advocate of catholic social teaching – concerning the ethical aspects of social insurance. In a contribution which anticipated some the catholic church's concerns about the 1951 Mother and Child Scheme, Coyne spoke of the danger that 'some very powerful body, say the State, operating though an impersonal bureaucracy' might merely transfer citizens from the 'bondage of poverty and insecurity into the much more de-humanising bondage of regimentation by card-indices, a cold and cruel form of slavery'. Coyne also expressed fears that a comprehensive system of social insurance would result in 'certain incentives being lacking which Nature uses to call forth certain healthy qualities, moral values, in men'. It might also spell the end for charitable bodies such as the Society of St Vincent de Paul and the Sick and Indigent Roomkeepers' Society (Coyne, 193). While Fr Coyne's critique concentrated on philosophical issues, B.F. Shields, professor of commerce at UCD, pointed out that introducing a Beveridge-style scheme to Ireland would absorb an estimated 28.9 per cent of national income against 15.2 per cent in Britain. Since this would be an impossible burden, Shields attempted to draft a more modest plan. However his scheme provided for extremely low levels of unemployment benefit pensions set at less than half the British basic rate and children's allowances which would either exclude the first two children in a family or subject all recipients to a means test. An addendum to the symposium from R.J.P. Mortished also came to the conclusion that the Irish Free State could afford only a meagre social security system. Mortished echoed Coyne when he referred to 'social security with its suggestion of the servile state'. He suggested that the Irish state should give priority to raising total output, as opposed to redistributing the existing national income (Mortished, 897). Although the paper presented by John Collins gave no indication of the Department's views, in the course of a written comment on an earlier paper about services for mentally defective schoolchildren, Collins had argued that the best hopes for improvement lay with voluntary agencies, as opposed to placing additional statutory obligations on local authorities (Clifford, 156).

When the Society held another symposium on social security in 1949 to discuss the Irish government's White Paper, the views expressed differed little from those in 1943. Most contributors were highly critical of the proposals contained in the White Paper, regarding them as evidence of a 'tendency to enhance the importance of the work of the State and to weaken the sense of personal responsibility (Eason, 283) or as an 'elaborate and costly and, to my mind, an unnecessary pretence of an insurance scheme set up in order to, as is said in the White Paper, "safeguard the self-respect" of a certain minority in the community and in order to avoid having to use the term "public assistance" or "public help" and in order to avoid having to apply a Means Test' (Coyne, 194). Joseph Johnston condemned the White Paper as 'inspired by a desire "to keep up with the Joneses" – up in Northern Ireland' (Johnston, 620). In the ensuing discussion, P.S. O'Hegarty, a former Secretary of the Department of Posts and Telegraphs condemned the proposals as 'another step on the road to totalitarianism'.

Ronan Fanning has noted that the Statistical Society was 'the only intellectual forum outside the service at that time where civil servants could make a contribution', citing T.K. Whitaker as his source.[50] Patrick Lynch has claimed that the Society offered members of the Department of Finance the opportunity to express in public views which diverged from the official Finance line as expounded by the secretary, J. J. McElligott.[51] Such opportunities would scarcely have presented themselves if the Society was known as a place where partisan political views were commonly aired. From 1927, when Fianna Fáil entered Dail Éireann, until 1938, the views of the government and opposition differed radically on the merits of economic self-sufficiency and this may have limited the possibilities for civil servants to express opinions, though it does not appear to have restricted the outspoken Joseph Brennan. From 1938, however, a consensus emerged between the major political parties on the key elements of social and economic policy. Consequently, by the 1940s the Society may have offered greater latitude to civil servants. On most issues, such as social security however, the civil servants did not express a judgment as to the merits or feasibility of implementing new policies. However, on one notable occasion, the symposium on Full Employment, Patrick Lynch and T.K. Whitaker, both officials in the Department of Finance, dissented from the Department's official line.

Opening the discussion, Patrick Lynch judged that many of the remedies recommended in the British White Paper would prove of little value in solving the problem of Irish unemployment. The British report concluded that cyclical fluctuations were the primary cause of unemployment, whereas in a predominantly agricultural country such as Ireland, the main problem was one of 'chronic under-investment'. Lynch acknowledged that 'a proper direction of the Irish economy will imply increased State intervention', in the form of economic planning, adding that a major ingredient of the Irish government's post-war planning – the rural electrification scheme – would actually increase the problem of providing full employment, by releasing additional labour from agriculture. Lynch concluded that there was a need to accept 'the Keynesian analysis of the economic system': he mentioned the potential value of 'the two-budget system' (capital and current budgets) and 'the advantages of budgeting on the national income as a whole and not on one-quarter of it' (Lynch, 737). Speaking towards the end of the discussion, Whitaker referred to the question of full employment in an international sense, and the relevance of the two reports under discussion to Irish circumstances. His assertion that 'demand is an inherently unstable quantity and that positive action by Governments is necessary to maintain and stabilise it'; and that 'it is now widely accepted that unemployment is a more intractable problem' than inflation, were at variance with the views generally expressed within the Department of Finance. However, Whitaker made these comments in the course of a general discussion of full employment. When he referred specifically to the Irish economy, he adopted a more conservative line.

Like Patrick Lynch, Whitaker noted that Irish circumstances differed from those in Britain and the United States: the level of Irish unemployment was much more dependent on the state of agriculture than on cyclical fluctuations in heavy industries. Consequently he claimed that 'we have not to contemplate the same degree of State control as they [economies such as Britain and the United States] will necessarily have to face in the interests of full employment'. He claimed that most Irish unemployment was short-term, resulting from 'seasonal causes, lack of training and inadequate diversification of industry'. Given the high volume of emigration, it represented 'a residue, a domestic core consisting largely of unemployables, perhaps, rather than unemployed'. Whitaker warned those who favoured increasing domestic investment in order to provide employment, that unless the jobs created were as productive as those available overseas, employment would only increase if people were forced to take up lower-paid jobs (Whitaker, 1296). While there has been a tendency for historians to emphasise Whitaker's divergence from the orthodox views favoured by the Department of Finance, his insistence that the return on domestic investment must equal the return on foreign investment was wholly in keeping with the official Department of Finance line. This was an important topic, because as a result of the views expressed in the minority reports of the Banking Commission, and the apparently sharp increase in Irish external assets during the war years, the government was under pressure to use these external assets to fund domestic investment, almost irrespective of the return on capital. Whitaker's contribution to the symposium suggests that he subscribed to a more rigorous and more restrictive approach to public investment than Patrick Lynch. By suggesting that the main problem facing the Irish economy was under investment and by calling for increased investment in agriculture and industry – but only if it yielded an adequate return – Whitaker anticipated a key ingredient in his 1958 report Economic Development.

The reference to Economic Development points to the fact that it is extremely difficult to draw a clear line between the socio-economic issues that preoccupied the Society during the Emergency years, and those that came to the fore in the decade or so after the war had ended. Despite the problems which the

Emergency posed for the Society, such as a shortage of paper, which meant that the discussions which followed the various papers – often the most instructive item – had to be omitted, the first 25 years after the establishment of the Irish Free State were very fruitful for the Society. It benefited considerably from establishing close links with the administrative elite of the new Irish state, though at times this also proved a constraint. In 1944, Lieutenant-Colonel Edgeworth proposed that the Council establish a sub-committee to study the problem of unemployment. The Council instructed the honorary secretary to inform Edgeworth that, while such committees fell within the terms of the Society's constitution, it was 'doubtful if in the present instance suitable members of the Society could be induced to join the Committees; in particular the many civil service members would be precluded from taking part'. It suggested that he present a paper to the Society, which would include a proposal to establish an informal study group on this subject. Yet when he submitted a paper, it was rejected. The Council suggested that the topic was better suited to a symposium.[52] Edgeworth's contribution to the symposium on full employment suggests that he believed that full employment could be attained only under an elaborate system of economic planning (Edgeworth, 295). Whether the Council's action smacks of censorship, or was merely an attempt to limit the amount of space devoted to the views of an eccentric member, it is difficult to say.

The late 1930s and the 1940s saw a marked increase in the proportion of papers employing more discriminating statistical techniques. These included T.J. Kiernan's pioneering effort to calculate Irish national income from expenditure data (Kiernan, 657), and George Duncan's estimation of the demand curve for wheat in 1934, which used regression and coefficients of correlation. Roy Geary, the first member to present papers which used these techniques (Geary, 360, 361), described Duncan's as 'just the kind of paper which this Society wants' (Duncan, 252). By 1940 the Society was able to draw on emerging statistical expertise in fields such as medical, social and life insurance. Some papers on these themes – notably Barry's use of regional life tables and D.H. Shaw's analysis of mortality among lower income families – prompted vigorous discussion (Barry, 45;

Shaw, 1127). By the mid-1940s the days when interested amateurs presented papers to the Society were numbered. This renaissance was a consequence of independence – which resulted in an expansion in the number of Irish civil servants and in the volume of official statistics – and of moves towards self-sufficiency. Until the 1930s, Irish life assurance business had been written by offices based outside Ireland, which meant that no specific Irish actuarial data existed (Honohan, 562). If we exclude reports on meetings of the International Institute of Statistics, the papers contain few references to international development in either statistics or in economics. Nevertheless, the Society was probably less insular than Irish intellectual and academic life as a whole; unlike the arts and humanities, statistics and social inquiry was relatively unaffected by censorship, and some members were in contact with international statistical organisations. In presenting research which appeared to indicate that there was an association between illness and poverty, and also holding symposia where speakers signalled their distrust of increased state involvement in the provision of social welfare, the Society encapsulated the contradictory attitudes that were characteristic of Irish society during these years.

NOTES TO CHAPTER THREE

[1] Black, *Centenary History*, p. 149.
[2] Council Minutes, 15 March 1920; 27 April 1920.
[3] Black, *Centenary History*, pp. 32-33, 42.
[4] For details see Tom Garvin *1922: The Birth of Irish Democracy* (Dublin, 1996), pp. 169-73.
[5] Mary Kotsonouris, *Retreat from Revolution. The Dail Courts, 1920-24* (Dublin 1994), p. 127.
[6] Statistical and Society Inquiry Society of Ireland. Centenary 1847-1947 Proceedings, pp. 24-25.
[7] For details, see Daly, *Industrial Development and Irish National Identity, 1922-39* (Dublin 1992), p. 21.
[8] Council Minutes, 3 July 1924.
[9] Council Minutes, 22 January 1925.
[10] Daly, *The Buffer State*, pp. 96-102, 529.
[11] Barrington's only formal education was at national schools in County Clare.
[12] Daly, 'Formation of an Irish nationalist elite'.
[13] Kotsonouris, *Retreat from Revolution*. In 1940 Meredith was appointed to

the Supreme Court.
[14] L.M.Cullen, *Eason & Son. A History* (Dublin, 1989), p. 389.
[15] Council Minutes, 25 September 1925.
[16] Council Minutes, 19 June 1925.
[17] Daly, *The Buffer State*, p. 209.
[18] Council Minutes, 22 January 1925; 19 February 1925.
[19] Black, *Centenary Volume*, pp. 43-44.
[20] Daniel Hoctor, *The Department's Story* (Dublin 1971), p. 133.
[21] Peter Solar, 'The agricultural trade statistics in the Irish Railway Commissioners' Report', *Irish Economic and Social History*, 6 (1979), pp. 95-101.
[22] Hoctor, *The Department's Story*, p. 56.; Oldham,1021. The first report on Irish trade carried out under Adams's direction was 1906 Cd. 2722; *The Agricultural Output of Ireland 1908* (Department of Agriculture and Technical Instruction for Ireland), Dublin 1912.
[23] Because of the absence of a customs barrier betweeen Great Britain and Ireland the statistics on external trade had to be estimated on the basis of information obtained on a voluntary basis from the postal authorities and shipping companies. My thanks to Tom Linehan for this information.
[24] Kieran A. Kennedy, Thomas Giblin and Deirdre McHugh, *The Economic Development of Ireland in the Twentieth Century* (London, 1988) p. 183.
[25] Patriarca, *Numbers and Nationhood*, p. 231.
[26] Cormac O Grada has described them as 'probably unparalleled anywhere for scope, detail and reliability', C. Ó Gráda, 'Supply Responsiveness in Irish Agriculture during the Nineteenth Century' *Economic History Review*, 2nd series, 28 (1975), p. 312. For a detailed, and occasionally critical,account of nineteenth-century Irish agriculture statistics, see Michael Turner, *After the Famine. Irish Agriculture, 1850-1914* (Cambridge 1996), pp. 217-26.
[27] My thanks to Tom Linehan for alerting me to this.
[28] John A. Murphy, *The College. A History of Queen's /University College Cork* (Cork, 1995), p. 254.
[29] The publication of J.J. Webb's book, *The Guilds of Dublin* (Dublin,1929) is evidence of the interest shown in this subject during the 1920s.
[30] I am indebted to William Murphy for this observation.
[31] They included Arthur Griffith; see Daly, 'Frugal comfort', pp. 88-89.
[32] Daly, *Industrial Development and Irish National Identity*, pp. 106-16, 121.
[33] Thomas Barrington, Obituary, *Journal of the Statistical and Social Inquiry Society of Ireland*, xv, p. 114.
[34] John W. O'Hagan, 'An analysis of the relative size of the government sector: Ireland, 1926-52, *Economic and Social Review*, 12, no. 1, pp. 22-23.
[35] Council Minutes, 7 April 1932.
[36] Council Minutes, 19 January 1938; 17 February 1938.
[37] National Library of Ireland, Brennan Papers Ms 26336.
[38] For details, see Deirdre McMahon, *Republicans and Imperialists. Anglo-Irish Relations in the 1930s* (London, 1984).
[39] Maurice Moynihan (ed.), *Speeches and Statements by Eamon de Valera 1919-73* (Dublin, 1980), pp. 154-55.
[40] Ó Grada, *Ireland. A New Economic History*, p. 383.

[41] Fanning, *Finance*, p. 359.

[42] D. V. Glass, *Population Policies and Movements in Europe* (Oxford: Oxford University Press, 1940).

[43] Daly, *The Buffer State*, pp. 265-68; 283-84.

[44] Barrington, *Health, Medicine and Politics*, pp. 153-54

[45] Eamonn McKee, 'From precepts to praxis: Irish governments and economic policy, 1939 to 1952', Ph.D. UCD 1987.

[46] Barrington, *Health, Medicine and Politics*, p. 129

[47] For details, see Barrington pp. 137-42.

[48] S 11296; Daly, *The Buffer State*, pp. 279-86, 290-95.

[49] Council Minutes 19 January 1944. This was granted on payment of a fee of 5 guineas, provided that full acknowledgement was made to the Society and the handbook did not retail at more than two shillings and sixpence.

[50] Fanning, *Finance*, p. 384.

[51] A comment to the author.

[52] Council Minutes 18 January 1944 and 8 February 1944.

CHAPTER FOUR

Post-War Ireland

In October 1947, the Society held centenary celebrations. The government allocated £120 towards the cost, and donations of £150 and £110 were received respectively from the Irish Banks' Standing Committee and from Arthur Guinness. Many individuals and firms made smaller contributions, though few contributions from companies exceeded £5, and the Council regarded this first effort to raise money from the corporate sector as something of a failure. The celebrations were concentrated in a four-day period, from 6 to 9 October, in the expectation that European statisticians who had attended the Washington meeting of the International Institute of Statistics – the first major post-war gathering of statisticians – would break their return journey in Ireland.

The prospect of overseas guests presented some practical difficulties. In July 1947, Patrick Lynch suggested that the Centenary Committee should make arrangements to obtain ration cards in advance, so that foreign visitors would not be required to make personal applications at garda stations.[1] In the event, there were few foreign visitors: in his presidential address Roy Geary explained their absence as due in part 'to the difficulties of the times', and to the competing attraction of a series of statistical congresses in North America, which had lasted for 6-8 weeks. However, the Royal Statistical Society, the Italian government, the National Statistical Institute of Madrid, the Hungarian Official Statistical Service and the Hungarian Statistical Society sent representatives.

Arranging the programme for the commemorative meeting required a measure of local diplomacy. It was originally proposed that Joseph Brennan, George Duncan, George O'Brien and Roy Geary would each read papers. By June 1947, however, J.C.M.

Eason reported to Joseph Brennan that George O'Brien was becoming 'a little "difficile"— he is peeved over the whole matter'. Eason suggested that Brennan try to placate him. O'Brien declined to read a paper, and a proposed paper by George Duncan on the reconstruction of international trade also vanished from the programme for inexplicable reasons.[2] Ultimately only three papers were read: by Roy Geary, who was president during the centenary year, (Geary, 363) Joseph Brennan (Brennan, 99), and by the distinguished Italian statistician Corrado Gini (Gini, 377). Members and visitors were entertained in Áras an Uachtaráin, Trinity College, Iveagh House and Guinness's Brewery. Sean Lemass, Minister for Industry and Commerce was the guest speaker at the centenary banquet.

LINKS WITH NORTHERN IRELAND

The centenary celebrations reinvigorated the Society. By 1949, membership stood at 238, the highest number since its foundation. In 1944, the Council had decided that candidates for membership, who were not known to any member of the Council – either personally or by repute, would be invited to submit the name of an ordinary member as a proposer.[3] This indicates that hitherto the membership had come from a limited circle. In the early 1950s, the Society made serious efforts to establish a branch in Belfast. Although the connections with Belfast dated from the middle of the previous century, these appear to have been tenuous, and there were never more than a handful of members with addresses in Ulster in the years before 1920. Consequently partition did not result in any loss of members.

By the 1930s, the Barrington Trust lectures constituted the Society's only significant contact with Northern Ireland. One lecturer was appointed annually for the province of Ulster. These lectures were generally restricted to Northern Ireland, though on at least one occasion a lecture was organised in County Donegal. However towns such as Carrickmacross and Ballybay (Co. Monaghan) were regarded as part of the Leinster lecture circuit. There appears to have been less demand for lectures in Northern Ireland than in other regions, and it proved more difficult to ring the changes on lecturers, as was the practice in other areas. In

1932 the President of the Society, J.C.M. Eason met the Vice-Chancellor of Queen's University in an effort to revive interest in the programme.[4]

With the exception of James Meenan's paper, which examined the preliminary findings of the 1937 Northern Ireland Census, and the contributions by Dr James Deeny on poverty and ill-health in Lurgan and Belfast, Northern Ireland scarcely featured in the Society's proceedings during the years 1922-47. There was no attempt to examine the implications of the tariff protection for cross-border trade, for example, perhaps because the subject was politically controversial. In 1951, when Norman Cuthbert of Queen's University Belfast, presented estimates for national income in Northern Ireland for the years 1938-47, Roy Geary, opening the discussion, lamented the fact that the Society had been unable to arrange a meeting in Belfast (Cuthbert, 204). In 1952, on the suggestion of Queen's University economists K.S. Isles and Charles Carter, the Council decided to establish a Belfast branch, which would be represented on the Council by a vice-president and one ordinary member.[5] This suggestion may have been prompted by the fact that the British Association was holding its annual meeting in Belfast. By the 1953/54 session, the Society had fifty-four members with Northern Ireland addresses, a far cry from the nine members of 1949/50.

The Society's growing interest in Northern Ireland may have been further stimulated by the fact that partition had become a more important political issue in Dublin. One of the factors behind the decision to establish the official Irish News Agency in 1950 was a desire to publicise the evils of partition throughout the world. The all-party Mansion House anti-partition conference also kept the issue to the fore. Although the Society played no part in such an overtly political campaign, the 1950s saw a significant increase in the number of papers relating to Northern Ireland. Among the topics examined were the economic future of the province (Nugent, 943); the composition of public expenditure (Robson, 1086); the Northern Ireland trade union movement (Bleakley, 78); the Northern Ireland Housing Trust (O'Brien, 953); and estimates of the province's gross domestic product (Carter and Robson, 133). In 1954, the Society's symposium, which was held in Belfast examined the economic prospects for the United Kingdom economy, with special attention to Northern Ireland (Black, 74; Cuthbert, 203). In 1951, both Roy Geary and Joseph Johnston, the current president, deprecated efforts to draw comparisons between the two Irish economies. Johnston claimed that such comparisons were 'apt to be misleading' because of differences in policies and in economic circumstances. It is also possible that he feared the political inferences that might follow. In fact UCG economist Labhrás Ó Nualláin had presented a comparison of both economies in 1945/46 (Ó Nualláin, 1034). An examination of agricultural output and productivity in Northern Ireland and in the Irish Republic reflected unfavourably on the latter, and drew attention to the costs imposed by Irish independence. In 1949, Louis Smith suggested that the agricultural sector in Northern Ireland had benefited considerably from the province's political status, which gave it access to the protected British market, though Smith also suggested that the powerful marketing boards established by the Northern Ireland government since 1924 had contributed to Northern success (Smith, 1161). In 1966, E.A. Attwood estimated that the volume of agricultural output in the Republic would be 50 per cent higher than its present level if farms in the South had expanded at a similar rate to those in Northern Ireland (Attwood, 11). However, the political implications of this finding were probably less serious in 1966 than in the early 1950s; the 1965 Anglo-Irish Trade Agreement had secured free entry to the British market for Irish exports, and Irish agriculture anticipated that membership of the EEC would soon mean higher prices for its produce .

Once the initial enthusiasm associated with the establishment of the Belfast branch had subsided, it began to face some difficulties. In October 1952, the government of Northern Ireland refused to grant John Oliver, a principal officer in the Ministry for Health and Local Government permission to have printed a proposed paper, which he had read to the Society, and the Council determined that his oral presentation would not rank as a full meeting.[6] Unfortunately we do not know the subject of Oliver's paper, but, given his interests, it probably related either to housing or to public health.[7] Although Dublin-based civil servants also had to seek permission to have their papers published – in January 1949 for example, the Council Minutes noted that T.K. Whitaker would have to obtain permission to communicate his forthcoming paper on Ireland's External Assets (Whitaker, 1295) – there is no evidence to suggest that this presented serious difficulty. It proved much more difficult to attract contributions from Belfast-based civil servants. Perhaps there was some suspicion of a Dublin-based Society and so the Northern branch became much more reliant on academics for its survival. In 1957, at the suggestion of Charles Carter, the Council agreed to transfer its holdings of British Parliamentary Papers to the library at Queen's University Belfast on permanent loan.

Charles Carter was one of the most active members of the Belfast section, and his departure in the late 1950s to take up a position in Britain proved a serious blow. In 1959, R.D.C. Black – who had written the history of the Society in 1947 – informed the Council that the departure of Professor Carter, and the probable departure of Peter Robson, had thrown the survival of the Belfast section into doubt. Meetings attracted poor attendances and papers could be obtained only by approaching possible authors, who were often not members of the Society. Consequently it proved difficult to reject an unsatisfactory paper. Dr Black suggested that all Northern members should be informed about the present difficulties, with the aim of encouraging those who were interested in the branch's survival to come forward and offer papers. The Council approved Black's suggestion that no programme of meetings should be offered in Belfast during the 1959/60 session, unless a satisfactory response was obtained.[8]

Some months later Black reported that the circular had brought a disappointing response. It might prove possible to carry on for a further year by holding meetings 'of a discussion type'; he also suggested that the Society explore the possibility of holding joint meetings with the Irish Association – a non-party political and non-sectarian association, founded in 1938 which sought 'to make reason and goodwill take the place of passion and prejudice in Ireland, north and south'. Although Joseph Johnston, a long-standing member of the Statistical Society, was President of the Irish Association from 1954 until 1963, there is no evidence that the two organisations held joint meetings.[9]

The Council also suggested that it would arrange to have any papers that seemed of particular interest to a Northern Ireland audience, re-read in Belfast.[10] In April 1961, Black reported in gloomy tones that it had proved possible to organise only one paper in Northern Ireland during the current session. In addition, the Society had arranged two discussion meetings, but plans for two further sessions had collapsed. In the light of the small membership, he believed that it was possible to hold only one or two meetings a year in the province. However, Black's prognosis proved to be unduly pessimistic; in particular he underestimated his ability to sustain the Northern branch almost single-handedly. By October 1961 he was in a position to announce that three papers had been planned for the coming session, and for the remainder of the decade the Northern branch offered an average of three or four papers annually. In addition, the Society managed to recruit a succession of distinguished Barrington lecturers for the province, including Norman Cuthbert, William Black, K. Samas, John Simpson, C.W. Jefferson and Michael McGurnaghan.

Although the Belfast branch continued its independent lecture series, the Council Minutes suggest that contact between the Ulster members and the remainder of the Society was limited during the 1950s and 1960s. The growth of civil unrest in Northern Ireland in the late 1960s seems to have alerted the Council to the relative isolation of its Belfast branch. In April 1971, the Council considered a proposal to hold a joint meeting of the Dublin and Belfast branches at Ballymascanlon, near Dundalk, County Louth; however in September Black reported that 'in the present circumstances' the prospects for such a meeting were not 'too bright' – a comment which reflects the growing violence during that summer. The Council decided that it should be left to Professor Black to initiate a joint meeting. When Black again raised the prospect of holding a north/south meeting in the autumn of 1973, the Council minuted that it would serve 'to renew personal contact between the people concerned'. The recently established annual meetings of Irish economists from north and south, which were being held at Ballymascanlon at Easter, appeared to offer an appropriate opportunity and Louden Ryan, Whately professor of political economy at Trinity College Dublin, agreed to explore the possibility that one evening of that conference would be dedicated to a paper presented by the Society on a topic of interest to members from both north and south. This proposal received strong support from Garret FitzGerald, now Minister for Foreign Affairs and a member of the Council: he suggested that a paper might be presented by an official from his Department.

In a further effort to strengthen north/south ties, the Council discussed the possibility of circulating copies of the papers presented in Belfast to all members, though this proposal was abandoned because of the Society's financial difficulties. It was also agreed that one of the forthcoming Council vacancies should be reserved for a member from Northern Ireland. Such efforts should be seen in the context of deteriorating conditions there: the 1973/74 Barrington lecture series was disrupted because of the fuel crisis and disturbances associated with the loyalist workers strike. In September 1974, Black again expressed fears that the Belfast branch could not survive: meetings rarely attracted an audience of more than 20, and an insufficient supply of papers had forced the Society to accept some of mediocre quality. A further threat came from the proposal at that time to establish a Belfast branch of the Royal Statistical Society. Although the Council agreed to hold a special meeting which would be 'mainly concerned' with the problems of the Northern Branch, it appears that the topic became subsumed into a wider concern with the future of the Society as a whole.

Although the Belfast branch did not fully live up to expectations, the links established during the early 1950s proved of long-term importance. Moreover they were forged at a time when contacts between north and south were extremely limited; this applied particularly to contact between government officials. By publishing papers on matters of common interest, such as the performance of agriculture, the organisation of publicly funded housing, and hospital services, in an uncontroversial atmosphere, the Society was in a small way anticipating the type of developments that were put in train at a more official level following the O'Neill-Lemass talks of 1965.[11]

THE SOCIETY DURING THE 1950S

In 1954, the Society, whether unwittingly or otherwise, opened its own personal chink in the Iron Curtain by responding warmly to an invitation to form a close and friendly relationship with the Yugoslavian Statistical Society, which had been constituted in 1953.[12] The Yugoslavian Society was duly added to the list of corresponding societies, though in 1955 the Council turned down an invitation to send a delegate to Belgrade for its third annual general meeting. This contact does not appear to have attracted public attention, unlike the proposed 1952 soccer match between the Irish Republic and Yugoslavia, which the Football Association of Ireland cancelled following a protest from the catholic archbishop of Dublin, Dr John Charles McQuaid. (In 1955 the Irish and Yugoslav soccer teams played a match at Dublin's Dalymount Park, despite Dr McQuaid's intervention, though on government advice President Seán T. O'Kelly did not attend.)[13] More conventionally, in March 1953 the Council acknowledged a letter of congratulation from Cardinal Dalton, Archbishop of Armagh, who was a long-standing member, on its affiliation to the International Institute of Statistics.

Council meetings throughout the early 1950s were dominated by financial problems. In 1952, the Belfast section mooted the possibility of admitting group members at a higher charge. However the Council was not enthusiastic, citing the disappointing experience in raising subscriptions from businesses during the centenary year.[14] An application for financial assistance to the Department of External Affairs was turned down because the Society did not meet the criteria of the cultural relations budget. Charles Carter explored the possibility of obtaining money from the Carnegie Trust, the Rockefeller Foundation and the Nuffield Foundation, only to discover that in all cases the Society was ineligible. With these options excluded, the Council began to view more favourably the prospect of admitting group members, and in 1955, following a proposal by J.C.M. Eason, it agreed to bring a constitutional amendment to this effect before the annual general meeting.

The first group members, admitted in the autumn of 1956, included the Central Bank and leading commercial banks, together with the prominent Irish manufacturing companies. These included firms such as Arthur Guinness, W. and M. Goulding and J. and L. Goodbody, whose existence predated the foundation of the state, together with many of the largest companies established under the protectionist regime of the 1930s, such as Irish Dunlop, Irish Ropes and Irish Worsted Mills. The Congress of Irish Unions and semi-state companies such as Aer Lingus, Bord Failte, the Agricultural Credit Company and the Industrial Credit Company also affiliated. Many corporate members were probably recruited as a result of the extensive commercial connections of the then president, Dr J.P. Beddy, formerly chief executive of the ICC, and first chairman of the Industrial Development Authority. The windfall provided by group membership left the Society with surplus funds, which the Council invested in stock. By the autumn of 1960, the Council was expressing concern that the Society had accumulated an excessively healthy credit balance, and it asked for suggestions as to how this should be spent. It was eventually decided to use the money to give better service to members, by printing and circulating papers in advance – a service which had been introduced and terminated on several occasions during the Society's history.

From the 1940s, proceedings reflected a growing division between members whose interests lay in statistics and quantitative economics, and others who classified themselves as qualifying for membership under the category of 'Social Inquiry'. By the 1950s, the papers presented to the Society dealt almost exclusively with economic topics. There was a substantial decline in the number of papers dealing with medical or medico-social topics, and if we exclude the perennial topic of population, few sessions examined social issues.

In 1953, the journal *Administration* was founded by a small group of civil servants based in the Custom House. Although the Society did not regard public administration as one of its central concerns – in 1944 it had rejected a request from F.C. King that it establish a sub-committee which would be dedicated to studying public administration[15] – many of the articles published in early issues of *Administration*, on topics such as adult education, forestry, public enterprise and turf development, would not have been out of place in the Journal of the Statistical and Social Inquiry Society.[16] In 1955, Tom Barrington, the editor of *Administration*, and son of Thomas Barrington who had been an active member of the Society in the 1920s, requested permission to reprint occasional papers of the Society in *Administration*.

Although the Council was unwilling to give a general commitment, it intimated that it would favourably consider requests to reprint specific papers. Barrington subsequently requested permission to reprint a paper on the Irish Family by R.C. Geary and one by J.J. McElligott on revaluation (Geary, 356; McElligott, 795).[17] When the Institute of Public Administration was established in 1957, the Society began to hold occasional joint meetings with the IPA. What appears to have been the first took place in November 1959 when Padraig Ó hUiginn (then an official in the Department of Local Government) provided a comparative analysis of housing conditions in Ireland and in other countries of western Europe (Ó hUiginn, 1008).

NATIONAL ACCOUNTS, STATISTICS AND ECONOMIC PLANNING

At the banquet marking the centenary of the Statistical Society in October 1947, Seán Lemass, Minister for Industry and Commerce, the parent department of the government's statistical service, spoke in optimistic tones about the growing importance of statistics as an aid to economic planning, and as a mechanism for helping to determine the direction of government policy, and perhaps ultimately a government's electoral fate. Lemass claimed that statistics were becoming 'the ammunition of political warfare ... the rise and fall of the balance [of payments] can put Governments out of office, or, as our present experience tells us, force them into action which affects every man in the most intimate way, in his food, in his home and in his work'. Roy Geary's presidential address to the centenary gathering referred confidently to the potential offered by recent developments in economic statistics, notably the emergence of national accounts, and the use of time-series data for economic forecasting. At this time Geary was attached to the Department of Applied Economics at Cambridge, where he was very much in touch with international developments in this field. Although Geary's paper anticipated the optimistic tone of Lemass's speech some days later, he was more conscious of the practical difficulties which such developments would entail. Geary believed that 'The best solution is to make the administrator statistics-minded and to find some way of giving the statistician a closer insight into current problems of administration' (Geary, 363).

Taken in isolation, these statements appear to suggest that the dominance of statistics, economic planning and forecasting was now assured, both within the Society and in the Irish public service. The decision in 1949 to establish a separate Central Statistics Office seemed to point in the same direction.[18] However this would not be correct. Indeed Kennedy and Dowling suggest that the deflationary Budget of 1952 was introduced at a time when up to date statistics would have indicated that the trade position was showing considerable improvement.[19] Although all applicants for Marshall Aid were required to submit an economic development plan – the Long-Term Recovery Programme published in 1949 – and participants in the Marshall Plan automatically became members of the Organisation for European Economic Co-operation, which required that they submit regular forecasts for future growth and balance of payments deficits, the Irish submission under these headings appears to have been largely cosmetic. T.K. Whitaker noted that 'no one who took part in preparing the Recovery Programme (and that includes myself) ever looked on it as a development programme, but rather as an exercise that had to be undertaken to persuade the Americans to give us Marshall Aid.'[20]

Within the Society the battlelines were firmly drawn between statistics and 'social inquiry', with the latter activity regarded as an innumerate exercise. Roy Geary's presidential address of 1947 can be viewed as the second round in a long-running debate, which began with the presidential address, entitled 'Economic Relativity', presented by George O'Brien at the opening of 1943/44 session. Professor O'Brien had deprecated his qualifications for presiding over meetings of a statistical society. He claimed that he had managed 'to slip in' under the category of social inquiry. His paper set out to minimise the scope and purpose of economics, and its ability to cure social maladies; he suggested that economic laws were not absolute, rather that they were relative and constantly changing. As to the relationship between economics and statistics, O'Brien emphasised the primacy of deduction, with statistics being limited to the subordinate role of arranging data, and verifying the results of deductive reasoning. Without the deductive framework provided by economics, he claimed that statistics was in danger of 'degenerating into mere historicism or a study of comparative institutions'; undue reliance on statistics also carried the risk that arguments would be oversimplifed. Roy Geary, replying, stated that he disagreed with 'almost every word' in this section of the paper. He, in turn, accused economists of oversimplification, and suggested that the principal use of texts on economics was 'as repositories of information, historical, descriptive, statistical'. He also claimed that O'Brien was unaware of the analytical potential offered by modern statistical methods. Geary believed that the most useful function that an economist could perform was to define the types of statistics to be collected, and in agitating 'loud and long for more, better and fresher statistics'. He also suggested that 'the remarkable degree of stability of economic statistics' suggested that the future was not as unpredictable as O'Brien had suggested (O'Brien, 947). Geary referred in passing to this exchange in the course of his 1947 presidential address, remarking that 'in our Society there is no tradition of sacrosanctity for presidential addresses' (Geary, 363).

The battle was joined once more in 1952 on the occasion of a symposium on national income. The first official estimates of Irish national income were published in 1946; they related to the year 1938.[21] A White Paper published in 1952 provided a continuous series for the years 1944-50.[22] The Society had played a pioneering role in publicising the first unofficial estimates of national income; three of the four seminal articles on this subject were presented at its meetings: T.J. Kiernan's estimates of national expenditure for the year 1926, and George Duncan's estimates of national income covering the years 1926-40 (Kiernan, 658; Duncan, 256, 257). Kiernan also published an estimate of national income for 1926 in the 1933 issue of the *Economic Journal*. Duncan's estimates of national income for the years 1926-38 were a revised version of data he had provided for the Banking Commission. He concluded that 'Allowing for the bias of the price indices, it cannot be confidently stated that the ten years preceding the present war saw any measurable improvement in the real social income of this state.' This assessment appeared to provide irrefutable evidence of the failure of the economic policies pursued by the Fianna Fáil government after 1932. Ernest Blythe, Minister for Finance in the Cumann na nGaedheal governments of 1922-32, was among the respondents to this paper, though he refrained from comments of a political nature (Duncan, 256). However, more recent estimates suggest that Duncan painted an unduly pessimistic picture of the Irish economy during the 1930s. Kennedy et al. suggest a growth rate of 10 per cent over the period 1931-38, and a correspondingly lower rate of growth for the years 1926-31.[23]

The 1952 symposium provided the first opportunity for the Society to consider official estimates of national income. Originally scheduled for December 1951, it was postponed because it proved difficult to secure sufficient speakers.[24] Opening the discussion, M.D. McCarthy of the Central Statistics Office examined the methodological difficulties involved in integrating government accounts with national income accounts. He noted that the most useful function that the Society could perform was to provide a forum that would critically examine the conventions on which the estimates were based. McCarthy's paper was not limited to discussing the technicalities of compiling national accounts; like Geary in 1947, he was interested in the possibility of using the data generated as a basis for determining economic policy. In particular, he emphasised that a national accounts framework opened up the possibility of determining the secondary effects of any policy (McCarthy, 768). This paper, and comments from Roy Geary, in the discussion following the symposium, indicated that the Central Statistics Office (CSO) had ambitions to produce a Leontief input-output table for Ireland, though these were not fulfilled. Indeed when the Programme for Economic Expansion was prepared in the late 1950s, a national accounts framework could not be used, because the necessary statistics were not available; in particular, the accounts of public authorities had not yet been remodelled on the basis of national accounts.[25]

The symposium gave rise to mutual recriminations between economists and the central statistics office. In his contribution, TCD economist George Duncan, 'an early player of this game' — calculating national accounts – remarked that Dr McCarthy had spoken 'rather slightingly of the universities and economists of this country'. Duncan replied that the Economics Department of Queen's University Belfast was the only one in Ireland 'which has even a hope of organising research on the factual side of the economy' He contrasted the frugal resources at his disposal with the lavish sums available to the Statistical Branch of the Department of Industry and Commerce – 'scarcely less than one-half the gross income of my University'. Such badinage concealed a much deeper argument concerning the relative merits of inductive and deductive reasoning, which went to the heart of the Society's origins. Despite, or perhaps because of, his being 'an early player', Duncan emphasised that his intellectual interests did not lie in econometrics – 'and that is as it should be'. He also disparaged the contribution that economic forecasting had made to the management of the wartime British economy (Duncan, 258).

Commenting on the symposium, Geary referred to the 'profound differences' which existed between himself and Professor Duncan over the role of statistics in economics; he also rebutted Duncan's dismissal of the practical value of British economic forecasts. Geary ended by questioning the value of 'pure economics for the solution of the practical economic problems which beset us. … When economists have to deal with these problems we do not hear much about marginal utility, imperfect competition, utility and the rest: they look to the statistics like the rest of us, and what they write is indistinguishable from what the statistician writes, if he can only write as well.' According to Geary, Irish economists would be made welcome in the Central Statistics Office: 'We offer them a place on the statistical band-wagon (or Juggernaut chariot, if you will), but if they continue to sulk in their tents we must travel alone' (1223). Ronan Fanning noted that a copy of these exchanges found their way into the papers of Patrick McGilligan, who served as Minister for Finance in the first inter-party government, 'which not only established the Central Statistics Office but which initiated the most dramatic shift in direction of government economic policy (and of how that policy was formulated) since independence'.

Geary used his presidency as an opportunity to promote papers which made use of modern statistical techniques, and, contrary to the Society's traditions, to invite distinguished speakers from outside Ireland. In March 1949, Gerhard Tintner of the Department of Applied Economics at Cambridge read a paper on the 'scope and methods of econometrics' (Tintner, 1254). Fanning noted that no university-based economist contributed to the discussion.[26] However when J.R.N. Stone, director of the National Accounts Research Unit of the Organisation for European Economic Co-operation, spoke on the subject of 'Recent Developments in National Income Research throughout the World' in March 1950, the speakers included Professors Duncan and UCD economics lecturer, James Meenan.[27]

Although Geary's presidency was dominated by sessions devoted to quantitative economics, including an important paper by Brendan Menton on theories of adjustment of the balance of payments under fixed exchange rates (Menton, 860), the triumph of quantification was by no means complete. In March 1950, George Duncan read a paper on Marshall Aid which is noteworthy for containing no statistics whatever (the only numbers refer to dates). Geary described the session as 'essentially an economists' evening'. Duncan concluded that the Marshall Plan was necessitated not by economic but by political conditions, and that Europe would have been capable of economic recovery without such aid – a judgment which, interestingly, anticipates the views expressed much later by Alan Milward, one of the leading experts on this subject.[28] Geary countered that 'irrefutable statistics are there to show that in the O.E.E.C. countries and in all the countries with which they have traded, the indices of real production, real consumption per head, industrial productivity, etc. have shown a most impressive increase since 1946 and this increase must be attributed to Marshall Aid' (Duncan, 253).

Geary was succeeded as president by Joseph Johnston and Johnston by James Meenan. Both men were much less sympathetic to statistics and econometrics. In 1957, Meenan, who was then president, claimed to note a shift in the 'pendulum of the Society' away from statistics, which had been dominant under Geary's presidency towards social inquiry (Meenan, 851).

THE IRISH ECONOMY IN THE POST-WAR WORLD

In the immediate aftermath of World War II, with Europe suffering from a significant shortage of food, it seemed that agriculture would be the key sector in the post-war Irish economy, and this view remained a central tenet of economic policy until the 1960s. A prosperous agricultural sector was dependent on two factors: access to profitable export markets, and higher productivity on Irish farms. From the 1940s, the Society provided a forum for numerous sessions which examined the productivity of Irish agriculture. Although other outlets existed for such research, such as the *Journal of the Department of Agriculture*, they tended to reach a more specialist audience consisting primarily of agricultural experts. The Society was an important bridge between agricultural scientists and statisticians, economists and public servants. During the Emergency years, Michael Murphy of the Faculty of Dairy Science in UCC presented a series of papers which analysed the output and operating costs of farms in County Cork (Murphy, 922-25). Murphy's work was followed by studies in a similar vein conducted by Bob O'Connor – a future president of the society and an active member for almost fifty years – on the performance of farms in County Roscommon (O'Connor, 984, 985). Both Murphy and O'Connor suggested that there was a considerable variation in productivity between farms that were of similar size and similar rateable valuation. This indicated the importance of the human factor, and the need to provide education in farm management.

On nine of the twenty Roscommon farms which kept accounts for the year 1945/46, family workers earned less than the statutory agricultural wage and half the farms were incapable of providing adequate remuneration for a farmer, his wife and an inheriting son. This was presumably the 'paper lately read before the Society', which prompted a letter of protest to the Council from the Minister for Agriculture, James Dillon, in January 1949. The Council deprecated the Minister's remarks, but felt that no action could be taken.[29] In fact O'Connor's follow-up study, which he presented to the Society in February 1950, confirmed his earlier findings. One speaker remarked that it had revealed a 'very disturbing state of affairs'; others welcomed the insights which Murphy and O'Connor had provided into the problems of collecting data on the economics of individual farms. Geary announced 'that the trail blazed so ably by Professor Murphy and Mr O'Connor would be followed during the coming 12 months by official statisticians'. The planned programme of official farm surveys was being carried out because the researches of Murphy and O'Connor 'had shown the practicability of those surveys and in large measure how they should be conducted' (O'Connor, 985).

The findings of Murphy and O'Connor suggested that a continuing exodus from rural Ireland was almost inevitable. Joseph Johnston attempted to evade this unpalatable dilemma in a utopian paper, which advocated the creation of large co-operative farms – an Irish form of collective farm. He claimed that these would provide substantial employment and be extremely productive (Johnston, 611). In contrast to the strong empirical basis of the papers by Murphy and O'Connor, Johnston cited no statistics, and his paper was singularly unscientific in its conclusions. A 1956 paper by Geary on 'Variability in Agricultural Statistics on Small and Medium-Sized Farms in an Irish County', showed that, whereas output per man was higher on larger farms, 'the density of manpower and of each agricultural statistic, even of dry cattle, decline with increasing farm size'. In addition, agricultural output per acre was lower on larger farms.

Geary confirmed earlier research by Murphy and O'Connor which showed that there was a high variation in output and in family income between farms of similar size and similar rateable valuation in the same county. His research indicated that there was an undoubted conflict between the goal of maximising total agricultural output – best done on smaller farms —and the aim of achieving higher output per agricultural worker. 'Meeting under the shadow of the 1956 Census figures' – which was to show a continuing high rate of population decline – Geary suggested that Irish agricultural policy should aim at maximising employment and output per acre (not per man), and at preventing a decline in the numbers working on the land: conclusions that echo the difficult trade-off which was characteristic of post-Famine Ireland (Geary, 366).

By comparison with the considerable attention devoted to agriculture, the Society showed little interest in industry, or in the economic potential of the manufacturing sector. Between 1922 and 1960 only four papers related to manufacturing industry. In 1935, C.P. McCarthy examined the structure of the boot and shoe industry in the Irish Free State (McCarthy, 765); during the

1948/49 session, a paper by Louden Ryan showed that tariff protection rose five-fold between 1926 and 1936, though more recent research suggests that this exaggerated the level of protection (Ryan, 1104).[30] During the years 1953-55, two papers examined the prospects for the Northern Ireland linen industry (Black, 74; Larmor, 669).

TOWARDS ECONOMIC DEVELOPMENT

Although the transfer of cabinet and department files to the National Archives means that it is now possible to trace in greater detail the changes in macroeconomic policy during the years 1948-59, the Society's Journal remains the most important printed source on this subject and in some respects the most important single source. The Journal contains several important contributions from T.K. Whitaker, who is generally credited with the key role in transforming the Irish economy during the late 1950s. Through its pages we can trace the evolution of a thought-process, which culminated in the publication of Economic Development in 1958.

A general election held in January 1948 led to the formation of a coalition government (generally known as the first inter-party government), which included representatives of all political parties in Dáil Éireann except Fianna Fáil. Socio-economic issues played a major role in the election campaign, as other parties attacked the government over the state of the Irish economy, the level of emigration, the housing shortage and inadequate social services. By 1948, the shortage of supplies which had bedevilled the immediate post-war years had eased, and with Marshall Aid providing temporary relief from the chronic shortage of dollars, plus additional funds for domestic investment, the inter-party government embarked on a major programme of public expenditure. A paper by J.C.M. Eason in 1947 examined the composition of public expenditure in 1929/30, 1939/40 and 1945/46 (Eason, 277). Four years later he provided a highly critical analysis of the rise in public expenditure which had taken place since 1948 (Eason, 282).

Whitaker, who replied to both papers, adopted a much less dogmatic approach to public expenditure than the overly simple

'Treasury' or 'Finance' view favoured by the then Secretary of Finance, J.J. McElligott. In 1947, speaking in decidedly Keynesian tones, Whitaker emphasised that 'on the general question of budget deficits and State debt, it is well to remember that modern economic theory does not in all circumstances condemn debt that is not financially productive. If national resources in men and materials are not fully employed, a budget deficit – financed by credit creation – may be the only means of lifting the economy to a higher level of activity' (Eason, 277). By 1951/52, however, with public expenditure accounting for 41.3 per cent of GNP, against a figure of 33.5 per cent in 1949/50, and with most of the increase devoted to social, i.e. non-productive, purposes,[31] Whitaker's tone had hardened. He described public capital expenditure as 'a gamble on what the future has in store'. According to Whitaker, higher investment in housing would be justified if the future was uncertain, and it seemed probable that it would bring higher inflation and a shortage of imports, resulting in 'a forced tightening of belts'. If, however, 'less disorderly conditions prevailed, a more careful approach to capital development would be preferable'. Whitaker believed that 'we are living beyond our means, saving too little and consuming too much' (Eason, 282).

Many people maintained that the problem of insufficient savings could be surmounted by repatriating Ireland's external assets. These had risen considerably in monetary value (though by much less in real terms) during the war years. Clann na Poblachta, one of the parties in the first inter-party government, had favoured such a policy since its foundation.[32] When Whitaker read a paper on the subject of external assets in April 1949, the Clann's views were expressed in a moderate tone by Arnold Marsh, who suggested that 'we [presumably the Irish people] had an obvious right to control the[ir] disposition' of the external assets, which were in the hands of the State or the Central Bank – amounting to £102m, or 25 per cent of the total, according to Whitaker's calculations. Marsh 'did not think it could be considered too much of an excursion into revolutionary socialism if the commercial banks also, including all that operated within the State, were required to invest a proportion of their funds in Irish securities'. Even the Taoiseach, John A. Costello, a member of Fine Gael, appears to have had some sympathy with such views.[33]

In these circumstances it seems probable that Whitaker's paper was designed to disabuse of such opinions certain influential sections of Irish society. He emphasised that, contrary to popular belief, there was no net investment abroad by Irish citizens in normal times; the value of overseas assets had risen owing to forced savings, or an inability to obtain imports during the first and second world wars. Furthermore, the real value of Irish assets had not risen significantly in real terms during the years 1940-45, and they had been depleted by almost one-third as a result of heavy trade deficits in 1947 and 1948. With three-quarters of sterling assets in 1949 held either by private individuals or by commercial banks, the government had little control over the pattern of external investment. Sterling assets ensured that the Irish currency could maintain parity with sterling. On this occasion, probably as a result of the international payments problems of the years 1947 and 1948, Whitaker set more stringent conditions for repatriating these assets than those he outlined in 1944 (Whitaker, 1295); the repatriated capital should be used only to fund additional investment (i.e. not as a substitute for domestic savings) and the investment must result either in higher imports or reduced exports: 'The net long-term effect on the balance of payments is the ultimate test' (Whitaker, 1294).

During the course of the 1952 symposium on national accounts, Whitaker engaged in an amicable debate with Patrick Lynch on the appropriateness of Keynesian policies to Irish circumstances. Lynch, who was by then a lecturer at UCD, had formerly served in the Department of Finance and in the Department of the Taoiseach, where he acted as an economic advisor to John A. Costello.[34] Whitaker proved much more sceptical than Lynch about the benefits of Keynesian economics in Irish circumstances; he pointed out that the assumption that the propensity to consume was less than unity, i.e. that expenditure was less than income was inconsistent with the evidence from Irish national accounts; in other words, his view was that consumption exceeded income. He concluded that Ireland presented a case which was 'as unlike the text-book illustrations of Keynesian theory as it would be possible to devise'. It had 'an unstable economy in which the expansive effects on income and employment or such increases as have occurred in domestic investment have been lost through an excessive propensity to consume, which has spent itself mostly on imports rather than in activating increased domestic production.' Whitaker believed that additional income and employment could be created 'if we spent less on imports and produced more at home' (Lynch, 738; Whitaker, 1296). James Dillon TD, Minister for Agriculture in the first inter-party government, criticised this aspect of Whitaker's argument, on the grounds that it seemed to favour the domestic market over exports.

Several elements of this symposium anticipate the paper which Whitaker read on 25 May 1956 on the subject of 'Capital Formation, Saving and Economic Progress'. Although this paper has been described as beginning the 're-assessment of Ireland's economic condition',[35] a close scrutiny of the Society's Journal suggests that the process had begun at a much earlier date. Whitaker again emphasised the need to raise savings in order to finance a higher level of capital formation, and once more he dismissed the possibility that the Keynesian multiplier would provide a painless or 'quasi-magical' mechanism for raising Irish national income. In this lengthy paper, Whitaker emphasised that priority should be given to investments which would bring about increased output in agriculture and industry, if necessary at the expense of investment in social amenities such as housing. He also suggested that native and foreign industrialists should be encouraged to establish industries that would prove capable of competing in export markets, and that 'tariff protection may have to give way to other stimuli, such as grants towards the capital cost of factories or technical training', a statement which anticipates the direction of industrial policy after 1956 (Whitaker, 1293).

In retrospect, it seems interesting that Whitaker discussed the question of savings and investment at length without referring to monetary policy. This reflects the comparative lack of interest in monetary policy as a tool of economic management in the immediate post-war years,[36] and it is consistent with the approach taken in Economic Development. It also suggests an unwillingness to stray into a potentially controversial field. In his 1956 paper, Whitaker was content to chart recent changes in Irish holdings of external assets; he steered clear of proposals that would entail major changes in the investment practices of Irish banks. The fact that Whitaker was involved in regular and apparently secret discussions with the commercial banks on the provision of funds for public capital expenditure would obviously have limited his freedom to comment on this matter.[37]

In 1957 however, Norman Gibson, an economics lecturer at Queen's University Belfast, argued that an integrated economic and money policy was essential if the Irish Republic wished to follow an expansionary economic policy. This would entail giving the Central Bank much greater control over the monetary system. He specifically suggested that the net external assets of the commercial banks should be transferred to the Central Bank, which should become the government banker. Gibson's proposals must be seen in the context of a 45 per cent decline in the net external assets of Irish banks during the years 1947-56. The problem was aggravated by an exceptionally high balance of payments deficit in 1955 consequent on a decision by the Irish Banks' Standing Committee not to raise interest rates in line with the rise in the British bank rate – a decision apparently taken at the behest of the Minister for Finance, but without the approval of the Central Bank – which Gibson described as 'a voice "crying in the wilderness"'. Patrick Lynch, proposing a vote of thanks, described the paper as 'controversial and outspoken'. He believed that it provided 'a means of educating public opinion on real issues rather than on phantom prejudices'. According to Lynch, 'too much of the informed discussion of Irish banking and credit has tended to be either esoteric or reticent and timorous'. Lynch appears to have been broadly in sympathy with the contents, unlike several other speakers. Replying to the discussion, Norman Gibson remarked that 'some – perhaps most' of the audience 'disagree[d] entirely with what I have said'. No senior civil servant or official of the Central Bank is recorded as taking part in this discussion (Gibson, 374).

It may be significant that this controversial topic was examined by an academic economist who lived in Belfast. Addressing the British Association for the Advancement of Science in Dublin in September 1957, James Meenan, president of the Society, suggested that, while it would have been pleasant to have presented a paper on the balance of payments, he was precluded from doing so by the Society's rule against topics 'which are likely to produce discussions connected with party politics'. According to Meenan, 'the balance of payments has too recently been the stuff of Irish party politics'. In its place he spoke on the 'Political Economy of Development', a paper which had much more in common with George O'Brien's 1943 lecture on 'Economic Relativity' than with recent developments in applied economics. Nevertheless, Meenan anticipated several themes that later emerged in Economic Development: that it was becoming 'more rather than less difficult for the State to fulfil its two self-imposed aims of creating the conditions for greater production and of establishing a way of life that is so distinctive as to support political separatism'. On a more controversial note, Meenan suggested that the growing involvement of the state in economic matters reduced the field of action for the economist, leaving him to survey 'a shrunken world'. Although this paper was delivered to a distinguished audience that included Professor James Meade and Ursula Hicks, the ensuing discussion suggested that they had little worthwhile advice to offer about the Irish economy. Meade asked why New Zealand had perhaps the highest per capita income in the world, whereas Irish income per capita was one of the lowest in Europe, given that both had free entry for agricultural produce to the British market. Hicks rambled on about market gardening, arable cultivation on the Dublin hills, and 'a magnificent ram' that she had 'met on Clare Island', which had been purchased with the aid of a government grant (Meenan, 851).

This session can be read as indicative of the paralysis concerning the future direction of the Irish economy, which is said to have characterised the 1950s. The prevailing mood of pessimism was fuelled by widespread interest in the pathological condition of the Irish population, specifically the persistence of emigration, and the Irish affinity for late marriages and a high rate of permanent celibacy. Ironically, this concern with a low rate of nuptiality and late marriages seems to have reached its peak at a time when the marriage rate was beginning to rise; however, emigration had also increased. In 1948, the first inter-party government established a Commission on Emigration and other Population Problems, whose members included many active members of the Society, including Duncan, Meenan, Geary and M.D. McCarthy. William Honohan, a future president of the Society, acted as secretary. As Liam Ó Buachalla remarked when the Society held a symposium to discuss the findings of the Commission, 'for those who have been giving thought to these questions of population and emigration, the Report contains little that is new' (Ó Buachalla, 970). Perhaps for this reason – and because some of the most interested members were excluded from contributing, since they had been members of the Commission – the symposium was uneventful. The Report of the Commission on Emigration did not appear until 1954. The delay was caused by unsuccessful efforts to achieve an agreed report.[38]

The majority report concluded that the primary cause of high emigration and a low rate of marriage was economic: specifically low living standards and lack of employment. This interpretation that can be traced back to many of the papers presented to the Society from the 1930s. Such views ran strictly counter to the views expressed by many politicians and religious leaders; according to Éamon de Valera emigrants were misguidedly deserting Ireland for living conditions of indescribable horror in English cities.[39] The findings of the Commission were widely publicised, with the *Irish Independent* reprinting the text in extenso over two weeks. This was an occasion when ideas that had long been common currency within the Society reached a wider public. In contrast to the critical reception given to the majority report of the Banking Commission, which also embodied the predominant views of members of the Society, the Commission's findings appear to have been widely accepted, though without enthusiasm.

If the symposium on the Commission on Emigration exuded a certain sense of *déjà-vu*, this was certainly not the case in 1959 when the Society organised a symposium on economic development, which considered three publications: Economic Development, the Third Report of the Capital Investment Advisory Committee, and the Programme for Economic Expansion. On this occasion, too, a substantial amount of the contents of these reports, such as the recommendation that priority be given to investing in agriculture and industry in preference to investment in housing and social services, had been anticipated by papers to the Society. With the exception of some detailed comments from Louis Smith concerning estimates of future demand for fertiliser, the discussants avoided technical matters, such as projected rates of economic growth and of public capital expenditure. Most historians have suggested that the principal significance of Economic Development was psychological, and both the contributions of R.D.C. Black and P. Lynch concentrate on this point. Black's remark that the Irish economy since independence was primarily adapted to securing independence rather than economic progress anticipates a later argument made by Joseph Lee.[40] Lynch claimed that Economic Development 'had captured the imagination of the young people between the ages of 18 and 21 who had become increasingly impatient with oracular generalisations'.

Although other speakers praised the reports, they seemed unwilling to accept some of the clear and often painful choices that had been presented. Thus Labhrás Ó Nualláin demanded a specific development plan for the west of Ireland, though Whitaker had insisted in Economic Development that the only criteria to be applied should be the rate of economic growth, irrespective of the number of jobs provided or their location. Ó Nualláin in contrast argued that it was 'no selling point' to state that national income would double within 35 years: 'What the public is interested in are employment figures and production targets.' A representative of the manufacturing sector reminded the audience of 'our duty to protect existing industries' and to ensure that any assistance offered to new exporting firms 'must not be to the detriment or prejudice of established concerns', despite clear statements in the reports that the Irish economy must move towards free trade (Thompson, 1245). Donal Nevin, speaking on behalf of the trade unions, emphasised the need to create employment and to retain a balance between projects that gave an economic return and socially desirable schemes. He also wanted a more prominent role for public enterprise (Nevin, 928). Paddy O'Keeffe, editor of the *Irish Farmers' Journal*, implicitly rebutted the recommendation that agricultural policy should concentrate on producing more cattle, when he expressed regret that the White Paper had written off the export market for eggs. He provided a list of intensive agricultural enterprises that should be developed (O'Keeffe, 1009). A similar, if rather anecdotal, lifeline was thrown to intensive agricultural enterprises by Professor Joseph Johnston, who was now running a smallholding on land in County Laois that had once formed part of the estate of Henry Grattan (1199). Such harking back to discredited economic policies showed that, despite the warm welcome given to Economic Development, the conversion to a new strategy for economic development was by no means complete.

During the 1950s, as in earlier decades, the Society attempted to present reasoned economic explanations for many of the problems which Irish society was confronting. In rejecting panaceas, such as appropriating Irish external assets, in highlighting the dangers posed by an uncritical expansion of public investment, and in suggesting that the continuing fall in the population was a reflection of dissatisfaction with existing living standards, and not the result of a national death-wish, it offered little comfort to those who sought easy solutions or scapegoats for Ireland's economic condition. In many respects the publication of the reports of the Commission on Emigration and Economic Development marked the Society's apotheosis. Both reports reiterated an analysis that had been aired, and indeed refined, within the Society over many years. By the late 1950s, these views had apparently been adopted by many politicians, and by a significant number of the wider public. Archbishop Whately would have been envious.

NOTES TO CHAPTER FOUR

[1] NLI Brennan Papers, Ms 26403.
[2] Ibid.
[3] Council Minutes, 13 October 1944.
[4] Council Minutes, 7 April 1932, 25 May 1932, 30 September 1932.
[5] Council Minutes, 29 April 1952, 23 September 1952.
[6] Council Minutes 27 October 1952.
[7] John A. Oliver, *Working at Stormont*, (Dublin 1978).
[8] Council Minutes, 3 April 1959.
[9] Paul Bew, Kenneth Darwin and Gordon Gillespie (eds), *Passion and Prejudice. Nationalist-Unionist Conflict in Ulster in the 1930s and the Founding of the Irish Association* (Belfast 1993), pp. vi, 113.
[10] Council Minutes, 17 August 1959.
[11] National Archives, Department of Foreign Affairs. Possibilities of Practical Cooperation with Northern Ireland following Talks 1965 (96/.3/15).
[12] Council Minutes, 12 February 1954.
[13] Dermot Keogh, *Twentieth-Century Ireland. Nation and State* (Dublin, 1994), p. 228.

14 Council Minutes, 29 April 1952, 23 September 1952.
15 Council Minutes, 10 January 1944.
16 Garret FitzGerald, 'Four Decades of Administration', *Administration. Cumulative Index*, volumes 1-40 1953-1992. (Dublin, 1994).
17 Council Minutes, 11 March 1955 and 14 May 1955.
18 Fanning, *Finance*, pp. 517-18.
19 Kieran A. Kennedy and Brendan R. Dowling, *Economic Growth in Ireland. The Experience since 1947* (Dublin, 1975), pp. 210-15.
20 Quoted in Fanning, *Finance*, p. 406.
21 Kieran A. Kennedy, 'The National Accounts for Ireland in the Nineteenth and Twentieth Centuries' *Scandinavian Economic History Review*, XLIII, no. 1 (1995), pp. 101-14.
22 Tables of National Income and Expenditure, 1938 and 1944-50 (Pr. 350). 1952.
23 Kennedy, Giblin and McHugh, *Economic Development of Ireland*, pp. 48, 118-19.
24 Council Minutes 15 December 1951
25 Garret FitzGerald, *Planning in Ireland*, (Dublin, 1968), p. 37.
26 Fanning, 'Economists and governments: Ireland 1922-52', in Murphy (ed.), *Economists and the Irish Economy*, pp. 150-52.
27 This paper was not printed. See note recording speakers in vol. xviii, pt. 3, p. 292.
28 Alan Milward, *The Reconstruction of Western Europe, 1945-51* (London, 1984).
29 Council Minutes, 22 January 1949.
30 D. MacAleese, *Effective Tariffs and the Structure of Industrial Protection in Ireland* (Dublin, 1971); Ó Gráda, *Ireland: a New Economic History*, pp. 407-08.
31 John O'Hagan, 'An analysis of the relative size of the government sector', p. 30.
32 Colman O'Sullivan, 'The IRA takes Constitutional Action: the History of Clann na Poblachta, 1946-65'. M.A. UCD 1995, pp. 189-91.
33 Daly, *The Buffer State*, pp. 350-51.

34 Fanning, *Finance*, pp. 457-58.
35 Basil Chubb and Patrick Lynch (eds), *Readings in Irish Public Administration Volume I. Economic Development and Planning*, (Dublin, 1969), p. 48.
36 Susan Howson, 'Money and monetary policy in Britain, 1945-1990', in Roderick Floud and Donald McCloskey, *The Economic History of Britain since 1700, vol. 3: 1939-1992* (Cambridge, 1994), p. 221.
37 Daly, *The Buffer State*, pp. 365-71.
38 National Archives, Department of the Taoiseach, S14219.
39 Daly 'Frugal comfort', p. 99.
40 J.J. Lee, *Ireland 1912-1985. Politics and Society* (Cambridge, 1989), pp. 511-687.

CHAPTER FIVE

The Age of Economic Growth, 1960-1997

THE ECONOMIC RESEARCH INSTITUTE

In retrospect the 1960s marked the peak of Irish confidence in all the values that the Society's founders held dear: the apparent ability of economics to transcend long-standing historic divisions of religion, politics and ethnicity, and the belief that economic progress was not only attainable, but that it would prove beneficial to all. Economic planning seemed to have triumphed, thanks to the record growth rates achieved during the years 1959-64 under the Programme for Economic Expansion . There was increased faith in the effectiveness of economic forecasting to effect even higher rates of growth, and the number of professional economists rose sharply as a by-product of the development of the Irish economy, and the emergence of a more developed public sector. Although the Society continued to provide an important forum for discussing economic and social questions, perhaps its most important contribution to the advancement of economic knowledge was to act as midwife to the Economic Research Institute.

In April 1959, F.H. Boland, Irish ambassador to the United Nations and a member of the Society since 1944, informed T.K. Whitaker that the Ford Foundation was disposed to do something that would be of economic benefit to Ireland. Whitaker suggested that there was an urgent need to establish an Economic Research Institute, in order to meet the growing need for more advanced economic research within Ireland. When it transpired that the Ford Foundation was reluctant to assist proposals which were directly sponsored by governments, and preferred to accept applications from universities, learned institutions or public-spirited citizens, Whitaker suggested that the Society take the initiative in applying to the Ford Foundation.

On 17 August 1959, the Council approved Whitaker's proposal

that it sponsor the establishment of an Economic Research Institute. Members noted that this project would further the ends of the Society, as laid down in its laws. In the Society's application to the Ford Foundation, dated 20 August 1959, which was drafted by Whitaker in his capacity as a joint honorary secretary of the Society, it was noted that the Society has 'within the limitations imposed by its resources and the voluntary character of its organisation, endeavoured since its foundation, to secure (in accordance with its Laws) the promotion of the study of statistics, jurisprudence and social and economic science.' Reference was made to the Society's longevity, its 'long history of public service', the fact that it drew membership from both parts of Ireland – minutes of the Council meeting of 17 August had suggested that efforts should be made to obtain some Northern sponsorship for the Institute – and its diverse and influential membership. In order to justify the case for an Economic Research Institute, the application referred to the Programme for Economic Expansion, and to the fact that economic research was essential in order to bring about 'a proper orientation of various schemes of economic development'. It was also suggested that the proposed institute should be an independent body. The letter of application was accompanied by a list of Council Members, indicating their wide range of academic, professional, business and public service connections, and by a list of suggested research topics that required urgent attention. Among the items which the Council regarded as needing urgent examination were the incidence of tariff protection; the factors affecting productivity in Irish industry; moves towards European integration; short-term forecasting; and the market for Irish livestock in the British market. All these topics were priorities for the Programme for Economic Expansion, and the list highlighted the close links which were envisaged between the proposed Institute and the implementation of the Programme. The application also reflected T.K. Whitaker's preference that the government's planning process should be monitored by an independent body.

Although Whitaker was undoubtedly the prime mover in the establishment of the Economic Research Institute, he received considerable support from other members of the Society, including the president, W.A. Honohan, M.D. McCarthy of the Central

Statistics Office, who prepared the memorandum and articles of association, and J.P. Beddy, who provided legal services. The provisional budget for the Institute was drafted by Roy Geary, who was at that time working at the United Nations Statistical Office in New York, and who became its first director. The only reservation entered against the proposal came from Dr Tom Walsh, Director of the Agricultural Institute, who feared that the new agency might duplicate its work. The Ford Foundation subsequently asked the Society to confirm that 'no part of the Institute's activities would be political in nature', a commitment which was very much in keeping with the Society's original constitution.[1]

The close association between the Society and the ERI was formally recognised when W.A. Honohan was nominated to represent the Society on the inaugural Board (in practice nearly all of the Board's members were active in the Society). With Roy Geary serving as the first director, the links between both bodies were assured. In October 1963 Geary informed the Council that he anticipated that ERI members would contribute at least one paper a year to the Society; he also suggested that meetings of the Society should be held in the Institute's lecture hall. However the Council believed that this premises was too small, and it rejected the proposal.[2] The Society continued to meet at Academy House until the beginning of the 1982/83 session when meetings were switched to the offices of the Economic and Social Research Institute at Burlington Road. The fact that ESRI Professor Bob O'Connor was president during that year may have prompted the move; Kieran Kennedy recalls that the decision taken in 1974 to hold meetings of the Society on Thursday evenings rather than on Friday meant that Academy House was not always available. The ESRI has continued to play an active role in the Society, contributing numerous papers, discussants and a substantial number of Council members over the years.

THE EXPANSION OF ECONOMIC AND SOCIAL RESEARCH

The establishment of the ERI was only one instance of the growing expertise and interest in economic and social research. From the 1960s the number of Irish graduates in economics and the social sciences who obtained post graduate training overseas appears to have risen sharply, or, alternatively an increasing number of economists were returning to Ireland on completion of their studies. One of the arguments that Whitaker advanced in favour of establishing an ERI, during the course of a lunch with members of the Ford Foundation, was the lack of outlets in Ireland for young Irish economists who had been trained abroad. Initially the ERI relied very heavily on foreign economists. Although this aroused hostile comment from Oliver J. Flanagan, TD and UCD economist John O'Donovan, it served to broaden the pool of economic expertise, and ERI economists such as C.E.V. Leser, a native of Germany, made a significant contribution to the Society.

Under the secretaryship of T.K. Whitaker and his successors, there was also a significant increase in the quality and quantity of economic research carried out in the Department of Finance, which resulted in a steady flow of papers to the Society. This trend, which began with the contributions of Whitaker and Brendan Menton in the late 1940s, is noteworthy: in the 1920s the Society's links with the public service were primarily with the Department of Industry and Commerce, presumably because it housed the statistical service. When T.K. Whitaker became governor of the Central Bank in 1969, he initiated a significant expansion in the bank's research activities. In 1969, Whitaker, then president of the Society, remarked on his sense of 'pride' at presiding over a paper by Thomas Hoare, an economist at the Central Bank (Hoare, 557). The following decades saw many other papers to the Society, presented by research economists of the Central Bank, on subjects such as monetary policy or macro-economic models. In November 1978, Professor Norman Gibson of the University of Ulster, replying to a paper on 'modelling the Irish economy', which had been presented by the research department of the Central Bank, commented on the 'increasing professionalism which has been evident in Irish economics for some years now' (Central Bank, 140).

The Society also attracted an increased flow of papers from officials working in state organisations such as the Industrial Development Authority, and from economists employed both in the private sector and by trade unions. Economists and statisticians from Northern Ireland also contributed a substantially greater number of papers than in the past. The long-standing relationship between the Society and the Central Statistics Office continued. In 1985, in the course of symposium on 'statistics for policy and research', Donal Murphy pointed out that personnel of the CSO contributed approximately 20 per cent of the papers presented to the Society (1231).

Although the expansion in the economics profession and the growth of specialisation undoubtedly enriched the Society, it also created a more competitive demand for papers, and for the scarce time and attention of economists and statisticians. During the 1960s Irish economists from north and south began to hold an annual conference. In January 1966, the Council gave John Simpson permission to read a paper on banking profits to this conference, which he had formerly presented to the Society (Simpson, 1148). Some years later, however, the Council rejected a proposed paper, because the author had already presented a virtually identical piece of research to the conference of economists. In April 1968, Louden Ryan drew the Council's attention to the moves that were underway to established an Irish journal of economics. As an alternative to establishing a separate journal, Ryan suggested that the Society expand its journal to two issues a year, which would enable it to publish some papers which had not been read before the Society. However, some Council members objected that this would alter the 'essential character of the Society'.

A small committee consisting of Louden Ryan, Roy Geary, Tom Linehan and Brendan Broderick, together with Michael Fogarty (director of the ESRI) and Bertram Hutchinson (a professor at the ESRI), was established to consider Ryan's suggestion. When a special Council meeting was convened in July 1968 to discuss this question, Ryan claimed that the membership and activities of the Society would suffer if a separate journal was established. Others argued that if it was decided to publish papers, which had not first been read in public to the Society, it would be necessary to set up a special editorial board, which would of necessity include representatives of the universities, the ESRI and the Society. If this were done, responsibility for the Journal would necessarily be shared between the editorial board and the

Society. One member of the Council argued that as a consequence, the Society might lose its identity, a view which was apparently shared by all the other members who were present, with the exception of Louden Ryan, though three absent members, Thekla Beere, Joseph Johnston and Professor J.R. Parkinson wrote letters supporting Ryan's proposal. While the majority of those present acknowledged that there was a need for a new journal, they were of the opinion that this should be organised by the universities and the ESRI. They also believed that the new journal would not adversely affect the Society.[3] The first issue of *The Economic and Social Review* appeared in 1970. In later years many of its contributors also read papers to the Society.

Whether the establishment of *The Economic and Social Review* had an adverse effect on the Society remains a moot point. In 1973, however, the Council noted that there was a need to tighten the procedures involved in accepting papers, and to insist on higher standards. The growth of alternative platforms for papers on economic and social issues meant that the Society no longer held a monopoly in this sphere. The ESRI organised regular seminars and by the 1980s many of the critical debates concerning the Irish economy were taking place at the annual, or biannual, conferences of economists. A proposal in 1975 to establish a Dublin branch of the Royal Statistical Society (which had long been a corresponding member of the Society) appeared to pose an additional threat; the president, Tom Linehan, and several Council members took steps to fend off this challenge. However in May 1974 the Council was informed that there were as yet no contributions in prospect for the coming session, and it was decided to invite a number of people to present papers, with the proviso that these would be submitted to referees in the normal manner.

The growth of competing conferences and societies and the heavy travel schedules of senior officials in the civil service, Central Bank and the universities made it more difficult to sustain attendance at meetings. In 1974, the Society decided to move its meetings from Friday to Thursday in an effort to attract a greater attendance. However a letter from the ever-perceptive R.D.C. Black, which began by voicing his concerns about the future of the Northern branch, raised a number of wider issues. Black queried whether the Society was 'appropriately organised' in view of the competition from other societies, the growing number of learned journals, and the difficulties in securing papers which appeal to a wide range of non-specialist members.[4] The Society was apparently suffering from the threats posed by growing specialisation, a process which had occasioned the collapse or redirection of similar organisations in Britain and the United States at the end of the nineteenth century. In 1986, Dermot McAleese noted:

> On the one hand, since there are more social science graduates than ever and more active interest among the public in such matters, the prospect for the development of our Society might be expected to be very favourable. Against this, however, is the fact that the Society now faces more intense competition than ever before from competing venues. While in former times the Society offered the public a unique opportunity of hearing scholars of the calibre of George O'Brien and Roy Geary, nowadays their successors could be found addressing the Dublin Economics Workshop, the ESRI Thursday seminar, the Industrial Studies Association, the IAUTE [Irish Association of University Teachers of Economics] conference, can be heard on radio and seen on television, can be read in our Journal, but also in *ESR* [*Economic and Social Review*], *IBAR* [*Irish Banking Review*], *Administration, Social Studies* and other publications outside of Ireland. Our problem is that there are too many outlets chasing too few papers (Black, 71).

Inflation, which was the subject of a symposium during the 1974/75 session (1211) forced the Society to double the sub–scription rate to £2 in October 1973. Although income from subscriptions rose from £1,028 in 1972/73 to £1,470 by 1974/75, private membership fell by over 25 per cent from the 1972/73 level of 388 and the Society's financial difficulties persisted. In an effort to offset the higher cost of printing and paper, in 1976 the Council decided that the ESRI and the CSO would produce the Journal, using the printing facilities available in the CSO. More intriguingly, in December 1974 the Council apparently accepted a proposal to delete law 16, which prohibited the discussion of topics connected with religious differences or party politics, a provision that had existed since the Society's foundation. Although there is no further reference to this matter in the Council minutes, the proposal was not carried by the Society, and the law drawn up by the Society's founders remains in operation.[5]

BARRINGTON LECTURES

The Barrington lecture series also suffered from the consequences of rising inflation and the growing number of competing attractions, notably television. In 1932 when Joseph Johnston lectured on 'Ireland and the World Crisis' in the County Monaghan towns of Carrickmacross and Ballybay, he attracted an estimated attendance of 100 at each lecture. During the same season, Professor Busteed, the Barrington lecturer in Munster, addressed audiences ranging from 50 to 100 people in Newmarket, Ballyclough, Skibbereen, Cork, Clonmel, Thurles, Tralee and Limerick.[6] Louis Smith recalls up to 100 people attending lectures in towns such as Tramore in the early 1960s, though on one occasion when his lecture clashed with a showing of the film, *The Quiet Man* in an adjoining hall, he found himself without an audience. According to Garret FitzGerald, his lectures tended to attract larger audiences in smaller centres such as Prosperous and Johnston County Kildare, than in bigger towns like Portlaoise, where alternative forms of evening entertainment were available. The lectures tended to be organised by the local Vocational Educational Committee, or by voluntary bodies such as Macra na Feirme and the Irish Countrywomen's Association. FitzGerald recalled that whenever he spoke about Economic Development, all the questions related to the price of fertiliser. FitzGerald recalls the Barrington lectures as 'great fun', and claims that they provided useful experience for a fledgling lecturer. Louis Smith remembers some dedicated listeners attending the same lecture in more than one location, because the question and answer session would be different. He regarded this as evidence of the lack of entertainment available in rural Ireland before the coming of television.

The series was temporarily suspended in 1961 following the death of E.C. Barrington. Initially the new trustees decided to appoint one lecturer instead of the previous four, in the hope that the higher fee would prove more attractive to prospective lecturers.

The trustees also suggested replacing the traditional programme of out-reach lectures with a series of lectures in large centres of population, preferably given in the universities. This proposal was not welcomed by Council. It noted that many other bodies, such as the Finlay Trust,[7] funded lectures of this type, and George O'Brien was dispatched to negotiate a compromise with the Barrington trustees.[8]

O'Brien does not seem to have succeeded in his mission, because in February 1963 the Council was informed that an Oxford-based economist had been selected to deliver the Barrington lectures at UCC, UCD and Queen's University Belfast. Council replied that the Society did not appear to have any useful role in this arrangement, and reiterated its preference for a lecture series carried out in rural areas.[9] This letter apparently proved effective, and in the autumn of 1963 three lecturers were appointed (a shortage of funds meant it was no longer possible to recruit four); the Council minutes specified that the lectures would be given in smaller centres of population. Norman Cuthbert (Queen's University Belfast), David O'Mahony (University College Cork) and Gerard Quinn (University College Dublin) were duly hired. In April 1964, O'Mahony reported that his lectures in Kilkenny, Thurles and Mallow had attracted small audiences, and he did not believe that his remarks had proved useful to those attending. For the future, he suggested that it was essential to enlist the interest of local bodies.

By 1966 the Barrington lectures outside Ulster had developed a distinctly agricultural flavour, with lecturers such as E.A. Attwood of the Agricultural Institute, and John Scully of the Department of Agriculture concentrating on themes such as the future of Irish farming and western development. Many of their successors, such as Michael Cuddy, Brendan Kearney, D. Nunan, Denis Lucey and Tom O'Dwyer chose similar themes, though Conor Ward's well-attended series of lectures on social policy and social research proved an exception to this pattern. The fee of £63 (originally 60 guineas) per lecturer had remained unchanged for many decades, and Council recommended that it be increased. When this proved impossible, it was decided that lecturers should in future only be required to deliver two lectures per session. However, inflation continued to take its toll, and it proved increasingly difficult to attract lecturers with the available money. Consequently, in 1984 the Council of the Society decided to replace the long-standing series of public lectures with a prize for a paper on 'economic policy and analysis of current interest in Ireland'. The competition was limited to candidates who had graduated within the past ten years. The first Barrington prize lecture, by Deirdre McHugh, was read before the Society in May 1985 (McHugh, 803).

TRANSITIONS

In 1976, the Council made a presentation to Roy Geary on the occasion of his seventy-fifth birthday.[10] As Kieran Kennedy notes, when he read his last paper, on profit-sharing, to the Society in March 1982 (Geary and Dempsey, 367), he created two records: 'in his 86th year he was the oldest person ever to have read a paper to the Society, and the time span since his first paper to the Society was a record 57 years'.[11] Although Geary remained active in the Society until his death on 8 February 1983, other long-standing members drifted away. In the autumn of 1962, George Duncan submitted a letter of resignation to the Council, but he was persuaded to serve for a further year.[12] In 1966, Joseph Johnston explained that he had attended very few meetings in recent years, because 'The Society has gone all econometric and papers are usually incomprehensible to a person of my limited understanding of mathematical matters' (Attwood, 11). There may have been an element of pique behind this statement: when Johnston submitted a paper to the Society in 1964 on the topic of 'consumer demand as a basis for credit', Roy Geary and T.K. Whitaker both agreed that it should be rejected. Johnston was informed that since 'the topic and treatment pertained more to philosophy than to economics' it did not fall within the scope of the Society; Geary's comment to Whitaker was predictably less diplomatic.[13]

In 1973, Thekla Beere, became the Society's first, and to date only, woman president. Since Beere, a former secretary of the Department of Transport and Power and the first woman to serve as secretary of an Irish government department, also chaired the

Commission on the Status of Women, it was appropriate that the
Society held a symposium on the Commission's Interim Report
on Equal Pay during her presidency. The session was memorable,
both for the rigorously argued critique of the economics of equal
pay presented by Paddy Geary and Brendan Walsh, and for the
colourful encapsulated account that one speaker gave of the
lifestyle of the six hundred lake-dwelling Tchambuli, who

> ... have built their houses along the edge of one of the loveliest
> of New Guinea lakes, which gleams like polished ebony, with
> a back-drop of the distant hills behind which the Arapesh life.
> In the lake are purple lotus and great pink and white water lilies,
> white osprey and blue heron. Here the Tchambuli women,
> brisk, unadorned, managing and industrious, fish and go to
> market: the men, decorative and adorned, carve and paint and
> practice dance-steps, their head-hunting tradition replaced by
> the simpler practice of buying victims to validate their manhood
> (1217).

This contribution suggested that the Society's ability to attract the
occasional eccentric offering had not entirely disappeared, despite
the proliferation of high-quality and increasingly professional
contributions.

From the 1970s, the papers presented to the Society show a
growing awareness of international developments in economic
theory, and in the extent to which conditions in Ireland were
comparable to other western economies: evidence that the greater
openness within the Irish economy extended to intellectual activity.
A typical example is Kieran Kennedy's 1992 presidential address,
which discussed the convergence of living standards in Ireland
with those in other EC countries. At the beginning of his paper,
Kennedy referred to two recent issues of the *Journal of Political
Economy* and the *Quarterly Journal of Economics*, both dealing
with the recent developments in the literature of economic growth
(Kennedy, 653). The number and range of works cited in the
typical paper rose substantially, particularly the number of
references to mainstream international journals. Econometrics
came very much to the fore, a development that was not welcomed
by all members. If we recall the distinctions that men such as
George O'Brien and James Meenan had previously drawn between

the statistical and social inquiry branches of the Society, by the mid-1960s it appears that statistics had triumphed.

Advances in social research lagged behind developments in economics. In 1969, Michael Fogarty, the director of the ESRI, informed the Society that 'Whereas economists, taking their basic map for granted, can proceed to pick out on it areas on which more light needs to be cast in the light of prospective practical needs, the social scientists (if I may give them that label for short, with apologies to the economists) have much more of their groundwork still to do' (Fogarty, 330). This lag reflected the fact that economic issues took precedence during the Lemass government of the early 1960s, and the underdeveloped status of social research in the Irish universities. A separate department of social science was not established at University College Dublin until 1964; the first professor was appointed in 1966, coincidentally the year when the remit of the Economic Research Institute was extended to include social research.[14] During the 1960s the proportion of papers presented to the Society that could be classified as social inquiry remained relatively low. The chronic preoccupation with demography had receded temporarily, presumably because the classic Irish problems of emigration and late marriage were disappearing, and the more novel implications of population increase were not yet apparent. Nevertheless, the small number of papers, which could be classified under social inquiry, such as Conor Ward's 1968 survey of life in a new Dublin suburb (Ward, 1286), or the papers by Monica Nevin, which documented the socio-economic background of undergraduates at Irish universities, (Nevin, 931-32) had assumed a more statistical form.

Although economic themes remained dominant, the 1970s saw a growing number of papers on social issues. These were often concerned with the relationship between economic development and social behaviour, as in David Rottman's paper on the changing pattern of crime in the Irish Republic (Rottman, 1093). A 1973 paper by Kent and Sexton, which examined the influence of social factors on the physical growth and development of Dublin children, echoed the findings of several papers from the 1940s, in showing that children from large families and from lower socio-economic groups remained at a physical disadvantage, despite the rise in living standards (Kent and Sexton, 655).

Papers on economics topics reflected the changing preoccupations of Irish government and society. Although agriculture remained important, with several papers discussing the prospects offered by EEC membership, and later contributors examining the sector's subsequent performance and future potential, (e.g. Embleton, 298) it received proportionately less attention than in the past. By comparison, industrial policy attracted much greater interest, because from the 1960s industry was regarded as the key sector in the success or failure of an overall employment policy.

While many papers deal with topics that were of interest to all western economies, such as inflation in the 1970s, unemployment and the resurgence of monetarism in the 1980s, and membership of the European Community and economic integration, successive issues of the Journal also reflect the changing nature of the Irish economy and society. Thus the growing interest in exchange rate policy was a consequence of the 1979 break in the link between the Irish pound and sterling. Similarly the renewed preoccupation with demographic forecasting from the 1970s, and with the participation of women in the labour force during the 1980s, reflects the rapid changes taking place within Ireland in these spheres.

Monetary policy was the subject of several important papers. This reflected both the emergence of a more active monetary policy within Ireland, and the growing economic expertise and interest in research among the staff of the Central Bank. When Tom Hoare presented a paper in 1969 on an Irish monetary market, T.K. Whitaker, president of the Society and governor of the Central Bank, used the occasion to highlight the extent to which Central Bank already performed many of the functions of a money market (Hoare, 557). A paper by Brendan Dowling during the 1973/74 session provided a historical account of the evolution of monetary policy since 1949, and a more critical assessment of the controls exercised by the Central Bank (Dowling, 245). Membership of the European Monetary System in 1979 provided an obvious subject for a symposium in 1980 (1208), and for a 1987 paper by Patrick Massey, which reviewed the Irish experience of EMS. Massey came to the conclusion that Ireland, a small open economy, should maintain a fixed exchange rate with a larger economy; he further argued that 'as long as the UK remains outside the EMS ... membership will pose problems for Ireland', an assessment that remains valid in the late 1990s.

Although both Massey and the participants in the 1980 symposium concentrated on the strictly economic aspects of monetary policy, as Joe Durkan, replying to Massey's paper, noted, 'The basis of our membership [of EMS] was almost certainly more political than indicated in the paper. Governments were obsessed with being "good Europeans", whatever that means, and with some primitive notions of financial and economic independence' (Massey, 840). This point was forcefully illustrated in Seán Cromien's comments on the occasion of the 1980 Symposium, when he noted that 'Entry into the EMS was a sign that the Irish economy had come of age. As in the case of the human being, this stage in an economy brings responsibilities as well as certain freedoms with it' (1208). In retrospect, such comments are often as valuable as the elaborate econometric equations which form the core of many papers.

ECONOMIC PLANNING, FORECASTING,
ECONOMIC MODELLING

Ireland's conversion to economic planning is generally dated to 1958, and the publication of Economic Development. Yet as Fanning and Bradley note, 'while it [Economic Development] may be based on theoretical and empirical analysis of the economy, it was not specified, estimated, or more importantly, tested in the manner that is possible with macroeconometric models' (Bradley, 88). In 1964, however, the Second Programme for Economic Expansion adopted what appeared at first sight to be a much more technical approach towards economic planning, and there was a growing interest in developing quantitative models of the Irish economy, whether as tools for medium-term planning or for the purpose of short-term forecasting. In a series of papers, ranging from Geary's input-output model in 1964 (Geary, 365), through the 1978 progress report on the Central Bank's macroeconometric model (140), FitzGerald and Keegan's detailed account of the Model-80 model in 1982, (323), and Fagan and Fell's 1991 paper (302), it is possible to trace the developments in the techniques used for economic forecasting and planning within the Irish economy. The process is superbly summarised in Fanning and Bradley's 1982 paper (88).

The Society's traditional role as a place where civil servants could speak with some freedom about government policy took on a new dimension as officials often presented unpublished economic data, or provided their audience with a glimpse of the methodological problems involved in economic forecasting; a practice which made the Society something akin to a testing station for new economic models. Thus in December 1964, Dr Brendan Menton of the Department of Finance read a paper on the subject of short-term forecasting, which contained estimates for the main aggregates of national income and expenditure for 1964. During the course of this paper, Menton remarked that the Department of Finance prepared unpublished short-term projections for the Irish economy 'at least twice and often three times a year'. Although Menton assumed full responsibility for the estimates presented in his paper, and described them as having 'no official standing', it would be naive to assume that they differed significantly, either in methodology or in detail, from those being developed within the Department of Finance. One speaker remarked that the section of the paper which outlined the Department of Finance's methods of short-term economic forecasting, 'pulls back the curtain from the Department of Finance and allows one to see the machinery at work' (859). This can be seen as an instance where Finance divulged information to an interested audience, without giving this information full official sanction.

This process was repeated in 1973 in yet another paper presented by officials from the Department of Finance (Cavanagh and Mooney, 139). When Roy Geary outlined an input-output decision model for Ireland in January 1964, during the ensuing discussion T.K. Whitaker (then secretary of the Department of Finance), noted that Geary had presented the Society with 'a synthesis of a series of confidential papers produced over the past year or so and made available to the Department of Finance' (Geary, 365). In 1967, in the course of a discussion on a paper by C.E.V. Leser, Geary produced unofficial data on changes in Gross Domestic Product by sector over the previous decade, emphasising that, while they had been provided by Brendan Broderick of the Central Statistics Office, that the organisation 'is not to be regarded as officially responsible' (Leser, 709). This tendency to use the Society as a forum for off-the-record briefings on economic matters may reflect an effort to overcome some of the excessive secrecy, of which the Irish civil service is regularly accused. In 1973, when Terry Baker of the ESRI asked why Finance would not publish its short-term economic forecasts, Seán Cromien suggested that Finance feared that too much weight would be placed on such estimates, which were 'no more than a series of integrated guesses' (Cavanagh and Mooney, 139). Members of the Society would presumably have been more conscious of the tentative nature of such estimates than the general public.

By the 1960s the earlier debate within the Society over the relative merits of statistics and innumerate 'social inquiry' seemed to have given way to a less ideological, and more technical discussion concerning the most appropriate methods of economic forecasting, and specifically the relative merits of econometrics, and a more informal approach. When Roy Geary outlined an input-output model of the Irish economy in 1964, he suggested that the macro-economic, national accounts approach goes 'a certain distance in defining the problems, essentially political, facing a planning authority'. The ensuing discussion threw considerable light on the views about economic planning and economic forecasting of T.K. Whitaker, then secretary of the Department of Finance. Both Whitaker and Geary agreed on the importance of the capital-output ratio as a tool for determining policy; Geary's model suggested that it would be necessary to achieve a lower capital-output ratio if the country was to achieve the target rate of economic growth. However they agreed on little else. Whitaker undoubtedly preferred a more intuitive and less rigid form of planning than input-output (Geary, 365).

In February 1964, one month after Geary's paper, Louden Ryan outlined an alternative method of economic planning: the iterative method, which was being developed under his direction within the Department of Finance. This involved making a succession of approximate estimates of the magnitude of different subheadings and running cross-checks. Ryan's paper was subsequently reproduced by the government as Appendix 5 to

Part II of the *Second* Programme for Economic Expansion, an indication that this method carried official sanction.[15]

Unlike the input-output model (if properly specified), the iterative method did not automatically expose inconsistencies between the assumptions and the projected outcome. Ryan noted that the model contained a large number of judgments, 'not all of which are of a narrow, economic kind'. He also remarked that more formal input-output style models were not without major drawbacks: these arose from initial errors in constructing the model, which often could not be readily identified. Ryan emphasised the contrast between the precise methods of the formal model and the 'indeterminate character of much of the material to which the model must be applied'. The discussion that followed Ryan's paper focused on the relative merits and shortcomings of both methods of economic planning: Garret FitzGerald favoured the iterative method, whereas Leser of the ERI asserted that the shortcomings of the formal model were overstated, though in a conciliatory tone he suggested that both had their rightful place. Leser and Geary's preference for a Dutch-style input-output model as the basis for economic planning was a minority point of view.

Garret FitzGerald and TCD economist Alan Tait both raised several intriguing and potentially controversial points. FitzGerald wondered how the target annual growth rate of 4.14 per cent for the years 1964-70 had been determined, in the light of a suggestion that this figure was only a transposition to Irish conditions of the overall growth target, that the OECD had set for member countries. Was it simply a coincidence that the sectoral targets, (apparently determined individually) added up to this magic figure, or had some sector(s) been regarded as a residual? Tait believed that the public service had drawn up forecasts of probable growth rates for public expenditure, investment and imports, 'leaving huge a residual composed of exports and personal expenditure'. He suggested that the Second Programme assumed that the rate of personal consumption could be influenced by policy, though he wondered if this would prove possible, given the openness of the Irish economy and the moves towards freer trade (Ryan, 1105).

In the course of his presentation, Louden Ryan remarked that in most planning exercises 'there appeared to be some built-in factor making for pessimism'; in fact, the planning exercise associated with the Second Programme appears to have suffered from excessive optimism. Several of the points raised in the discussion following Ryan's paper were examined in greater detail in a 1978 paper by Katsiaouni, which included a detailed critique of the methodological flaws contained in the Second and Third Programmes. In particular, he criticised 'the widespread complacency that the methodology of the Second and Third Programmes was beyond theoretical reproach' (Katsaiouni, 634). Yet the discussion at the Society in February 1964 – which is not listed in Katsaiouni's bibliography – suggests an early awareness of the Programme's inherent shortcomings in the ranks of the Society.

Papers presented by Geary, Ryan and Menton indicate that during the 1960s the Department of Finance favoured informal methods of economic planning, rather than econometric models. Even proponents of more quantitative methods, such as C.E.V. Leser, acknowledged that 'how to use econometric relations to best advantage in short-term forecasting is a difficult one which still awaits a solution' (Menton, 859). In a 1965 paper, J. McGilvray prepared a set of inter-industry coefficients for 1956, projected them to 1958, and compared the projections with the actual outcome. He concluded that the model was 'too unstable to be used with any confidence for projections or forecasts of the future economic structure', and that consequently a more empirical approach would be preferable. In the ensuing discussion, Maurice Doyle of the Department of Finance (a future secretary) was highly dubious about the merits of using an input-output model. He noted that 'by effectively begging the question of home production versus competitive imports the projects were robbed of much predictive value'; furthermore, he argued, given that most of the growth in Irish industrial output was coming from new industries, which were not included in a historic input-output table, and from sectors such as chemicals, metals and engineering where the data were known to be extremely weak, the exercise was of limited use. Doyle warned of the 'danger of building an inverted pyramid of mathematical expertise on a foundation of statistics which were not designed to take the load' (McGilvray, 798). While some of this scepticism may reflect a wish to avoid confronting the harsh realities which an input-output model might reveal, it was also realistic in the light of the limited technology then available. In 1964, Roy Geary tested his input-output model on the Agricultural Institute's one computer. Although Finance was making greater use of econometric techniques by 1973, they were employed only as 'supplementary aids'. Cavanagh and Mooney stated that 'the basic procedure by which the forecasts are formulated is still essentially of an informal nature' (Cavanagh and Mooney, 139).

Paradoxically, Irish competence in model-building and faith in the procedure would seem to have grown during the 1970s and early 1980s, at a time when the process was being questioned elsewhere. Nineteen seventy-three marked the end of a long phase of post-war growth throughout the developed world. In Ireland, as Noel O'Gorman and Carroll showed, the origins of many of the undesirable fiscal trends, which have been regarded as a hallmark of the post-1973 period, such as the growing share of GNP attributable to taxation and public expenditure and rising public debt, can be traced back to the 1960s, though their impact became much more pronounced with the decline in the growth rate (Carroll and O'Gorman, 130). Although symposia in 1974 on inflation (1216) and in 1975 on full employment (1214) reflect a preoccupation with the economic problems of the mid-1970s, it is difficult to pinpoint any paper, with the possible exception of that by Fionán Ó Muircheartaigh, which examined the implications of government policy during these years, particularly the sharp increase in public expenditure (Ó Muircheartaigh, 1031). Introducing their 1982 paper which discussed the characteristics of the MODEL 80 model of the Irish economy, John FitzGerald and Owen Keegan suggested that constructing a formal model of the Irish economy – a process which entailed 'setting down one's prejudices in algebraic format' – would assist in the formulation of policy by 'acting as a stimulus to logical thinking'. This model provided more detailed specifications for the government sector than for the private sector in order to enable it to be used to estimate the effects of changes in fiscal policy. However when Paddy Geary opened the discussion on this paper, he commented on the 'widespread dissatisfaction with the performance of macroeconometric models' which had developed in the US during the 1970s, and the existence of widely-differing views among economists concerning the true structure of an economy. Paddy Geary commented on the 'curious serenity' evident in FitzGerald and Keegan's paper, 'as though untouched by the battles which raged around its subject' (FitzGerald and Keegan, 323).

Ironically, the next paper read to the Society consisted of a retrospective examination of the various models of the Irish economy devised during the previous twenty-five years. The authors concluded that 'to date they [economic models] have, in their own right, provided very little empirical or conceptual knowledge of the Irish economy'. They also conceded that it had proved 'very difficult to combine the two goals of a regular forecasting tool and of an analytical instrument in one macro-econometric model'. Nevertheless, Connell Fanning and John Bradley agreed with FitzGerald and Keegan that such models would play an increasing role in Irish policy research, even suggesting that they could form the basis for discussing economic and social policies with 'social partners'. In a statement that would have been widely supported by the Society's founders because it echoed their belief in the power of scientific argument, they suggested that a more open approach towards econometric modelling, including the possibility of specifying models which reflected alternative perspectives of the economic system, would make it easier to achieve a consensus on economic policies. They also urged that

there should not be a monopoly of information or methodology, i.e. no advantages due to using unpublished data; unknown adjustments to published data, uncertainty as to methods of calculation and 'barriers to entry' to the process. Ultimately economic policy is about politics and this unavoidable uncertainty combined with the interest-group process inherent in a democratic society is a potential source for the misuse of macroeconometric models of the economy (Bradley and Fanning, 88).

In 1991 a large audience heard Gabriel Fagan and John Fell summarise the various techniques that were now available for short-term economic forecasting, including structural econometric models, time series and qualitative or judgmental forecasting. The authors concluded that Irish forecasting continued to be dominated by the judgmental approach. Although Fagan and Fell argued the merits of using more formal methods of forecasting, they ultimately came down in favour of an eclectic approach, applying different methods to different series. The discussion prompted by this paper was a reprise of many earlier sessions, with speakers divided between those, like John FitzGerald and Patrick Honohan, who offered 'a stout defence' for the value of a large-scale structural econometric model (Honohan emphasised that it was more valuable as a means of simulating changes in policy than as a tool for short-term forecasting) and one of the country's most experienced forecasters, Joe Durkan explaining why judgmental forecasting remained dominant in Ireland: in his opinion, it produced the best results, though he made occasional use of econometric models (Fagan and Fell, 302).

STATISTICS AND STATISTICAL SERVICES

The plea, which Fanning and Bradley made in 1982, for wider access to statistical information reflects an ongoing theme within the Society. In the 1950s Geary had begged economists to make use of the resources of the Central Statistics Office (1223). From the 1960s, however, although the volume and range of statistical data rose steadily, the growing interest in applied economics led to an insatiable appetite for even more information, though the Society does not appear to have made any formal protest at the government's decision to cancel the 1976 Census. The emergence of a more advanced economy and in particular the emergence of industries and services which needed highly-educated labour, led to demands for data on topics such as participation rates in education and estimates of the future size and characteristics of the labour force. Equally, the gradual emergence of a more independent monetary policy forced the Central Bank to generate new statistical series, both for its own needs, and to meet the demands of economists. EEC membership brought comparative statistics on an immense range of social and economic indicators.

The 1973 Household Budget Survey, the first to collect data from both rural and urban households, provided important information on a variety of social trends, such as ownership of cars and houses (Murphy 909). This survey also made it possible for the first time to draw some firm comparisons about income distribution in Ireland and in other OECD countries, and to examine the redistributive effects of taxation and public expenditure (Nolan, 936).

The Society continued its long-standing role of publicising the findings of various official inquiries, both old and new, such as the 1973 Household Budget Inquiry (Murphy, 909), the 1981 Census (Garvey, 351), and the new monthly banking statistics, first published by the Central Bank in 1983 (McEvoy, 796). Discussions on topics such as sensitivity of weights for the Consumer Price Index (Murphy, 909), or the use of a sample selection of returns from the 1981 census to elicit additional information on specific topics (Garvey, 351), provided the Central Statistics Office with informed comments from the users of statistics. At the same time the Society highlighted the potential value of linking disparate statistical series (Nolan, 936). Another key function was to provide a critical evaluation of widely used statistical measurements, particularly those that were regularly cited uncritically in political debate. Thus in 1968, at a time when achieving a maximum growth rate remained 'the sacred cow of economic policy', Brendan Broderick of the CSO exposed some of the fragile assumptions on which official estimates were based (Broderick, 106).

In an important paper presented in 1988 entitled 'What is the Best Measure of Employment and Unemployment in Ireland', Donal Garvey outlined the methodology employed in the Labour Force Survey, and explored the complexities involved in defining terms such as 'employed' or 'unemployed'. One senior civil servant, Paddy Teahon (subsequently secretary to the Department of the Taoiseach), used the occasion to speak about the differences between the numbers unemployed and at work, as measured by the Labour Force Survey and by the Live Register, and the implications which the data posed for policy makers (Garvey, 352). By the mid 1990s, this topic, first aired within the relatively rarified ranks of the Society had become part of the wider public debate on unemployment. In 1983, following a paper on the 1981

Census, members argued at some length that there was an urgent need for an annual Labour Force Survey (Garvey, 351). While it is impossible to trace the precise impact of such discussions on the production of Irish statistics, they were not without influence.

Meetings of the Society provided a regular forum where producers and users of statistics – the title of Jerry Sexton's presidential address in 1989 – met, though the encounters were not always amicable (Sexton, 1122). The most adversarial session took place in 1985 on the occasion of a symposium devoted to 'Statistics for Policy and Research', which was organised in response to a recent government paper on the Central Statistics Office. This report, which examined how the future demands of Irish society for statistical information could best be met, reflected the pressures which the government statistical service faced in meeting the needs of a modern society, in particular the proliferation of organisations that were generating statistics, and the need for a co-ordinating agency. The White Paper assigned this function to the Central Statistics Office.[16] The symposium also raised questions about the relative roles of statisticians and economists: should statisticians become involved in interpreting data, or merely act as 'fact gatherers', leaving others with the responsibility for making policy. John Blackwell used the occasion to argue the case for a central funding body for social science research (1231). The discussion saw a reprise of elements of the 1952 exchange about the relative contributions to knowledge and research made by the universities and the CSO (1223).

Sexton's 1989 presidential address, when he noted that 'in recent years at any rate, much more had been said about the activities of producers of statistics than of users' can be regarded as a continuation of this debate, Sexton examined in some detail how the activities of producers, and the needs of users of statistics could best be reconciled. He also drew attention to the importance of anticipating future changes in the demand for statistical information. Before the establishment of the National Statistics Board in 1986, no permanent structure existed to facilitate planning and identify future priorities. Sexton remarked that identifying priorities for statistical investigation had long been a function of the Statistical Society, whether formally, as when the Society responded to government requests for suggested changes to the

Population Census, or informally when members suggested the need for new data in the course of papers or discussions (Sexton, 1122). Although many members appointed to the National Statistics Board were active in the Society, the Statistical Society was not formally represented on the new Board. More surprisingly, it was not among the many professional bodies which made submissions to the National Statistics Board, in response to their request for views about future priorities.[17] In many respects the new Board was fulfilling a role that previously had been carried out by the Society in a more informal manner. This is yet another instance where the emergence of a more developed, and more statistically minded economy tended to reduce the traditional role of the Society.

POPULATION, THE LABOUR FORCE, EMPLOYMENT AND INDUSTRIAL POLICY

During the early 1950s, the Central Bank earned the unenviable nickname of the Banshee of Foster Place, as a result of its repeated warnings about the unhealthy state of public finances;[18] warnings which largely went unheeded until the crisis year of 1956. With hindsight, the Society performed a similar function, though in less apocalyptic tones, by repeatedly highlighting the changes that were taking place in the size and dependency rate of the Irish population, and the emerging role of women within the labour force. Although the statistical projections became more complex, the subject had been a long-term interest of the Society. In 1971, Knaggs and Keane presented a series of estimates of the population of Ireland in 1996, which ranged from 3.5 to 4.1m, depending on various assumptions. The figures had been generated by a computer model devised by the Central Statistics Office. As Brendan Walsh noted in the discussion after this paper, even the projections that assumed a rapid decline in fertility indicated that in 1996 Ireland would have a higher dependency ratio than any other European country (except Albania); if fertility declined at a more gradual pace, the dependency ratio would continue to rise (Keane and Knaggs, 636). Roy Geary recalled that when he had presented a paper to the Society in 1935, which proved that it would be impossible for the Irish population to regain its pre-Famine level during this century (Geary, 358), he was 'duly savaged for lack of patriotism' by a contemporary periodical. This paper by Knaggs and Keane indicates that the future prospects for the Irish economy appeared difficult, because of the high level of dependency, even before the 1973 oil crisis had inflicted a serious shock to the international economy, resulting in a decline in the rate of economic growth and in the prospects for increasing employment.

In 1977, Keating presented projections for the population in 1981 and 1986, which pointed towards the first signs of a decline in the dependency rate. His paper also charted the fall in fertility, which could be dated to the availability of the contraceptive pill in the 1960s (Keating, 639). Although statisticians, economists and many policy makers were undoubtedly aware of the implications, firstly of the rising dependency rate, and secondly of the fall in fertility, there is little indication that such consciousness percolated into the wider society until many years after these trends were first identified. The time-lag in the transmission of knowledge about the Irish economy appeared as important in the 1980s as it had been in the 1940s and 1950s.

A similar point came be made about the participation of women in the labour force. As Boylan and Foley have shown, the Society expressed considerable interest in the question of female employment throughout the nineteenth century,[19] though members were much more concerned about the employment difficulties facing single middle-class women than with the status of the daughters, wives and sisters of rural labourers and small farmers. From 1970, a succession of papers examined prospective trends in Irish female participation rates, in the light of developments taking place in other western economies (Walsh, 1273). The topic was discussed both in papers which concentrated on women, and as a component of papers relating to Irish demography. In 1971, Knaggs and Keane indicated that 'With many conflicting factors affecting the female participation rate, including on the one hand longer periods of education, earlier marriages, higher marriage rates and earlier retirement, and on the other more employment opportunities for women, single and married, it is difficult to predict the overall participation rate to within ten per cent' (636).

In 1973, Walsh and Whelan applied the techniques devised by

leading American experts on female labour supply, such as Mincer and Cain, in order to establish the factors which determined the participation of Irish women in the labour market. For married women, the important variables were the number of dependent children, potential income as measured by educational attainment, and a husband's attitude. Whereas job opportunities influenced the participation of single women, they did not appear to be a determining factor in the case of married women (Walsh and Whelan, 1275). Although the 1975 symposium on increasing employment made no reference to women (1214), Donal Garvey's 1983 paper, based on a sample from the 1981 Census, highlighted the rising participation rate among married women (Garvey, 351). Because of these papers, and others such as that by Drew on part-time working in Ireland (Drew, 249), the Journal ranks as a key source of information on the economic role of women in late twentieth-century Ireland.

Before the 1960s the Society had shown little interest in industrial development. However the paramount role assigned to industry in the Second Programme for Economic Expansion, together with Leser's 1967 paper, which emphasised that if Ireland followed a similar pattern of development to other comparable economies, industry would become the leading sector, led to greater interest in industrial policy. At a time when Irish attitudes towards the process of economic growth were generally optimistic, Leser suggested that the prospect of achieving sustained growth in industrial output seemed rather uncertain for countries starting from Ireland's level of industrialisation, and that success would be heavily dependent on the effectiveness of government policy, and on investment from abroad. He also suggested that the experience of other countries indicated that heavy industry offered the prospect of more rapid economic growth (Leser, 709).

The debate over the 1969 Buchanan Report on regional development, which recommended that new industrial investment should be concentrated in the Cork and Limerick regions in order to achieve the highest possible expansion in employment,[20] exposed the gulf between rhetoric and realism concerning the prospects for industrial development, and the political costs involved in achieving the maximum possible rate of industrial growth. In practice the government ignored the recommendations contained in the Buchanan Report. When the Society debated the matter eighteen months after the publication of the Report (an apparently longer gap than normal in such circumstances), sociologist Rev Liam Ryan asserted that it offered 'a somewhat drastic solution to a *national problem* which in any case seems to be now under control and no solution at all to a regional problem of Connaught and the North-West whose decline is hastened rather than halted by the recommendations of the Buchanan Report'. He concluded by urging that 'The process of recovery should be allowed to run its course' (1100).

Such complacency about the performance of the Irish economy did not survive for long after 1973. In 1975, when Ireland, in common with most western economies was in recession, the Society held a symposium on increasing employment in Ireland, which attracted an extremely large attendance. Kieran Kennedy emphasised that Ireland's problem was not solely attributable to the recession. Indeed international recession had only aggravated the long-term difficulties presented by an expanding labour force, falling employment in agriculture, and a low level of net employment growth in manufacturing industry, despite record levels of 'job approvals' by the Industrial Development Authority. This was one of the first occasions when questions were raised in public about the relationship between 'job approvals' and jobs actually provided, and about the nature of job losses in manufacturing industry — topics which became central to subsequent reviews of industrial policy (1214).

In 1980, Frances Ruane, replying to a paper on industrial policy, remarked that 'economics as a discipline has relatively little to say about much of the Trojan work done by the IDA (Mc Keon, 811). However, from the 1970s the Society could claim to have done much to remedy this apparent shortcoming, by devoting regular sessions to examining aspects of the Authority's strategy. Thus in 1972 Dermot McAleese gave a largely positive account of the contribution which foreign-owned industries had made to employment, output and capital inflow (McAleese, 756). The IDA also used the Society as a forum for revealing aspects of its internal procedures, in much the same fashion as the economic forecasters of the Department of Finance had been doing for many years. Thus in 1980 John McKeon explained the criteria that the

IDA used to evaluate industrial projects and to determine the appropriate level of financial assistance. The discussion following this paper raised a host of crucial issues, such as the opportunity cost of labour hired by grant-assisted firms, and the appropriate level of grant assistance (McKeon, 811). These topics were subsequently examined in considerable detail by the Telesis report on industrial policy, which was the subject of a lively symposium in 1982 (1215). Ten years later, in 1992, the Society held another symposium to explore the findings of the Industrial Policy Review Group, the so-called Culliton Report. By this stage the debate over industrial policy had moved beyond the details of specific incentives provided to industrialists, and was highlighting macro-economic issues, such as the general competitiveness of the Irish economy and the quality of the labour force (1209). A noteworthy feature of the 1982 and 1992 symposia and the 1975 symposium on full employment is the absence of contributions from the Department of Industry and Energy and the Department of Industry and Commerce, the Departments which were primarily responsible for determining industrial policy. Whereas civil servants appear to have been willing to debate the technicalities of short-term or medium-term forecasting, they were much less willing to engage in discussions over future policy respecting industry and education.

Most nineteenth-century statistical societies devoted considerable attention to education, in part because the subject generated readily-accessible data; Ireland was an exception, presumably because any serious examination of educational matters carried a real danger of entering the proscribed subject of religion. This position did not change until the 1960s. A speaker at the Society's 1966 symposium on the White Paper Investment in Education claimed that this was only the second talk on the Irish educational system given to the Society (1219). A paper read by T. Ó Raiftearaigh of the Department of Education in 1958/59 had looked at developments in Irish education since 1922 (Ó Raiftearaigh, 1036). However, with the publication of Investment in Education, which highlighted the relationship between successful economic development and the educational system, and a growing awareness of the need to plan for higher participation rates in both second and third-level education, the subject began to assume a much more important place within the Society. The inclusion of questions on educational experience in the 1966 Census is evidence of this. In 1971, William Hyland of the Department of Education discussed the types of data that were needed to assist the state in planning for future educational services (Hyland, 587). Other papers examined the need to plan for an expansion in the numbers with qualifications in science and technology (Franklin and Johnston, 335).

During the course of the 1966 symposium, Dr K. Milne, who spoke about the Church of Ireland and Education, noted that there was not a sentence in Investment in Education that was critical of one- and two-teacher schools per se; the White Paper had also largely ignored the question of the Irish language. Although Milne raised a number of potentially controversial topics, such as the restrictions imposed by the Catholic hierarchy on Catholics attending TCD, the symposium was rather lack-lustre. Most contributors spoke on behalf of specific interest-groups. The absence of a speaker from the Department of Education was particularly disappointing, because, as several speakers noted, changes in educational policy had already overtaken some of the conclusions reached in the Report (1219). The 1981 symposium on the White Paper on Education was a much livelier affair, with Dale Tussing of the ESRI and A.C. Barlow of UCC both criticising the White Paper for failing to discuss the critical issues facing Irish education. Tussing raised questions about accountability, planning, denominational segregation and class stratification (1234). In broaching topics such as the impact of religion on Irish schools, and unequal access to educational resources, the Society, like the Irish people, was beginning to examine important topics, which it had hitherto tended to avoid.

CONCLUSIONS

In his introduction to R.D.C. Black's centenary volume in 1947, Roy Geary noted that 'it is fascinating to observe how in each generation the studies under Society auspices reflected the public interests of the time'. A review of the Society's Journal provides evidence both of changes in methodology and standards of scholarship within the social sciences in Ireland, and the dominant topics of contemporary interest. As already noted, the discussions that follow the presentations are often at least as valuable, and sometimes more revealing than the actual papers, particularly when they may signal future directions in economic and social policy. This is also true of the symposia, which have become a regular feature of the Society. Indeed a list of the dates and subjects of symposia would provide a useful barometer of current interests and they frequently provide an admittedly impressionistic, but still valuable index of attitudes among various interested parties. The 1987 Symposium on privatisation of state assets suggested that, while there was no groundswell of support for privatisation, several speakers were conscious of the need to achieve greater competitiveness within state-owned companies: – a foretaste of the direction of future policy towards state-owned companies. Although Seán Cromien, secretary of the Department of Finance, who was one of the contributors, stated an intention to limit his remarks 'to considerations of a general nature', without discussing the merits or otherwise of privatisation, he indicated that 'the level of Exchequer support provided heretofore [to commercial state bodies] cannot continue' (1226).

The 1983 symposium outlined the case for reforming the tax system on the lines recommended by the report of the Commission on Taxation, together with the views of employers and the trade unions on this subject. On this occasion remarks by Seán Cromien of the Department of Finance, to the effect that the Department had determined that the figures on which the Commission's proposals for tax reform were based, were unrealistic, together with the comments both by Cromien, and by Eithne FitzGerald (an economist and a member of the Labour Party), that the Commission's proposals would hit the poorer sections of the community, suggested, correctly, that its recommendations were unlikely to be implemented (1233). Although papers to the Society provide a rigorous and scientific analysis of a specific problem, the sessions generally take some account of wider political dimensions. Thus during the course of the 1982 symposium on industrial policy (the Telesis Report), Kieran Kennedy warned that a policy of favouring some industrialists at the expense of others, which had apparently been successful in

South Korea might not be acceptable in a democracy such as Ireland (1215).

A 1991 paper on alcohol policy by Daniel McCoy is evidence of the continuity provided by the Society, when he reprises many of the arguments found in papers to the Society during the nineteenth century about the need to control the consumption of alcohol and the most appropriate methods of achieving this (McCoy, 773). Although McCoy's paper lacks the moralising tone favoured by Victorian members such as Haughton (518, 523) or Daly (208), he would share their belief in the need to control alcohol. Perhaps one of the most striking links with the past emerges from a reassessment of the long-standing tension between statistics and social inquiry, or between quantitative and qualitative research (Black, 71). A casual glance through recent issues of the Journal might suggest that quantitative methods had not only triumphed, but that they had assumed a complexity and sophistication that earlier members of the Society would regard as inconceivable. Yet in 1995, in a paper with the intriguing title, 'Econometrics and Truth', John Frain came to the conclusion that 'Econometrics, or more precisely, the application of statistics to quantitative economic analysis, is now in a state of flux'. The flux was a consequence both of the rapid developments that were taking place in the discipline, but also by growing doubts about its predictive powers. The issues, raised by Frain, echo some of the doubts expressed by Galton over one hundred years ago about the predictive value of statistics. Yet, whereas in the 1870s the slightest whiff of uncertainty threatened to destroy the scientific credentials of statistics, by the late twentieth-century it is widely acknowledged that truth, or scientific laws, even in physics are no longer absolute, but merely relative. Consequently Frain came to the more reassuring conclusion that 'Economic theory is no different from other sciences' (Frain, 333).

While the Society lacked sufficient confidence to celebrate its fiftieth anniversary, its sesquicentennial sees it in a much more secure position, with a personal membership of almost 400, a figure which is close to its historic peak. The major difficulty now facing the Society is how to square the circle between retaining a broadly based membership, by producing papers that can appeal to people who are not necessarily specialists, while at the same time ensuring that the papers presented reach a high quality of technical excellence. Excessive specialisation and consequent fragmentation of disciplines is a serious problem, given the explosion of information and of advanced education in the late twentieth century. At the same time, it is even more important to view many contemporary socio-economic questions from a multi-disciplinary perspective. The Society provides an appropriate forum not only for multi-disciplinary discussions, but for bridging gaps between academia, business, the state, and other interest groups and a historical perspective, which suggests that many issues of concern in modern society, such as crime, the care of deprived children, and the nature of economic progress, are not new, but rather have antecedents stretching back for up to one hundred and fifty years.

NOTES TO CHAPTER FIVE

[1] Economic and Social Research Institute Archives: Origins of the ERI; Ford Foundation File. My thanks to the director Dr. Brendan Whelan for giving me access; to the ESRI Secretary John Roughan, and to Dr. Kieran Kennedy for drawing my attention to these files. See also Kieran A. Kennedy, 'R.C. Geary and the ESRI', *The Economic and Social Review*, vol. 24, no. 3, April 1993, pp. 225-45.

[2] Council Minutes, 1 February 1963.

[3] Council Minutes, 27 April 1968, 1 July 1968.

[4] Council Minutes, 6 February 1975.

[5] Tom Linehan, who signed the minutes of this meeting, has no recollection of this incident.

[6] Council Minutes of the Statistical and Society Inquiry Society of Ireland, 30 September 1932.

[7] A Trust established to fund an annual lecture at University College Dublin in memory of Rev. Thomas Finlay.

[8] Council Minutes, 7 October 1961, 28 September 1962

[9] Council Minutes 1 February 1963.

[10] John E. Spencer, 'Robert Charles Geary — an appreciation', *Economic and Social Review*, vol. 14, no. 3, April 1983, pp. 161-64.

[11] Kennedy, 'R.C. Geary and the ESRI', p. 242.

[12] Council Minutes, 28 September 1962, 1 December 1962.

[13] ESRI, T. K. Whitaker file.

[14] Kennedy, 'R.C. Geary and the ESRI, p. 239.

[15] For a description see FitzGerald, *Planning in Ireland*, pp. 71- 72.

[16] *A New Institutional Structure for the Central Statistics Office* Pl. 3483, 1985.

[17] National Statistics Board, *Strategy for Statistics, 1988-92* (Dublin, 1988).

[18] Maurice Moynihan, *Currency and Central Banking in Ireland 1922-60* (Dublin, 1975), p. 341.

[19] Boylan and Foley, *Political Economy and Colonial Ireland*, pp. 144,148-51; Timothy P. Foley, 'Public sphere and domestic circle: gender and political economy in nineteenth-century Ireland', in Margaret Kelleher and James H. Murphy (eds), *Gender Perspectives in 19th Century Ireland. Public and Private Spheres* (Dublin, 1997), pp. 21-35.

[20] Colin Buchanan and Partners, *Regional Studies in Ireland* (Dublin, 1969).

Index

Explanatory Note on Volumes

The Statistical and Social Inquiry Society of Ireland has passed
through several stages of development since the Dublin Statistical
Society was first established in 1847. These changes are reflected
in the publication of its Proceedings, the sequence of which is
given below.

When the date is given as e.g. 'September 1853', the paper was
published in pamphlet form prior to 1855. From 1855 to 1923, the
pages of the Journal are numbered consecutively. 1923 to 1927 is
numbered consecutively. 1928-29 is not paged at all. From 1930-
1942 the paging is for each Session.

TRANSACTIONS OF THE DUBLIN STATISTICAL SOCIETY (originally published as pamphlets)

Volume I   November 1847 to October 1849
Volume II   November 1849 to October 1851
Volume III   November 1851 to October 1854.

PROCEEDINGS OF THE SOCIAL INQUIRY SOCIETY OF IRELAND

Addresses and Reports from 1851 to March 1855, when this
Society merged with the Dublin Statistical Society. The addresses
and reports were published as separate pamphlets.

JOURNAL OF THE DUBLIN STATISTICAL SOCIETY

This Journal began in January 1855, and was published in Parts
and paged in Volumes.

Volume I	Parts I to VII, 1855-56
Volume II	Parts VIII to XVII, 1857-60
Volume III	Parts XVIII to XXV, 1861-63.

JOURNAL OF THE STATISTICAL AND SOCIAL INQUIRY SOCIETY OF IRELAND

Volume IV	Parts XXVI to XXXIV, 1864-68
Volume V	Parts XXXV to XXXIX, 1868-70
Volume VI	Parts XL to XLIX, 1870-76
Volume VII	Parts L to LV, 1876-79
Volume VIII	Parts LVI to LXIII, 1879-86
Volume IX	Parts LXIV to LXXIII, 1885-93
Volume X	Parts LXXIV to LXXX, 1894-1900
Volume XI	Parts LXXXI to LXXXVI, 1900-06
Volume XII	Parts LXXXVII to XCII, 1906-12
Volume XIII	Parts XCIII to XCVII, 1912-19
Volume XIV	Sessions 73rd to 83rd, 1919-30
Volume XV	Sessions 84th to 90th, 1930-37
Volume XVI	Sessions 91st to 95th, 1937-42
Volume XVII	Sessions 96th to 100th, 1942-47
Volume XVIII	Sessions 101st to 105th, 1947-52
Volume XIX	Sessions 106th to 110th, 1952-57
Volume XX	Sessions 111th to 115th, 1957-62*
Volume XXI	Sessions 116th to 121st, 1962-68**
Volume XXII	Sessions 122nd to 126th, 1968-73*
Volume XXIII	Sessions 127th to 131st, 1973-78*
Volume XXIV	Sessions 132nd to 136th, 1978-83*
Volume XXV	Sessions 137th to 141st, 1983-88*
Volume XXVI	Sessions 142nd to 146th, 1988-93*

* Parts I to V in each case.
** Parts I to VI.

Notes:
1. 1942-52 – paging is for complete volume.
2. 1952 onwards – paging is for each Session.
3. Parts 1 and 2 of Vol. XXVII for the 147th and 148th Sessions, 1993-4 and 1994-5, have also been published.

Index to Articles by Author

References are to volume; page number; date; pt=part.

17   Bagenal, Philip H. *Report of the International Law Committee, on the impediments to the trade between the UK and America which exist in Dublin from the unsatisfactory state of the law as to Foreign Sailors*, vii, 209, 1878

18   Bagot, Charles E. *Management of Crown Lands in the Australian Colonies, and the Appropriation of the Revenues arising from them*, iii. 405, 1863

Bagot, John. *see* Statistical Papers

19   Bailey, W.F. *Baronial Guarantees under the 'Tramways Act, 1883'*, viii, 556, 1884

20   Bailey, W.F. *Fiscal Relations of the United Kingdom and Ireland, with special Reference to the State Purchase of Land*, ix, 69, 1886

21   Bailey, W.F. *Forestry in Ireland*, ix, 429, 1889

22   Bailey, W.F. *Future of American Agricultural Competition*, viii, 401, 1883

23   Bailey, W.F. *Government Valuation of Ireland: an Examination of its authority as a Standard of Value*, ix, 651, 1893

24   Bailey, W.F. *Ireland since the Famine: A Sketch of Fifty Years' Economic and Legislative Changes – Presidential Address*, xi. 129, 1902-3

25   Bailey, W.F. *Magisterial Reform: being some Considerations on the Present Voluntary System, and Suggestions for the Substitution of an Independent Paid Magistracy*, viii, 595, 1885

26   Bailey, W.F. *Primary Education: with a Review of the German, Irish and English Systems*, vii, 473, 1884

27   Bailey, W.F. *Prussian Agrarian Reforms of the Present Century: their Method and Extent*, ix, 477, 1890

28   Bailey, W.F. *Ulster Tenant-Right Custom: its Origin, Characteristics and Position under the Land Acts*, x, 12, 1894

29   Bailey, W.F. *Woods, Forests, Turf-bogs and Foreshores of Ireland. Opportunity for and advisability of establishing Government management and protection*, ix, 468, 1890

30   Bailie, J.C. *Symposium on the Present and Future of Inland Transport*, xix, 61, 1956-7

31   Baldwin, W.F. *Diminution of the National Wealth from Cattle Diseases*, v, 183, 1870

32   Barbour, Sir David M. *Bimetallism*, x, 100, 1895

54   Bastable, Charles F. *Some Economic Conditions of Industrial Development, with special reference to the case of Ireland*, viii, 461, 1884

55   Bates, Arthur H. *Extent to which the Principles advocated in Bentham's* Letters on Usury *have still to be adopted in the Laws of England and of Foreign Countries*, viii, 363, 1882

56   Bates, Arthur H. *Irish Linen Laws and Proposed Amendments thereof*, viii, 203, 1881

57   Bates, James and Bell, Maeve *Small Manufacturing Business in Northern Ireland*, xxii Pt 5, 162, 1972-3

58   Battersby, Frank S. *Amalgamation: being some considerations on Proposed Changes in the Relations of the Legal Professions in Ireland*, ix, 30, 1886

59   Battersby, Frank S. *Financial Crisis in the United States, 1893-94*, x, 34, 1894

60   Beddy, J.P. *A Comparison of the Principal Economic Features of Eire and Denmark*, xvii 189, 1943-4

61   Beddy, J.P. *The Future of Irish External Trade. Discussion*, xvii, 309, 1943-4

62   Beere, Thekla J. *Cinema Statistics in Saorstat Eireann*, xv, 83, 1935-6

63   Beere, Thekla J. *The Language Revivals in Finland, Norway and Wales*, xiv, 25, 1929-30

64   Beere, Thekla J. *Schemes for the Rehabilitation of Youth in Certain Countries, with Special Reference to Labour Service*, xvi, 33, 1938-9

     Bell, Maeve. *see* Bates, James

65   Bell, Robert *Investment in Northern Ireland*, xx, 22, 1958-9

66   Beveridge, John *Substitution of Stock for other Forms of Local Indebtedness*, viii, 227, 1881

67   Bigger, J.W. *Clean Milk*, xiv, 199, 1921-2

68   Birnie, J.E. and Hitchens, D.M.W.N. *Symposium on the Findings of the Industrial Policy Review Group*, xxvi Pt 4, 153, 1991-2

69   Black, Boyd *Collective Bargaining Structure in Northern Ireland: Dimensions, Determinants and Developments*, xxv Pt 2, 159, 1984-5

70   Black, R.D. Collison *Measurement, Measures and the Millennium: The Society's Activities in a Long Perspective*, xxv Pt 5, 163, 1987-8

Econometric Modelling: Modelling Aggregate Supply for a Medium-Term Macroeconomic Model, xxiv Pt 4, 85, 1981-2

89 Bradley, John and Fanning, Connell *Twenty-Five Years of Modelling the Irish Economy – Retrospect and Prospect*, xxiv Pt 4, 107, 1981-2

90 Bradley, John and Wright, J. *Two Regional Economies in Ireland*, xxvi Pt 5, 211, 1992-3

91 Brady, Francis W. *Publication known amongst Traders as the Black List*, ii, 473, 1860

92 Brady, G. and Geoghegan, B. *Road Freight Transport in Ireland, 1980*, xxiv Pt 5, 140, 1982-3

93 Brand, M. *Symposium on Geographic Information Systems: The Northern Ireland Geographic Information System*, xxvi Pt 3, 273, 1990-1

94 Bray, F. Sewell *Company Accounting*, xviii, 536, 1951-2

95 Brennan, Joseph *The Currency System of the Irish Free State*, xv, 23, 1930-1

96 Brennan, Joseph *Monetary Functions of Commercial Banks*, xvii, 62, 1942-3

97 Brennan, Joseph *The Population Problem. Broadcast Discussion*, xvi, 112, 1937-8

98 Brennan, Joseph *The Public Debt of the Irish Free State*, xv, 37, 1934-5

99 Brennan, Joseph *Some Aspects of Cheap Money*, Centenary Proceedings, p 31, 6-9 October 1947

100 Brennan, Peter *The Finance of Air Transport Services in Ireland*, xviii, 379, 1950-1

101 Bristow, John A. *State Enterprise and Economic Planning in the Irish Republic*, xxi Pt 3, 77, 1964-5

102 Bristow, John A. *Symposium on Local Government Reform*, xxvi Pt 3, 324, 1990-1

103 Brock, Catherine *The C.I.O. Industrial Survey*, xxi Pt 2, 176, 1963-4

104 Broderick, J.B. *An Analysis of Government Revenue and Expenditure in Relation to National Accounts*, xx Pt 3, 132, 1959-60

105 Broderick, J.B. *Classification of Multiple Causes of Death*, xix Pt 3, 159, 1954-5

106 Broderick, J.B. *Problems in Measuring the Growth Rate*, xxi Pt 6, 97, 1967-8

125   Campbell, James H.M. *Report on the Bankruptcy Law of Ireland compared with that of England and of Scotland*, vii, 429, 1879

126   Canavan, Rev. J.E. *Slum Clearance in Dublin*, xvi, 21, 1937-8

127   Cannon, Patrick F.G. *Symposium on Investment in Education*, xxi Pt 4, 67, 1965-6

128   Carey, G.C.R. *Air Pollution [Belfast 1961/65]*, xxi Pt 5, 48, 1966-7

129   Carre, Rev. Nathanial W. *Law of Marriage in its Bearing on Mortality*, viii, 289, 1882

130   Carroll, T.A. and O'Gorman, N.T. *The Dilemma of Irish Economic Development – Perspectives on the Evolution of Ireland's Public Finances and Economy from the Early 1960s to the Mid-1980s*, xxv Pt 4, 127, 1986-7

131   Carter, C.F. *Symposium on the Economic Outlook for 1954*, xix, 100, 1953-4

132   Carter, C.F. *Symposium on the Report of the Commission on Emigration and Other Population Problems*, xix, 104, 1955-6

133   Carter, C.F. and Robson, Mary *A Comparison of the National Incomes and Social Accounts of Northern Ireland, the Republic of Ireland and the United Kingdom*, xix Pt 3, 62, 1954-5

134   Carter, C.F. and Robson, Mary *Estimates of the Gross Domestic Product of Northern Ireland, 1950-56*, xx, 149, 1958-9

135   Carton, Richard P. *Decrees by Default in Civil Bill Courts in Ireland*, xi, 174, 1902-3

136   Casey, M. *Symposium on the Economic Implications of Peace in Ireland*, xxvii Pt 2, 121, 1994-5

137   Cassells, Peter *Symposium on the Privatisation of State Assets and State Commercial Companies*, xxv Pt 5, 61, 1987-8

138   Castletown, Lord, of Upper Ossory *A Plea for Tillage Farming on Co-operative Lines*, xi, 339, 1904-5

139   Cavanagh, C.F. and Mooney, P.J. *Trends in Short-Term Macroeconomic Forecasting for Demand Management*, xxii Pt 5, 133, 1972-3

140   Central Bank of Ireland – Research Department *Modelling the Irish Economy: A Progress Report on the Central Bank's Macroeconometric Model*, xxiv Pt 1, 1, 1978-9

141   Chambers, Derek *A Symposium on Increasing Employment in*

Assets and State Commercial Companies, xxv Pt 5, 53, 1987-8

198   Crowley, M.J. and Moran, M.A. *The Leaving Certificate and First Year University Performance*, xxiv Pt 1, 231, 1978-9

199   Crowley, P.G. *The Problem of Full Employment (Discussion)*, xvii, 452, 1944-5

200   Cruickshank, Margaret *Symposium on Geographic Information Systems: GIS and Machine Peat Extraction*, xxvi Pt 3, 295, 1990-1

201   Cunningham, E.P. *The Genetic Improvement of the Irish Cattle Population*, xxi Pt 4, 99, 1965-6

202   Curry, J. *Symposium on the Report of the Commission on Social Welfare*, xxv Pt 4, 1, 1986-7

203   Cuthbert, Norman *Symposium on the Economic Outlook for 1954: Trade and the Balance of Payments*, xix, 105, 1953-4

204   Cuthbert, Norman *Total Civilian Income in Northern Ireland*, xviii, 416, 1950-1

205   Daly, Edward D. *Crime, and how best to Attack it*, x, 333, 1897
206   Daly, Edward D. *Neglected Children and Neglectful Parents*, x, 350, 1898

207   Daly, Edward D. *Our Industrial and Reformatory School Systems in relation to the Poor*, ix, 523, 1891

208   Daly, Edward D. *The Struggle between the State and the Drunkard*, x, 268, 1897

209   Davis, E.E. and Fine-Davis, Margret *On the Relationship between Objective and Subjective Social Indicators: Implications for Social Planning in Ireland*, xxiv Pt 1, 91, 1978-9

210   Davis, R.G. *Income Tax Statistics*, xv, 49, 1934-5
211   Dawson, Charles *The Children Act and the Oldham League*, xii, 388, 1909-10

212   Dawson, Charles *The Dublin Housing Question – Sanitary and Insanitary*, xiii, 91, 1913

213   Dawson, Charles *Greater Dublin: Extension of City Boundaries*, x, 341, 1898

214   Dawson, Charles *The Housing of the People, with special reference to Dublin*, xi, 45, 1900-1

343   French, H.J.S. *Permanent Finance for Public and Private Companies*, xx Pt 4, 1, 1960-1

344   Friis, Henning *The Aged in Three Western Societies*, xxi Pt 4, 1, 1965-6

       Froggatt, P. *see also* Cresswell, W.L.

345   Froggatt, P. *One-Day Absence in Industry*, xxi Pt 3, 166, 1964-5

346   Galbraith, Rev. Joseph Allen *Decimal Currency*, May, Vol III, 1853

347   Gallagher, D.P. *The Oireachtas as a Natural Economic Council*, xiv, 1, 1928-9

348   Gallagher, M. and Unwin, A. *The Impact of Random Sampling on the Counting of Votes at Elections in the Republic of Ireland*, xxv Pt 2, 195, 1984-5

349   Garmany, J.W. *A Survey of Manpower: Londonderry, Coleraine, Limavady and Strabane – A Case Study*, xxi Pt 2, 55, 1963-4

350   Garmany, J.W. *The Universities and Management Training*, xx, 52, 1958-9

351   Garvey, Donal *A Profile of the Demographic and Labour Force Characteristics of the Population: Sample Analysis of the 1981 Census of Population*, xxiv Pt 5, 104, 1982-3

352   Garvey, Donal *What is the Best Measure of Employment and Unemployment in Ireland?*, xxv Pt 5, 185, 1987-8

353   Geary, Major H.L. *Importance of Industrial Education*, vii, 44, 1876

354   Geary, Patrick T. *A Symposium on Inflation: The Causes of Inflation*, xxiii Pt 2, 1, 1974-5

355   Geary, Patrick T. *A Symposium on The Interim Report on Equal Pay of the Commission on the Status of Women: The Economics of Equal Pay*, xxii Pt 4, 112, 1971-2

356   Geary, Robert C. *The Family in Irish Census of Population Statistics*, xix, 1, 1954-5

357   Geary, Robert C. *The Future of Irish External Trade. Discussion*, xvii, 309, 1943-4

358   Geary, Robert C. *The Future Population of Saorstat Eireann and Some Observations on Population Statistics*, xv, 15, 1935-6

359   Geary, Robert C. *Irish Population Prospects Considered from*

378   Glass, Colin J. *Factor Substitution and Demand for Labour in the Northern Ireland Engineering Industry*, xxii Pt 4, 156, 1971-2

379   Glass, J.C. and Kiountouzis, E. *A Study of Optimal Resources Allocation Models for the Northern Ireland Economy*, xxiii Pt 1, 125, 1973-4

380   Glenavy, Lord *Broadcast Discussion on Unemployment*, xvi, 94, 1939-40

381   Gogarty, John *A Symposium on The Interim Report on Equal Pay of the Commission on the Status of Women: Some Practical Considerations*, xxii, 4, 1971-2

382   Goodbody, Robert *Fluctuations in the Value of the Precious Metals and their effect on Trade*, vii, 238, 1878

383   Grace, E.A. *Accounting and Economic Decision*, xix Pt 1, 73, 1952-3

384   Graves, Arnold Felix *Reorganization of Irish Education Departments and the Appointment of a Minister of Education*, viii, 350, 1882

385   Gray, H.J. *The Economics of Irish Forestry*, xxi Pt 2, 18, 1963-4

386   Greer, Samuel M'Curdy *Bank Charter Act of 1844*, i, 335, 1856

387   Greer, Samuel M'Curdy *Government Purchase of Railways in Ireland: How can it be accomplished?*, v, 71, 1869

388   Greer, Samuel M'Curdy *Legal Impediments to the Cultivation of Trees in Ireland*, iii, 461, 1863

389   Greer, Samuel M'Curdy *Railway Reform: or the Policy of the Purchase and Management by the British Government of the Railways of the United Kingdom*, iv, 165, 1865

390   Greer, Samuel M'Curdy *Relation between Landlord and Tenant in Ireland*, April, Vol III, 1853

391   Grimshaw, Thomas Wrigley *Agricultural Statistics in Ireland*, ix, 439, 1890

392   Grimshaw, Thomas Wrigley *Child Mortality in Dublin*, Appendix, ix, 1889

393   Grimshaw, Thomas Wrigley *Irish Progress during the Past Ten Years, 1881-1890*, ix, 571, 1891

394   Grimshaw, Thomas Wrigley *Notes on the Statistics of Waste Lands in Ireland*, viii, 522, 1884

395   Grimshaw, Thomas Wrigley *Some Comparative Statistics of Irish Counties, Compiled from the Returns obtained*

to that of Personal Property, ii, 482, 1860

457 Hancock, William Neilson *Mortality of Children in Work-houses in Ireland*, iii, 193, 1862

458 Hancock, William Neilson *Mr. MacNeel Caird's Essay in 'The Cobden Club Series' on Local Government and Taxation in Scotland, considered with reference to the Suggestions it affords upon the following questions [roads, courts, rating, urban improvements]*, vi, 438, 1875

459 Hancock, William Neilson *Notes as to Proceedings of the State Charities' Aid Association of New York*, vii, 51, 1876

460 Hancock, William Neilson *Notice of a Plan for the Systematic Collection of Irish Economic Statistics*, May, 1848

461 Hancock, William Neilson *Notice of the Theory 'That there is no hope for a Nation which lives on Potatoes'*, April, Vol I, 1848

462 Hancock, William Neilson *Obituary Notice of the late Alexander Thom, J.P.*, viii, 5, 1880

463 Hancock, William Neilson *Obituary Notice of the late Most Rev. Richard Whately, D.D., Lord Archbishop of Dublin, President of the Society*, iv, 9, 1864

464 Hancock, William Neilson *Obituary Notice of the late Richard Hussey Walsh, L.L.D.*, iii, 181, 1862

465 Hancock, William Neilson *Official Report on the Statistics of Flax Culture in Munster and Connaught in 1865*, iv, 297, 1866

466 Hancock, William Neilson *Plan for extending the Jurisdiction for selling Incumbered Estates to cases where a Receiver has been appointed over a Life Estate*, i, 55, 1855

467 Hancock, William Neilson *Plan for obviating the identification of Luggage at Kingstown and Holyhead, and so accelerating the Through Traffic between London and Dublin*, ii, 485, 1860

468 Hancock, William Neilson *Plan of Applying the latest improvements sanctioned by Parliament in the Management of the Public Debt and of Town Finance to the Debts and Borrowing Powers of the Town Council of Dublin*, vi, 1, 1871

469 Hancock, William Neilson *Present Law of Landlord and Tenant, as exhibited in the recent decision of the Master of the Rolls in the case of O'Fay v. Burke*, ii, 345, 1860

and Insolvency in 1861, iii, 198, 1862
551   Heron, Denis Caulfield *Taxes on the Administration of Justice*,
       January, Vol II, 1851
552   Heron, Denis Caulfield *A Visit to Russia*, vi, 181, 1873
553   Hertz, Hartwig S. *Banks of Issue in Germany*, ii, 277, 1859
554   High Court of Justice – Queen's Bench Division *Commercial
       Cases*, xi, 379, 1905-6
555   Hillery, Brian *Symposium on Necessary Changes in Indus-
       trial Relations*, xxiv Pt 2, 54, 1979-80
       Hitchens, D.M.W.N. *see* Birnie, J.E.
556   Hoare, Thomas F. *International Economic Interdependence –
       The Commission of the European Communities' Meteor
       Model*, xxiii Pt 4, 175, 1976-7
557   Hoare, Thomas F. *Nature and Functions of an Irish Money
       Market*, xxii Pt 2, 1, 1969-70
558   Hogan, William *Advantages and Disadvantages of Indirect
       Taxation; and a Scheme for Direct Taxation which would
       be equitable and combine the advantages of an Indirect
       Tax*, December, Vol II, 1850
559   Hogan, William *Dependence of National Wealth on the
       Social and Sanitary State of the Labouring Classes*,
       February, Vol I, 1849
560   Holmes, Denis *The function of Marketing Research in the
       Distributive System*, xvii, 611, 1946-7
561   Honohan, Patrick, and Dunne, John *The Flow of Funds 1972-
       1977*, xxiv Pt 4, 175, 1981-2
562   Honohan, William A. *Irish Actuarial Data*, xvii, 381, 1944-5
563   Honohan, William A. *Irish Social Services, A Symposium.
       A Short Review of Irish and British Social Insurance
       Schemes*, xvii, 116, 1942-3
564   Honohan, William A. *Pension Fund Principles*, xvi, 19,
       1938-9
565   Honohan, William A. *The Problem of Full Employment.
       Discussion*, xvii, 453, 1944-5
566   Honohan, William A. *Providing for Old Age through Private
       Channels*, xx Pt 3, 178, 1959-60
567   Honohan, William A. *Symposium on the Government Green
       Paper 'A National Income-Related Pension Scheme':
       Financial Aspects*, xxiii Pt 4, 87, 1976-7
568   Hooper, J. *Statistics of Examinations*, xiv, 1928-9
569   Horgan, John J. *The Development of Local Government in*

621   Johnston, Joseph *Symposium on Social Security*, xviii Pt 3, 262, 1949-50
       Johnston, R.H.W. *see* Franklin, Genevieve
622   Johnston, William John *Coming Changes in Irish Local Government*, x, 366, 1898
623   Johnston, William John *The Land Purchase Problem*, xi, 396, 1905-6
624   Jones, Emrys *The Social Geography of Belfast*, xix, 1, 1953-4
625   Jones, R.M. and Slattery, D.G. *Some Aspects of (Net) Emigration from Northern Ireland*, xxiv Pt 1, 133, 1978-9
626   Jones, Thomas *Pauperism and Poverty*, xii, 358, 1909-10
627   Jordan, Rev. Thomas *Decrease of Pauperism, how far the work of the Poor*, ii, 73, 1857
628   Jordan, Rev. Thomas *Effects of Emigration: Can it be made a means of relieving Distress?*, i, 378, 1856
629   Jordan, Rev. Thomas *Present State of the Dwellings of the Poor, chiefly in Dublin*, ii, 12, 1857
630   Joyce, Alan *The Development of Yield Curves for the Irish Securities Market*, xxvi Pt 3, 109, 1990-1
631   Joynt, William Lane *Salmon Fishery and Fishery Laws of Ireland*, iii, 37, 1861

632   Kane, Sir Robert *Address at Opening of 5th Session*, November, Vol II, 1851
633   Kane, Sir Robert *Address at Opening of 20th Session*, iv, 355, 1867
634   Katsiaouni, Olympios *Planning in a Small Economy: The Republic of Ireland*, xxiii Pt 5, 217, 1977-8
635   Keane, Sir John *The Human Factor in Industry*, xvi, 47, 1940-1
       Keane, T. *see also* Keating, W.
636   Keane, T. and Knaggs, J.F. *Population Projections*, xxii Pt 4, 30, 1971-2
637   Kearney, Brendan and O'Connor, R. *Economic Issues in Irish Forestry*, xxvi Pt 5, 179, 1992-3
638   Keating, W. and Keane, T. *Irish Industrial Structures 1979-1985, A Longitudinal Analysis*, xxvi Pt 1, 181, 1988-9
639   Keating, William *Population Projections for the Years 1981 and 1986*, xxiii Pt 4, 113, 1976-7

660   Killeen, Michael J. *A Symposium on Increasing Employment in Ireland*, xxiii Pt 3, 50, 1975-6

661   Kilroy, J., Ryan, P.F. and Walsh, T. *A Half Century of Fertiliser and Lime Use in Ireland*, xix, 104, 1956-7

662   King, F.C. *Drifting to Absolutism?*, xix, 1, 1952-3

663   King, F.C. *The Problem of Full Employment. Discussion*, xvii, 443, 1944-5

664   Kingston, W.V. and Prendiville, B.J. *The Volume of Press Display Advertising in Ireland, 1957*, xx, 136, 1957-8

665   Kinsella, R.P. *The Measurement of Market Concentration in Irish Banking*, xxiv Pt 3, 31, 1980-1

       Kiountouzis, E. *see* Glass, J.C.

       Knaggs, J.F. *see also* Keane, T.

666   Knaggs, J.F. *Natality in Dublin in the Year 1955*, xx, 37, 1957-8

667   Lalor, Joseph *Use of Education and Training in the Treatment of the Insane in Public Lunatic Asylums*, vii, 361, 1878

668   Larcom, Thomas Aiskew *Address at conclusion of 3rd Session*, June, Vol II, 1850

669   Larmor, Sir Graham *Mechanisation and Productivity in the Linen Industry*, xix, 31, 1954-5

670   Law, Hugh *Peasant Proprietorship of the Channel Islands*, vii, 181, 1878

671   Law, Hugh *Remarks on Preceding Papers*, vii, 177, 1878

672   Lawrence, R.J. *Local Government in Northern Ireland: Areas, Functions and Finance*, xxi Pt 4, 14, 1965-6

673   Lawson, James Anthony *Address at Opening of 11th Session*, ii, 142, 1858

674   Lawson, James Anthony *Address at Opening of 16th Session*, iii, 284, 1862

675   Lawson, James Anthony *Address at Opening of 25th Session*, vi, 47, 1872

676   Lawson, James Anthony *Address at Opening of 26th Session*, vi, 169, 1873

677   Lawson, James Anthony *Agricultural Statistics of Ireland*, April, Vol III, 1854

678   Lawson, James Anthony *Commercial Panics*, May, Vol I, 1848

679   Lawson, James Anthony *Comparative Advantages of Direct*

Dublin, xii, 230, 1909

699   Lawson, William *The Social Legislation of 1904: Registration of Clubs (Ireland): Licensing (England): Applicability of it to Ireland*, xi, 325, 1904-5

700   Lawson, William *Social Problems and the War*, xiii, 344, 1917

701   Leathem, J. *Observations on the present method of contracting for the Mail Packet Service*, ii, 368, 1860

702   Lee, George *Hysteresis and the Natural Rate of Unemployment in Ireland*, xxvi Pt 2, 31, 1989-90

703   Lee, J. *An Analysis of Land Potential for Grazing in Ireland with Particular Reference to Farm Size Relationships*, xxiii Pt 1, 149, 1973-4

704   Leet, Francis L. *'Credit Power and Democracy' by Major C.H. Douglas, Considered*, xiv, 34, 1924-5

705   Leet, Francis L. *The Trade Statistics of the Irish Free State in 1924*, xiv, 128, 1924-5

706   Lentaigne, John Francis O'Neill *Address at Opening of 31st Session*, vii (Appendix), 1877

707   Lentaigne, John Francis O'Neill *Treatment and Punishment of Young Offenders*, viii (Appendix), 1881

708   Leser, C.E.V. *The Pattern of Personal Expenditure in Ireland*, xxi Pt 2, 1, 1963-4

709   Leser, C.E.V. *Problems of Industrialisation in Developing Countries and their Implications for Ireland*, xxi Pt 6, 1, 1967-8

710   Leser, C.E.V. *Recent Demographic Developments in Ireland*, xxi Pt 3, 179, 1964-5

711   Leslie, Thomas Edward Cliffe *Inquiry into the Progress and Present Conditions of Mechanics' Institutions* (2 parts), February & June, Vol III, 1852

712   Leslie, Thomas Edward Cliffe *Maritime Captures and Commercial Blockades*, i, 97, 1855

713   Leslie, Thomas Edward Cliffe *Self-Dependence of the Working Classes under the Law of Competition*, April, Vol II, 1851

714   Leslie, Thomas Edward Cliffe *Trades' Unions and Combinations in 1853*, May, Vol III, 1853

715   Levi, Leone *International Code of Commerce morally and judicially considered*, Social Inquiry Society, November, Vol III, 1851

necessary in the Present System of Sale and Mortgage of Land in Ireland, Social Inquiry Society, Vol III, 1853

734   Lucey, Brian M. *Profits, Efficiency and Irish Banks*, xxvii Pt 1, 31, 1993-4

735   Luke, Arthur E. *Structural Change in the Northern Ireland Economy*, xxiii Pt 4, 151, 1976-7

736   Lurgan Loan Fund Trustees *Report to the Commissioners of the Loan Fund Board of Ireland*, February, Vol I, 1848

737   Lynch, Patrick *The Problem of Full Employment. Discussion*, xvii, 438, 1944-5

738   Lynch, Patrick *Symposium on National Income and Social Accounts*, xviii, 503, 1951-2

739   Lynch, Stanislaus John *Land Purchase in Ireland: a Retrospect and a Forecast*, xiii, 1, 1913

740   Lynch, Stanislaus John *Suggestions for the Simplification of the Procedure in relation to the Sale of Land in Ireland*, viii, 606, 1885

741   Lyon, Stanley (1) *The Statistical Abstract; (2) The 24th Session of the International Institute of Statistics. Opening Address*, xvi, 1, 1938-9

742   Lyon, Stanley *The Census of Population, 1946*, xvii, 579, 1945-6

743   Lyon, Stanley *The Forthcoming Census of Population*, xv, 69, 1935-6

744   Lyon, Stanley *Irish Social Services: A Symposium. Unemployment – The Statistical Background*, xvii, 107, 1942-3

745   Lyon, Stanley *Natality in Dublin in the Years 1943, 1944, and 1945*, xviii, 57, 1947-8

746   Lyon, Stanley *The Organisation of Official Statistics in Saorstat Eireann and in some other countries*, xv, 29, 1932-3

747   Lyon, Stanley *The Population Problem. Broadcast Discussion*, xvi, 112, 1937-8

748   Lyon, Stanley *The Session of the International Institute of Statistics at Mexico, 1933*, xv, 43, 1933-4

749   Lyon, Stanley *Some Observations on Births in Dublin in the years 1941 and 1942*, xvii, 144, 1942-3

750   Lyon, Stanley *The Trade Statistics of the Irish Free State: Methodological Aspects*, xvi, 9, 1937-8

751   Lyon, Stanley *The Trade Statistics of the Irish Free State in 1924*, xiv, 94, 1924-5

804   McKenna, Peter John *Criminal Jurisdiction of Courts of Quarter Sessions in Ireland*, i, 276, 1856
805   McKenna, Peter John *Disposal of our Convicts*, ii, 19, 1856
806   McKenna, Peter John *Factory Education*, i, 78, 1855
807   McKenna, Peter John *Observations on Lord Brougham's Bill for the Further Amendment of the Law of Evidence, as well in Criminal as in Civil Cases*, ii, 362, 1860
808   McKenna, Peter John *Parnerships with Limited Liability*, June, Vol III, 1853
809   McKenna, Peter John *Partnership with Limited Liability*, i, 136, 1855
810   MacKenzie, Gilbert *Covariate Models for Accident Data*, xxv Pt 3, 71, 1985-6
811   McKeon, J. *The Economic Appraisal of Industrial Projects in Ireland*, xxiv Pt 2, 119, 1979-80
812   Mackie, John *Irish Free State Railway Accounts*, xv, 83, 1935-6
813   Mackie, John *Proportional Representation and the Irish Free State*, xiv, 311, 1926-7
814   Mackie, John *Some Suggestions for a Simpler and More Equitable Income Tax System*, xiv, 61, 1919-20
        McMahon, Thomas *see* Jennings, David
815   McMechan, William *Proposal for the more effectual prevention of Corrupt Practices at Parliamentary Elections, by enabling Revising Barristers (subject to Appeal) to determine concerning persons disqualified for bribery, treating, or undue influence*, ii, 421, 1860
816   McNamara, Brendan *Symposium on EEC Membership: The Impact of EEC Financial Assistance on Irish Economic Development since 1973*, xxv Pt 1, 221, 1983-4
817   McWeeney, Edmond Joseph *On Immunity against Infectious Disease, with Special Reference to Anti-Typhoid Inoculation*, xiii, 231, 1915
818   McWeeney, Edmond Joseph *Popular Endeavour against Tuberculosis: its Instruments, Methods, and Results*, xii, 62, 1906-7
819   McWeeney, Edmond Joseph *On The Recent Action of the State with Regard to Venereal Diseases*, xiii, 498, 1919
820   Maeren, Corr Vander *Universal Free Trade*, ii, 131, 1857
821   Maguire, J. *The Housing Problem in Ireland and Great*

    during the period 1841-1901, xi, 196, 1902-3

842   Matheson, Robert Edwin *Mechanism of Statistics*, Appendix, ix, 1889

843   Matheson, Robert Edwin *The Principal Results of the Census of the United Kingdom in 1901*, xi, 289, 1904-5

844   Matheson, Robert Edwin *A Review of the General Topographical Index of Ireland, 1901*, xii, 263, 1909

845   Matthews, A. *Symposium on EEC Membership. The Options for Further EEC Integration: An Irish View*, xxv Pt 1, 207, 1983-4

846   Matthews, A. *Symposium on Ireland, Europe and the Third World: Ireland, The Common Agricultural Policy and the Less Developed Countries*, xxv Pt 2, 149, 1984-5

847   Matthews, Alan *Common Agricultural Policy Reform and National Compensation Strategies*, xxvi Pt 1, 1, 1988-9

848   Mayne, Edward Graves *Foreign Systems of Registering Dealings with Land by means of maps and indexes*, Social Inquiry Society, Vol III, 1852

849   Meenan, James F. *The Future of Irish External Trade (Discussion)*, xvii, 309, 1943-4

850   Meenan, James F. *The Impact of the War upon Irish Economy*, xvi, 17, 1939-40

851   Meenan, James F. *The Political Economy of Development*, xx, 1, 1957-8

852   Meenan, James F. *Preliminary Notes on the Census of Population in Northern Ireland, 1937*, xv, 69, 1936-7

853   Meenan, James F. *Some Aspects of the Italian Corporative Organisation*, xv, 1, 1934-5

854   Meenan, James F. *Some Causes and Consequences of the Low Irish Marriage Rate*, xv, 19, 1932-3

855   Meenan, James F. *The Universities I – University College, Dublin*, xvii, 460, 1944-5

856   Meenan, James F. *The Universities II – Trinity College, Dublin*, xvii, 594, 1945-6

857   Meenan, James F. *The Universities III*, xviii Pt 3, 349, 1949-50

858   Menton, Brendan *Ireland and International Monetary Institutions*, xx, 80, 1957-8

859   Menton, Brendan *Short-Term Economic Forecasting*, xxi Pt 3, 15, 1964-5

860   Menton, Brendan *Theories of Adjustment of the Balance of*

882 Moloney, Sir T.F. *Recent Social Legislation in England*, xvi, 33, 1937-8

883 Moloney, Sir T.F. *The Treatment of Young Offenders*, xiv, 437, 1926-7

884 Monahan, James Henry *Functions of Grand Juries in Criminal Cases*, iv, 218, 1865

885 Monahan, James Henry *Suggestions for a Bill to regulate Sales of Property*, vii, 310, 1878

886 Monsell, Rt Hon William *Address at Opening of 22nd Session*, v, 53, 1869

887 Monsell, Rt Hon William *Does Ireland Suffer from Wrongs and Grievances not existing in the rest of the United Kingdom?*, vi, 347, 1874

888 Monteagle, Rt Hon Lord *Presidential Address at Close of 36th Session*, viii, 387, 1883

889 Montrose, J.L. *The Nature of Legal Sociology*, xix Pt 3, 122, 1954-5

Mooney, P.J. *see* Cavanagh, C.F.

890 Moore, Arthur *Registration of Births, Deaths, and Marriages in Ireland:- Observations on the late Government Bill of 1857*, ii, 424, 1860

891 Moore, Fletcher *Magistrates' Law and Suggested Increase of Jurisdiction and Powers*, ix, 671, 1893

892 Moore, Fletcher *The Re-afforesting of Ireland: the Advantages and Disadvantages*, viii, 440, 1883

893 Moore, Fletcher *Some Notes upon Light Railways and Tramway Guarantees in Ireland under the Tramways and Public Companies' Act, 1883, 46-47 Vic.cap.43, and Suggestions for a Different and Improved System of Guarantee*, ix, 512, 1891

Moran, M.A. *see* Crowley, M.J.

894 Morris, E.A. Montmorency *Canals and Waterways of Western Europe*, xi, 381, 1905-6

895 Mortished, R.J.P. *The Future of Irish External Trade. Discussion*, xvii, 309, 1943-4

896 Mortished, R.J.P. *The Industrial Relations Act, 1946*, xvii, 671, 1946-7

897 Mortished, R.J.P. *Irish Social Services – A Symposium. Addendum*, xvii, 141, 1942-3

898 Mortished, R.J.P. *Notes on the National Economic Councils of Germany and France*, xiv, 1, 1928-9

Branches of the Legal Profession, ix, 613, 1892

920 Murphy, Joseph John *A Suggestion on Coinage*, ix, 381, 1889

921 Murphy, Joseph John *Tenures and Taxation of India*, ii, 214, 1858

922 Murphy, M. *Financial Results on Mixed Dairy Farms in 1937-38*, xvi, 105, 1938-9

923 Murphy, M. *Financial Results on Mixed Dairy Farms in 1942-43 as Compared with 1938-39*, xvii, 269, 1943-4

924 Murphy, M. *Financial Results on Sixty-one West Cork Farms in 1940-41*, xvi, 60, 1941-2

925 Murphy, M. *Tables in Continuation of those Published in Paper entitled 'Financial Results on Mixed Dairy Farms in 1937-38'*, xvi, 90, 1939-40

926 Murray, C.H. *Some Aspects of the Industrial Capital Market in Ireland*, xx, 97, 1959-60

927 Neill, D.G. *Some Problems of Integration in the Hospital Service in Northern Ireland*, xix, 169, 1955-6

928 Nevin, Donal *Symposium on Economic Development*, xx, 129, 1958-9

929 Nevin, Donal *A Symposium on Increasing Employment in Ireland*, xxiii Pt 3, 64, 1975-6

930 Nevin, Donal *Symposium on the Report of the Commission on Emigration and Other Population Problems*, xix, 113, 1955-6

931 Nevin, Monica *A Study of the Social Background of Students in the Irish Universities*, xxi Pt 6, 201, 1967-8

932 Nevin, Monica *A Study of the Social Background of Students in University College, Dublin*, xxi Pt 5, 62, 1966-7

933 Nevin, T.E. *Symposium on Science and Irish Economic Development,* xxi Pt 5, 38, 1966-7

934 Nichol, Dr R.J. *Symposium on Future Demands for and Supplies of Energy: Costing Ireland's Energy Options*, xxiv Pt 1, 155, 1978-9

935 Nixon, J.W. *Work of International Labour Office*, xvi, 69, 1937-8

936 Nolan, Brian *The Personal Distribution of Income in the Republic of Ireland*, xxiii Pt 5, 91, 1977-8

937 Nolan, Francis *British Citizenship as opposed to American Citizenship,* v, 40, 1868

956	O'Brien, Murrough *Continental Land Banks and Land Registers*, ix, 192, 1887

957	O'Brien, Murrough *Description of the System of Registration and Transfer of Land Titles and Securities in the Canton Vaud*, ix, 448, 1890

958	O'Brien, Murrough *Economic Theory of Rent*, viii, 164, 1881

959	O'Brien, Murrough *Graduated Taxation in Switzerland*, ix, 163, 1887

960	O'Brien, Murrough *Note on the Operations of Some Swiss Land Banks*, ix, 316, 1888

961	O'Brien, Murrough *Recent Statistics of French Rural Economy*, ix, 363, 1889

962	O'Brien, Murrough *Sliding Scales for Rent: Value and Fair Rents: Annual and Capital Value*, ix, 278, 1888

963	O'Brien, Murrough *Some of the Difficulties in the way of Creating a Peasant Proprietary in Ireland*, vii, 161, 1878

964	O'Brien, Murrough *A Swiss Land Credit Bank*, viii, 578, 1885

965	O'Brien, Murrough *Valuation of Property for Taxation*, viii, 406, 1879

966	O'Brien, Murrough *Valuation of Real Property for Taxation*, vii, 223, 1878; vii, 385, 1879

967	O'Brolchain, R. *Examination of the Sickness Experience for the year 1935 of Persons Insured under the National Health Insurance Acts*, xvi, 53, 1938-39

968	O'Brolchain, R. *Irish Social Services, A Symposium. National Health Insurance*, xvii, 125, 1942-3

969	O'Buachalla, Liam *Some Reflections on the Social and Economic Organisation of Connemara*, xv, 31, 1936-7

970	O'Buachalla, Liam *Symposium on the Report of the Commission on Emigration and Other Population Problems*, xix, 117, 1955-6

971	O'Buachalla, Liam *Unemployment. Broadcast Discussion*, xvi, 94, 1939-40

972	O'Coineain, A. *The Future of Irish External Trade. Discussion*, xvii, 309, 1943-4

973	O'Connell, John J. *Measurement and Growth of the Food Production and Distribution Industry in Ireland*, xxiii Pt 4, 229, 1976-7

974	O'Connell, John Robert *Foundations of Colonial Self Government*, xiii, 419, 1917

Rearing Poor Orphans in Families, instead of placing them in the Workhouses, ii, 331, 1859

993　O'Hagan, John and Jackson, Arthur S. *Inquiry into the Taxes on Law Proceedings in Ireland*, Social Inquiry Society, Vol III, 1852

994　O'Hagan, John W. *An Analysis of the Growth of the Public Sector in Ireland, 1953-1977*, xxiv Pt 2, 69, 1979-80

995　O'Hagan, John W. *Export and Import Visitor Trends and Determinants in Ireland*, xxii Pt 5, 1, 1972-3

996　O'Hagan, John W. and Duffy, C. *Access and Admission Charges to Museums: A Case Study of the National Museum*, xxvii Pt 1, 125, 1993-4

997　O'Hagan, John W. and Waldron, P. *Estimating the Magnitude of Tourism in the European Community: Data Deficiencies and Some Results*, xxv Pt 4, 89, 1986-7

998　O'Hagan, Thomas *Address as President of Social Science Congress, Dublin, 1881*, Appendix, viii, 1881

999　O'Hagan, Thomas *Address at Opening of 19th Session*, iv, 229, 1866

1000　O'Hagan, Thomas *Address at Opening of 24th Session*, v, 219, 1870

1001　O'Hanlon, G. and Treacy, J. *An Analysis of Irish Farming in 1980 based on the Community Typology of Agricultural Holdings*, xxv Pt 2, 71, 1984-5

1002　O'Hare, Daniel *Symposium on the Idea of a University in the 1990s*, xxvi Pt 2, 129, 1989-90

1003　O'Hegarty, P.S. *The Future of Irish External Trade. Discussion*, xvii, 309, 1943-4

1004　Ó hEocha, Colm *The Science Budget*, xxii Pt 2, 120, 1969-70

1005　Ó hEocha, Colm *Symposium on Investment in Education*, xxi Pt 4, 92, 1965-6

1006　Ó hEocha, Colm *Symposium on the Idea of a University in the 1990s*, xxvi Pt 2, 125, 1989-90

1007　O'Herlihy, C. St. J. *Economic Studies in Northern Ireland Labour Statistics*, xxi Pt 2, 145, 1963-4

1008　Ó hUiginn, P. *Some Social and Economic Aspects of Housing – An International Comparison*, xx, 36, 1959-60

1009　O'Keeffe, P. *Symposium on Economic Development*, xx, 134, 1958-9

1010　Oldham, Charles Hubert *The Bearing on Industry of the Impending Changes in Irish Education*, xi, 1, 1900-1

sonal Income Tax in Ireland and the Social Valuation of Income 1946-76, xxiii Pt 4, 1, 1976-7

1032 O'Neill, Helen *Symposium on Ireland, Europe and the Third World: The Question of Aid*, xxv Pt 2, 137, 1984-5

1033 O'Neill, Henry *The Progress of Sanitary Science in Belfast*, xi, 35, 1900-1

1034 O'Nuallain, Labhras *A Comparison of the Economic Position and Trend in Eire and Northern Ireland*, xvii, 504, 1945-6

1035 O'Nuallain, Labhras *Symposium on Economic Development*, xx, 112, 1958-9

1036 O'Raifeartaigh, T. *Changes and Trends in our Educational System since 1922*, xx, 42, 1958-9

1037 O'Reilly, Liam *Estimating Quarterly National Accounts*, xxiv Pt 4, 1, 1981-2

1038 O'Reilly, Michael *State Debt Balance Sheets*, xx, 30, 1958-9

1039 O'Reilly, Myles *Symposium on Competition Policy*, xxvii Pt 1, 181, 1993-4

1040 O'Riain, Micheál *Cross Channel Passenger Traffic 1960-1980*, xxv Pt 4, 45, 1991-2

1041 O'Riordan, W.K. *Consumer Response to Price and Income Changes*, xxiii Pt 2, 65, 1974-5

1042 O'Riordan, W.K. *Induced Employment in the Marketed Services Sectors in Ireland 1975*, xxv Pt 2, 41, 1984-5

1043 O'Riordan, W.K. *Is Irish Public Sector Employment a Burden?*, xxvi Pt 2, 1, 1989-90

1044 O'Rourke, Kevin H. *Industrial Policy, Employment Policy and the Non-Traded Sector*, xxvii, 2, 61, 1994-5

1045 Orpen, E.R. Richards *The Problem of Full Employment, Discussion*, xvii, 444, 1944-5

1046 Orpen, J.R. *The Problem of Full Employment. Discussion*, xvii, 442, 1944-5

1047 Osborne, Rev. Henry *Prevention and Elimination of Disease, Insanity, Drunkenness, and Crime – A Suggestion*, x, 85, 1895

1048 Osborne, Robert William *Transfer of Land Considered in relation to the Rights of Judgment Creditors*, March, Vol II, 1850

1049 O'Shaughnessy, Mark S. *Criminal Statistics; especially with reference to Population, Education, and Distress in*

of the Deaf and Dumb, the Blind, and the Imbecile, iv, 26, 1864

1067   Pim, Jonathan *Partnerships of Limited Liability*, December, Vol II, 1851

1068   Pim, Joseph Todhunter *Condition of our Railways considered with Reference to their Purchase by the State*, iv, 370, 1867

1069   Pim, Joseph Todhunter *Foreign Commerce and Free Trade Policy*, viii, 238, 1881

1070   Pim, Joseph Todhunter *Is our Commercial Depression due to Free Trade, and would it be relieved by Limited Protection*, Appendix, vii, 1878

1071   Pim, Joseph Todhunter *Municipal Government and Taxation*, vi, 410, 1875

1072   Pim, Joseph Todhunter *Review of the Economic and Social Condition of Ireland*, x, 453, 1899

1073   Pim, William Harvey *Importance of Reformatory Establishments for Juvenile Delinquents*, February, Vol III, 1854

1074   Power, Con *Symposium on the White Paper on Educational Development*, xxiv Pt 3, 84, 1980-1
        Prendiville, B.J. *see* Kingston, W.V.

1075   Preston, Samuel P. *Some Economic Objections against the Custom of 'Fortuning' Daughters, that prevails amongst the farming classes in Munster*, vii, 425, 1879

1076   Quinlan, P.M. *A Dynamic Model of the Irish Economy*, xx Pt 5, 1, 1961-2

1077   Rea, Desmond *An Analysis of the University as an Organisation*, xxii Pt 4, 186, 1971-2

1078   Rea, Desmond *A Contemporary Definition of Personnel Management, Some of its Critical Assumptions and their relevance to the University Organisation*, xxii Pt 5, 36, 1972-3

1079   Rea, Desmond *A Discussion on Social Class Background with Special Reference to Students at Queen's University, Belfast*, xxi Pt 6, 152, 1967-8

1080   Rea, Desmond *The Financial Analysis of the Published*

1099   Ryan, F.W. *What the Worker should know*, xiv, 133, 1920-1
1100   Ryan, Rev. Liam *A Symposium on 'The Buchanan Report -
        Regional Studies in Ireland': Some Social Aspects*, xxii Pt
        2, 202, 1969-70
        Ryan, P.F. *see* Kilroy, J.
1101   Ryan, Pierce *A Symposium on 'The Buchanan Report –
        Regional Studies in Ireland': Land Use Implications*, xxii
        Pt 2, 194, 1969-70
1102   Ryan, Terence *A Symposium on Inflation: The Cure for
        Inflation*, xxiii Pt 2, 10, 1974-5
1103   Ryan, W.J.L. *Investment Criteria in Ireland*, xx Pt 5, 52,
        1961-2
1104   Ryan, W.J.L. *Measurement of Tariff Levels for Ireland for
        1931, 1936, 1938*, xviii, 109, 1948-9
1105   Ryan, W.J.L. *The Methodology of the Second Programme for
        Economic Expansion*, xxi Pt 2, 120, 1963-4

1106   Sadlier, T.U. *Varied Origins of the Irish People*, xv, 63,
        1932-3
        Sams, K.I. *see* Robertson, N.
1107   Samuels, Arthur Warren *The External Commerce of Ireland*,
        xii, 193, 1909
1108   Samuels, Arthur Warren *Financial Relations of Great Britain
        and Ireland – The Expenditure Account*, x, 292, 1897
1109   Samuels, Arthur Warren *Irish Private Bill Legislation – a
        Tribunal*, x, 379, 1899
1110   Samuels, Arthur Warren *Law of Divorce in Ireland*, ix, 186,
        1887
1111   Samuels, Arthur Warren *Private Bill Legislation for Ireland*,
        x, 238, 1897
1112   Samuels, Arthur Warren *Private Bill Procedure (The Scotch
        Act of 1899)*, x, 509, 1900
1113   Samuels, Arthur Warren *Scottish Private Bill Legislation in
        Working*, xi, 270, 1903-4
1114   Samuels, Arthur Warren *Some Features in Recent Irish
        Finance*, xii, 1, 1906-7
1115   Samuels, Arthur Warren *A Suggestion for the Removal of
        Taxes on Litigation in Ireland as a Condition of the
        Reduction of the Judicial Establishment*, x, 135, 1896
1116   Sapsford, D. *Symposium on Necessary Changes in Industrial*

where tenants have bought their holdings, and also to other Church lands where tenants have not yet bought their holdings, vii, 183, 1878

1136 Shaw Lefevre, George *Remarks on Preceding Papers*, vii, 177, 1878

1137 Sheehy, S.J. *Co-Responsibility and the Future of Irish Agriculture*, xxiv Pt 5, 1, 1982-3

1138 Sheridan, L.A. *National Insurance Adjudication*, xix, 29, 1955-6

1139 Shields, B.F. *An Analysis of Irish Transport Acts 1944 and 1950, and of the financial and operating statistics of CIE and the GNR Company 1945-51*, xix, 19, 1953-4

1140 Shields, B.F. *An Analysis of the Financial and Operating Statistics of the GSR Company and GNR Company, 1938-1944*, xvii, 541, 1945-6

1141 Shields, B.F. *An Analysis of the Irish Census of Distribution, 1951*, xx, 118, 1957-8

1142 Shields, B.F. *An Analysis of the Legislation, Published Accounts and Operating Statistics of the Great Southern Railways Co., 1924-37*, xvi, 87, 1937-8

1143 Shields, B.F. *Irish Social Services: A Symposium. Some Considerations Regarding the Cost of Social Security in Ireland*, xvii, 134, 1942-3

1144 Shields, B.F. *The Minimum Wage*, xv, 61, 1933-4

1145 Shields, B.F. *The Trade Statistics of the Irish Free State in 1924*, xiv, 110, 1924-5

1146 Sigerson, George *The Law and the Lunatic*, ix, 7, 1886

1147 Sigerson, George *Need and Use of Village Hospitals in Ireland*, viii, 340, 1882

1148 Simpson, J.V. *An Estimate of the Profits of Banking in Northern Ireland*, xxi Pt 4, 43, 1965-6

1149 Simpson, J.V. *An Investigation into the Employment Generated by New Industry Locating in Northern Ireland, 1951-1980*, xxv Pt 2, 1, 1984-5

1150 Simpson, J.V. *The Finances of the Public Sector in Northern Ireland, 1968-1978*, xxiv Pt 2, 99, 1979-80

1151 Simpson, J.V. *Population, Employment and Urbanisation Trends in Northern Ireland*, xxiii Pt 3, 120, 1975-6

1152 Sinclair, Sir Kenneth *The Port of Belfast*, xix, 37, 1956-7
Slattery, D.G. *see also* Jones, R.M.

1153 Slattery, D.G. *Estimating Irish Prices*, xxii Pt 1, 1, 1968-9

1174   Stanuell, Charles Atthill *The Government Management of Indian Railways*, xi, 244, 1903-4

1175   Stanuell, Charles Atthill *The Improvement of Dublin Harbour*, xii, 546, 1911-12

1176   Stanuell, Charles Atthill *The Industrial Awakening of Ireland*, xiii, 99, 1914

1177   Stanuell, Charles Atthill *International Time*, xiii, 26, 1913

1178   Stanuell, Charles Atthill *Irish Forestry and the Land Purchase Acts*, xii, 93, 1906-7

1179   Stanuell, Charles Atthill *The Practice of the Commercial Court*, xi, 365, 1905-6

1180   Stanuell, Charles Atthill *Report of the Vice-Regal Commission upon Irish Railways*, xii, 401, 1910-11

1181   Stanuell, Charles Atthill *Weights and Measures after the War*, xiii, 460, 1917

        Statistical Papers, Miscellaneous

1182   *An Examination into the Principles of Currency involved in the Bank Charter Act of 1844* (J.E. Cairnes), 1854

1183   *An Introductory Lecture on Political Economy* (W.N. Hancock), 1848

1184   *On the Economic Causes of the Present State of Agriculture in Ireland*, 1849

1185   *Elements of Jurisprudence, being selections from Dumont's Digest of the Works of Bentham* (ed. W.N. Hancock), 1852

1186   *Observations on the Present State of the Law Affecting Home Made Spirits in Bond* (John Bagot), 1853

1187   *Perfect Income Tax of 10%* (J.N. Hancock), 1855

1188   Stewart, D. *Dublin City Passenger Transport Services*, xix Pt 3, 136, 1954-5

1189   Stewart, J.C. *Company Tax – Effective Tax Rates on Profits*, xxiv Pt 3, 101, 1980-1

1190   Stewart, J.C. *Fiscal Incentives and Corporate Financing: A Flow of Funds Analysis 1964-82*, xxiv Pt 2, 97, 1985-6

1191   Stoker, Charlotte M.B. *Necessity for a State Provision for the Education of the Deaf and Dumb of Ireland*, iii, 456, 1863

1192   Stoney, Thomas Sadlier *Remarks on the Adjustment of the Poor Rate Taxation in Ireland*, February, Vol II, 1850

1193   Story, John Benjamin *Medical Inspection of Schools and School Children*, xii, 523, 1911-12

1194   Streight, R.L. *Symposium on the Present and Future of Inland*

1218   *International Dimensions in Corporate Mergers and Acquisitions – The Implications for Ireland*, xxvi Pt 1, 133, 1988-9

1219   *Investment in Education*, xxi Pt 4, 67, 1965-6

1220   *Ireland, Europe and the Third World*, xxv Pt 2, 125, 1984-5

1221   *Irish Social Services*, xvii, 107, 1942-3

1222   *Local Government Reform*, xxvi Pt 3, 303, 1990-1

1223   *National Income and Social Accounts*, xviii, 473, 1951-2

1224   *Necessary Changes in Industrial Relations*, xxiv Pt 2, 29, 1979-80

1225   *The Present and Future of Inland Transport*, xix, 61, 1956-7

1226   *Privatisation of State Assets and State Commercial Companies*, xxv Pt 5, 53, 1987-8

1227   *Report of Commission on Social Welfare*, xxv Pt 4, 1, 1986-7

1228   *Report of the Commission on Emigration and other Population Problems*, xix, 104, 1955-6

1229   *Science and Irish Economic Development*, xxi Pt 5, 35, 1966-7

1230   *Social Security*, xviii Pt 3, 247, 1949-50

1231   *Statistics for Policy and Research*, xxv Pt 3, 1, 1985-6

1232   *Structural and Cohesion Funds,* xxvi Pt 5, 135, 1992-3

1233   *Taxation*, xxv Pt 1, 1, 1983-4

1234   *White Paper on Education*, xxiv Pt 3, 71, 1980-1

1235   Synnott, Nicholas Joseph *Housing of the Rural Population in Ireland*, xi, 215, 1903-4

1236   Synnott, Nicholas Joseph *Over-Taxation and Local Expenditure in Ireland*, x, 404, 1899

1237   Synnott, Nicholas Joseph *Proposals for a New Labourers' Bill: an Attempt to solve the Rural Housing Question in Ireland*, xi, 411, 1905-6

1238   Synnott, Nicholas Joseph *The Proposed Re-Valuation of Land in Ireland: A Survey of its Meaning, Scope and Effect*, xii, 338, 1909-10

1239   Synnott, Nicholas Joseph *Re-Valuation of Ireland*, x, 528, 1900

1240   Synnott, Nicholas Joseph *Some Features of the Over-taxation of Ireland*, x, 251, 1897

        Systems: GIS and Machine Peat Extraction, xxvi Pt 3,
        295, 1990-1

1258   Torrens, Robert R. *Transfer of Land and the Registration of
        Title*, iii, 468, 1863

        Treacy, J. *see* O'Hanlon, G.

1259   Tussing, Dale A. *Symposium on the White Paper on Education:
        Accountability, Rationalisation and the White Paper on
        Educational Development*, xxiv Pt 3, 71, 1980-1

        Unwin, A. *see* Gallagher, M.

1260   Urlin, Richard Denny *Dwellings of Working Men in Cities,
        and the Efforts that have been made to Improve them*, iv,
        158, 1865

1261   Urlin, Richard Denny *Proposal for the addition to the Queen's
        Colleges of Junior Departments, intended to supply to
        some extent the want of Intermediate Education in Ireland*,
        iii, 187, 1862

1262   Urlin, Richard Denny *Recommendations of the Land Transfer
        Commission of 1869, considered with especial reference
        to their Applicability to Transfer of Land in Ireland*, vi,
        323, 1874

1263   Urlin, Richard Denny *Remarks on the Middle Class (Female)
        Emigration Society and Miss Rye's Visit to Otago*, iii, 439,
        1863

1264   Urquhart, William Pollard *Competitive Examinations*, iii,
        362, 1863

1265   Urquhart, William Pollard *Plan for the reduction and ultimate
        extinction of the National Debt*, i, 165, 1856

1266   Vance, Robert *English and Irish Analyses of Wages and
        Profits*, February, Vol I, 1848

1267   Vereker, Hon. John Prendergast *Absenteeism Economically
        Considered*, December, Vol II, 1850

1268   Vereker, Hon. John Prendergast *Economic Consideration of
        the Irish Judgment Acts*, March, Vol I, 1849

1269   Vincent, A.V. *Symposium on Science and Irish Economic
        Development*, xxi Pt 5, 42, 1966-7

Subject Index to Articles

High Court
    commercial cases, 1905. *see* 554
higher education
    analysis of university, 1971. *see* 1077
    management training, 1958. *see* 350
    performance in, 1970s. *see* 198
    personnel management, 1972. *see* 1078
    social background of students, 1966-8. *see* 931-2, 1079
    Trinity College, Dublin, 1945. *see* 856
    universities, 1949. *see* 857
    universities in the 1990s (symposium, 1989). *see* 1213
    University College, Dublin, 1944. *see* 855
    of women, late 19th c. *see* 108
historical statistics. *see* 545
Holland
    pig production, 1948. *see* 1120
hops, duty on, 1857. *see* 123
hospitals
    county infirmary statistics, 1884. *see* 780
    Dublin, 1870. *see* 836
    finances, 1955. *see* 499
    hospital system, 1857. *see* 790
    Northern Ireland, 1955. *see* 927
    village hospitals, 1882. *see* 1147
Household Budget Survey, 1973. *see* 909
Houses of Parliament. *see* parliament
housing
    1857. *see* 629
    1865. *see* 1260
    1881. *see* 307
    1899. *see* 270
    1900. *see* 214
    1909. *see* 698
    1913. *see* 212
    1914. *see* 146, 868
    1915. *see* 248
    1841-1906. *see* 841
    Artizans' Dwellings Acts. *see* 507
    committee report, 1914. *see* 171
    need for Labourers' Bill, 1905. *see* 1237
    Northern Ireland, 1952. *see* 953

quantitative planning
    agricultural applications, 1968. *see* 502
Queen's Colleges, 1862. *see* 1261
Queen's University, Belfast
    social class of students, 1967. *see* 1079

Radio Eireann
    listener research, 1953-5. *see* 331
railways
    commercial construction, 1867. *see* 902
    financial position of, 1866. *see* 440
    France, 1866. *see* 776
    government purchase proposed, 1860s. *see* 387, 389
    guarantees, 1883. *see* 893
    IFS accounts, 1935. *see* 812
    management in India, 1903. *see* 1174
    problem, 1919. *see* 642
    rates, 1883. *see* 267
    reform. *see* 372, 389, 604
    and the state, 1866. *see* 918
    and state purchase, 1867. *see* 1068
    statistics
        1849. *see* 908
        1924-37. *see* 1142
        1938-44. *see* 1140
        1945-51. *see* 1139
    USA, 1886. *see* 264
    Vice-Regal Commission, 1910. *see* 1180
reciprocity, 1879. *see* 770
regional input-output models
    problems of, 1974. *see* 543
regional studies. *see* Buchanan Report
Registration of Assurances Bill, 1891. *see* 825
Registration of Births, Deaths, Marriages, 1860. *see* 890
Registration of Clubs Act, 1904. *see* 699
Registration of Titles Commission, 1857. *see* 785
religious toleration
    for criminals, 1868. *see* 373
rent
    economic theory of, 1881. *see* 958

time, international, 1913. *see* 1177
Tipperary Bank, 1882. *see* 423
tobacco cultivation, 1884. *see* 1270
topographical index, 1909. *see* 844
tourism
    1900. *see* 1302
    in EC, 1986. *see* 997
    effects of, 1989. *see* 541
    trends and determinants, 1972. *see* 995
towns. *see also* housing
    codification of town law, 1873. *see* 903
    decline of country towns, 1931. *see* 251
    insanitary state, 1866. *see* 839
Towns Improvement Act (Ireland), 1854. *see* 400
trade. *see also* customs duties; protectionism
    1909. *see* 1107
    Anglo-Irish, 1775-1800. *see* 73
    butter, late 19th c. *see* 50
    commercial blockades, 1855. *see* 712
    comparative advantage of exports, 1969-82. *see* 1252
    effect of precious metals fluctuations, 1878. *see* 382
    export changes, 1919. *see* 1013
    free trade or protection, 1886. *see* 158
    future of (discussion, 1943). *see* 61
    Irish Free State statistics, 1937. *see* 285; 749
    Irish Free State, 1924. *see* 286, 705, 751, 833, 1028, 1137
    Irish Free State, 1937. *see* 260, 285, 750
    risks of free trade, 1883. *see* 150
    statistics 1909. *see* 1
    trader concentration, 1994. *see* 602
    United Kingdom - USA, 19th c. *see* 17
trade boards, 1919. *see* 977
Trades Union Congress
    address to, 1881. *see* 594
    law reforms sought, 1881. *see* 453
trades unions
    1853. *see* 714
    combinations, 1860. *see* 116
    Northern Ireland, 1950s. *see* 78
    organisation, 1925. *see* 900
    organisation, 1958. *see* 1084